DEMOCRATIC JUSTICE AND THE SOCIAL CONTRACT

DEMOCRATIC JUSTICE AND THE SOCIAL CONTRACT

ALBERT WEALE

OXFORD
UNIVERSITY PRESS

OXFORD
UNIVERSITY PRESS

Great Clarendon Street, Oxford, OX2 6DP,
United Kingdom

Oxford University Press is a department of the University of Oxford.
It furthers the University's objective of excellence in research, scholarship,
and education by publishing worldwide. Oxford is a registered trade mark of
Oxford University Press in the UK and in certain other countries

First Edition published in 2013
Impression: 1

Published in the United States of America by Oxford University Press
198 Madison Avenue, New York, NY 10016, United States of America

British Library Cataloguing in Publication Data
Data available

ISBN 978–0–19–968464–9

Printed in Great Britain by
CPI Group (UK) Ltd, Croydon, CR0 4YY

For Jan—once again

What people say is that to do wrong is, in itself, a desirable thing; on the other hand, it is not at all desirable to suffer wrong, and the harm to the sufferer outweighs the advantage to the doer. Consequently, when men have a taste of both, those who have not the power to seize the advantage and escape the harm decide that they would be better off if they made a compact neither to do wrong nor to suffer it.

Glaucon in Plato, *The Republic*, Book II, 358–9.

The ancient republics, being mostly grounded from the first upon some kind of mutual compact, or at any rate formed by an union of persons not very unequal in strength, afforded, in consequence, the first instance of a portion of human relations fenced round, and placed under the dominion of another law than that of force.

John Stuart Mill, *The Subjection of Women*, chapter 1.

For really I think that the poorest he that is in England hath a life to live, as the greatest he; and therefore truly, sir, I think it's clear, that every man that is to live under a government ought first by his own consent to put himself under that government...

...the main cause why Almighty God gave man reason, it was that they should make use of that reason.... I do not find anything in the Law of God that a lord shall choose twenty burgesses, and a gentleman but two, or a poor man shall choose none: I find no such thing in the Law of Nature, not in the Law of Nations. But I do find that all Englishmen must be subject to English laws, and I do verily believe that there is no man but will say that the foundation of all law lies in the people....

Colonel Rainborough, speaking in the Putney Debate on 'The Agreement of the People', 29 October 1647.

If I am not for myself, who is for me? And if only for myself, what am I?

Rabbi Hillel, *Chapters of the Fathers*, 14, *The Mishnah*.

CONTENTS

PREFACE AND ACKNOWLEDGEMENTS

This work offers a theory of democratic justice, that is to say a theory in which the principles of social justice for a political association are defined by the democratic procedures of that association. Provided collective decision making respects basic conditions of procedural democracy and takes place under circumstances in which the strength of the parties is approximately equal, it will generate principles of just obligation. One inspiration for the theory is John Stuart Mill's observation in *The Subjection of Women* that unjustifiable social inequalities arise from inequalities of power. Injustice then is an effect of unequal power at work in the basic institutions of society. According to Mill, the ancient republics of the classical Greek world were formed through social compacts among persons of roughly equal strength. As a result, relations among their members were governed by principles other than those of mere force. From this it is a short step to the claim that justice can be defined by the principles that would be agreed among persons entering a social contract in which their power of negotiation over the terms of that contract was approximately equal. When it functions well, political democracy is a system of government in which power is as equally distributed as it can be. In the same way that the ancient republics, with equal strength among their members, established a principle of social organization other than force, democratic procedures, in circumstances in which all parties to the contract enjoy a balance of power, provide one model for a just social contract. So some types of democratic procedure empirically model, that is to say stand as a representation of, a social contract. The theory of democratic justice is thus a social contract theory.

As Chapter 1 notes, social contract theories of justice go back to the Sophists and Epicureans of classical Athens and the Hellenistic world. Plato has Glaucon, his brother, state the idea in the second book of *The Republic*. Glaucon is made to expound the theory so that the Platonic Socrates can refute it (an expression of sibling rivalry perhaps?). Despite Platonic and Aristotelian objections, the idea of justice as the product of a social contract survived in the Hellenistic thought world, particularly among the Sophists and the followers of Epicurus. According to their view, justice is to be understood as a convention. As a principle of social organization, it derives its force from its coordinating the expectations of separate persons to their mutual advantage. In being conventional, principles of justice do not derive from an eternal natural law or from reasoning in terms of universalizable maxims. Instead, such principles are to be understood as constructions of human practical rationality under conditions in which persons of roughly equal power have to cooperate to mutual advantage in circumstances of limited altruism and moderate scarcity. Each party to the contract pursues his or her own good. The need for a social contract arises because the collective outcome of this pursuit is mutually self-defeating. The principles of justice are those principles that agents trapped in this dilemma could agree to their mutual advantage. To use the contemporary distinction, the theory is contractarian rather than contractualist. Since the mutual advantage of the associates is negotiated through democratic procedures, the theory may be called democratic contractarianism.

Social contract theory captures a key element in the logic of any viable society, namely the need to reconcile the existence of separate and competing interests with the need to secure common interests. Any viable society requires an implicit social contract in order to bring about this reconciliation, but not all such contracts are just. How could we know which social contracts were just and which unjust? To answer this question, in Chapter 2 we identify societies or social organizations in which the logic of contractual association among persons of roughly equal strength is exhibited. Empirical examples of such societies are to be found in common property resource regimes. The features that enable successful common property resource regimes avoid collective action failure in the context of pressing environmental constraints can also be interpreted as the conditions for a just social order.

What principles of economic justice are found in common property resource regimes? As Chapter 3 explains, a central principle is that producers are entitled to the full fruits of their labour, provided that all have access to the essential means of production on equal terms. The principle that all should receive the full fruits of their labour can be seen as a focal point agreement to mutual advantage in a situation in which the uncoordinated exercise of Hohfeldian liberties by each agent leads to mutually disadvantageous spillover effects for all. To be effective, principles of social justice must strike a balance between economic individualism and economic collectivism. The full fruits principle, resting on the equal access principle, may be contrasted with Locke's individualism, Rawls's collectivism and Gauthier's attempt to combine both an individual right to the appropriation of natural resources with collective control of the economic rent resulting from the social contract. The full fruits principle, when combined with equal access to the means of production, mean that economic advantages that accrue from luck are permissible. The problem of need is to be solved at a later point in the argument.

Contractarian accounts of justice often rely upon formal bargaining theory, using a deductive choice-theoretic account of rationality. However, as explained in Chapter 4, democratic contractarianism does not adopt this approach, but relies instead upon a concept of rationality in which choice is voluntary action arising from deliberation. Such deliberative rationality involves reflective distance, deliberative competence in the practical syllogism, the ability to understand particular specifications as elements of planned ends, including specifications that are novel, and the capacity of rational agents to give themselves normative self-direction. Practical public reasoning is also defeasible, meaning that it is liable to being altered by the discovery of unanticipated facts that render previous decision premisses unreliable. Consequently, political decision making should be sensitive to the limits under which general principles are to be applied, political design should take into account local information and political theory needs to model reflective and creative thinking in the design of solutions to collective action problems.

Common property resource regimes are small-scale societies in which participants can bargain and negotiate face to face with one another. How, then, can we use their experience to model principles applicable to industrial and post-industrial societies, regarded as 'great societies'? Some, like Hayek, have argued that we cannot. To transpose the principles of one type of society to the other type is to commit a category mistake. Another view is that it should prove no more difficult to model a just social contract in terms of common property resource regimes than it is to model a social contract by a hypothetical thought-experiment in which the potential members of society bargain or deliberate over the terms of their association. Chapter 5 suggests that both answers miss a trick. By understanding the 'great transformation' from small-scale to large-scale societies, we gain an understanding of what the distinctive features of justice are in large-scale societies. These features include the centrality of broad political representation where there is an inevitable plurality of interests; the relative contribution of markets and hierarchies in allocating returns to labour; and the transformation of interdependence in the household as it ceases to be the predominant unit of production.

The central problem in designing the political institutions of a great society is to make political decision making responsive to a plurality of interests and opinions, whilst simultaneously meeting standards of deliberative rationality. The solution to this problem of design is not to suppose that deliberation can generate consensus across the whole of society. Rather, as argued in Chapter 6, a system in which political parties are elected by proportional representation and policy is decided with the support of a majority of representatives in the legislature exemplifies one possible institutional design that satisfies the requirements of a just social contract. Even when shifting parliamentary-coalitions determine legislation or policy, political accountability is still possible, though it cannot be represented in the form of a consistent rank-ordering of a disinterested social planner. Instead, public deliberative rationality requires institutions to test and refine the decision premisses of authoritative political action.

Returns in the hierarchies of the modern corporation do not give workers the full product of their own labour, a principle that was a feature of common property resource regimes. As argued in Chapter 7, under some circumstances, denying workers their marginal product is to deny them justice. The marginal product principle is not challenged by the observation that there are increasing returns to scale in a modern economy that provide grounds for redistribution. Scale economies entail that workers should contribute to the common overheads required for production, not share their product with other producers. The marginal product principle is not even challenged by the principle of need, taken as an independent consideration of social justice, since redistribution on grounds of need in the modern welfare state is best understood as redistribution across the life-cycle among those who produce, rather than as redistribution from those who produce to those who do not. Moreover, the transformation of the household in a great society, with a life-cycle approach to redistribution, reveals the extent to which the labour of reproduction is a social responsibility. Finally, securing equal access to the means of production requires the widespread distribution of material and human capital.

Participants in a social contract need a sense of justice. Chapter 8 argues that a sense of democratic justice cannot come from identification with the principles that define the historic identity of a community, since traditional principles may need to be challenged in the name of justice. A just social contract must allow for self-assertion among equals. However, it cannot rely only on self-assertion. It also requires an understanding of the contribution that each has to make to the common enterprise. Yet there is no reason for thinking that rational contractors will always find a prudential reason for abiding by the terms of a social contract. In consequence, there is a need for governance, to monitor and enforce performance, if the mutual assurance of cooperation on which the social contract rests is to be secured. Since social justice requires democracy, pride in a just social order is only possible among those who contribute to that social order. In a democracy, only citizens who contribute to the maintenance of the social order can say with Rabbi Hillel: if I am not for myself, who will be for me and if only for myself, what am I?

So the leading propositions offered of the democratic theory of justice can be stated as follows. Justice can be represented as a convention among persons of equal strength for their mutual advantage. The political procedures of some societies, one example of which is common property resource regimes, model a social contract for justice. Such societies show that a justifiable principle of economic appropriation is that producers are entitled to the full fruits of their labour, provided that all political associates have equal access to and control over the essential means of production. The rationality of the social contract is a deliberative non-deductive form of rationality that requires associates to understand how their common ends can be specified in practice whilst allowing that agreed decision premisses can be overturned by new evidence. Neither considerations of method nor of substance prevent the principles of common property resource regimes being applied, with due modification, to great societies, and indeed the development of great societies enables us to understand what a democratic social contract entails. The political equality of each associate is consistent with majority rule when representative political parties enter into shifting coalitions with each other. Economic justice links work and reward, sometimes requiring the modification of market transactions arising from organizational and other imperfections. Needs are met by institutions that spread income across the life-cycle. To have a sense of democratic justice in such a political economy requires one to understand oneself as a cooperating partner in a scheme of mutual advantage so long as effective governance provides the requisite assurance of cooperation from others.

A number of the claims offered in this book are ones that I endorsed before I started working on the project. To me it has long seemed a useful heuristic device to think of societies as though they involved an implicit social contract, not least because any viable society has to balance the claims of the individual and the collective. I had also thought for some time that practical rationality was defeasible, although I did not have an inkling of how the idea might be developed and how extensive its implications might be. Earlier work on environmental policy in Europe had convinced me that policy making involved essential reference to intellectual paradigms that constituted decision premisses. I had been attracted to an empirical approach to social contract theory by the work of Brian Barry, and his approach tied in with my more general conviction that the type of analysis characteristic of comparative political science, involving typologies of institutional forms, had received insufficient attention in the theory of justice. I also thought that, though institutions mattered and their evaluation ought to be a prime task of normative political theory, one could not understand how democracies might flourish without seeing the role played in that flourishing of a civic culture based on a sense of justice.

However, an equal number, if not more, of claims advanced in the present work are ones that, before writing, I would have rejected completely or held only half-heartedly. Although convinced that the empirical method was a viable approach to justice, I did not think this meant that democratic decision making modelled a social contract. Instead, I thought that one would derive justifiable principles of democracy from a social contract, without fully realizing that I was thereby committed to presupposing a veil of ignorance in a necessarily hypothetical social contract. My initial prejudices also led me to think that justice could not adequately be modelled on principles of mutual advantage, so my preferred mode of theory was contractualist rather than contractarian. This preference seemed to dovetail with that strand of deliberative democracy that stressed public reasoning as discussion on the merits of the case rather than bargaining and mutual accommodation. Lingering pre-Enlightenment and rationalistic sentiments led me to reject the idea that justice could be a mere convention. I certainly rejected the claim that economic justice required that workers be entitled to the full fruits of their labour, and I did not realize that the theory of justice could deal with the centrality of the household to human life only by understanding its historical transformation.

Because working on this project has required me to give up a number of important prior prejudices, I have wondered at times whether I could expound a theory that seemed so out of balance with my long-held considered judgements. But theoretical reflection means nothing unless you are prepared to treat some of your intuitions as misguided prejudices to be rejected. So I have adopted the strategy of pursuing my *idée fixe*—that justice can be understood by reference to empirical social contracts in which the power of the parties is equalized—to the best of my ability, in order to see to what principles and conclusions it might lead. I am comforted by the thought that as great a political theorist as John Stuart Mill thought the idea worth stating. Indeed, rereading his work with this idea in mind makes one realize just how central to his thinking is the need to rectify inequalities of power. Whether, in pursuing my *idée fixe*, I shall be led, like the character in Berlioz's *Symphonie Fantastique*, to the fatal gallows with the critics taking their role in the witches' Sabbath only time will tell. Political theorists are a hard-headed bunch, so where I have made mistakes, it will soon be apparent.

In an earlier draft, I offered a series of interpretations of key texts in modern social contract theory as a way of locating my own approach. However, I found it impossible to keep to this plan. I had a great mass of material and, in trying to compress that material between the same covers as the present work, I ended up saying either too much or too little. So I have taken out that interpretative material and I hope to publish it as a separate monograph. It currently has the working title *Modern Social Contract Theory.* Its central thesis is that, although hypothetical social contract theory is offered as a method of political ethics, it can be formulated in such varied ways that first-order disagreements about justice and democracy are simply displaced onto second-order disagreements about how to model the hypothetical contract. A sketch of this argument, which I draw upon in the present work, can be found in my 'Contractarian Theory, Deliberative Democracy and General Agreement', in Keith Dowding, Robert E. Goodin and Carole Pateman (eds.), *Justice and Democracy: Essays for Brian Barry* (Cambridge: Cambridge University Press, 2004), pp. 79–96.

If you write about the social contract, you should acknowledge the extent to which your individual effort depends upon the public goods that are the preconditions for any productive activity. In my case, I thank the United Kingdom's Economic and Social Research Council (ESRC) for awarding me a Professorial Fellowship between January 2009 and March 2012 (RES-051-27-0264-A) for a programme of work on 'Social Contract, Deliberative Democracy and Public Policy'. Naturally a successful award is likely to make anyone well disposed to the body that provides the money. Despite that, I hope my view will not be discounted if I say that the Professorial Fellowship scheme, by encouraging a programme of work and not a single project, is both ambitious and displays a commendable willingness on the part of the ESRC to take risks. I should also like to put on record that I have always found the staff at the Council to be courteous and effective, and I am particularly grateful to my case officer, Chris Wyatt, for dealing with the inevitable complications of a large award in such a helpful, timely, and efficient manner.

If the ESCR is the agent, the UK taxpayer is the principal. No one should write on social justice without realizing that goods have to be produced by work. During my own working life I have been fortunate in having a succession of posts at five excellent universities, posts that have been both personally satisfying and economically well rewarded. I will defend to any taxpayer who asks the importance to a society of financing academic research in the social and political sciences that is speculative and theoretical. But I also always try to bear in mind that publicly funded research is paid for by some portion of the difference between the figures at the top left and at the bottom right portions of each taxpayer's pay-slip. I hereby record my gratitude.

As well as supporting a significant proportion of my own salary, the ESRC award also provided monies for replacement teaching, a PhD studentship, and research assistance. Deborah Savage covered some of my teaching with real commitment at the same time as conducting her own research, never an easy feat. Nick Martin took up the challenge of writing a PhD on liberal neutrality and the public benefit test for charities in a way that has exceeded my expectations. Aude Bicquelet provided the initial research assistance on the programme drawing on our earlier joint work on the computer-aided text analysis of political reasoning, a small sample of which is referred to in the present work. I am grateful for her enthusiasm and I hope that she and I can return, in the not too distant future, to the challenges and opportunities that the new methods of text analysis present. Sarah Clark has worked on the public policy implications of the research programme. She has been indefatigable, combining a remarkable lucidity of mind with an exemplary commitment to working out the significance of social values for public policy. Quite apart from her intellectual contribution, she has always made me feel, whenever I have talked to her about this work, that the project was worthwhile, for which I am particularly grateful.

With complete disregard for the proper courtesies of life, I inflicted earlier drafts, sometimes very rough earlier drafts, of this book on those willing to read it. I am grateful to those who gave me written comments, including Peter Bloom, Cécile Laborde, Sue Mendus, Ian O'Flynn, and Laura Valentini. John Horton was kind enough not only to provide written comments on one very early draft but also to spend a morning, followed by a pub lunch, discussing where it could be improved. Robert Sugden read a version and helped me greatly in correspondence to understand the logic of economies of scale. In one conversation, Joseph Raz alerted me to the significance of non-monotonic reasoning and in another conversation Thomas Baldwin was able to reassure me that I was not too far off the mark in understanding the significance of the key ideas. Malcolm Schofield took me through social contract theory in classical Greek political thought, passing on some important references. An anonymous referee pressed me hard, and rightly, on a number of points, not least the need to think about how to apply principles developed in small-scale societies to large-scale ones. Matt Matravers, originally an anonymous referee, provided comments that were insightful, challenging, and encouraging at the same time. If I am now a genuine constructivist, it is due to him.

I owe a special debt to Richard Bellamy. He and I always joke how we have chased one another around the UK university system in successive posts. I am particularly grateful to him for the role he played in recruiting me to University College London. I am also indebted to him for both his comments on successive drafts and his own work on political constitutionalism. The Department of Political Science and School of Public Policy at UCL has turned out to be a wonderful place at which to work. I am grateful to David Coen, who followed Richard Bellamy as head of department, for his support.

I have given sundry papers and talks related to the main thesis of this book at various universities, including Essex, Exeter, Newcastle, UCL, and LUISS in Rome. On each and every occasion I was both flattered by the interest shown in the ideas and challenged by the criticisms. I am grateful to all participants. I thank Marit Boeker, Michael Freeman, and Iain Hampsher-Monk for their written comments following presentations.

Claudia Landwehr was kind enough to invite me to present an early version of the ideas at the conference on 'Democracy and Justice in Distribution Conflicts' held by the Section on Political Theory and the History of Ideas of the German Political Science Association at the University of Frankfurt am Main in March 2010. She then arranged for a German translation to appear, as 'Gesellschaftsvertrag und demokratische Deliberation', in a book for which she edited with Regina Kreide and Katrin Toens with the title *Demokratie und Gerechtigkeit in Verteilungskonflikten* (Baden-Baden: Nomos Verlagsgesellschaft, 2012). I am extremely grateful to her.

My thinking on externalities was greatly prompted by returning to the origin of the concept in the work of Alfred Marshall when I was preparing a paper now published in a *Festschrift* for my friend and sometimes collaborator, Gerd Wagner, as '"Eigentum verpflichtet": A Social Contract Analysis', in Rüdiger Hahn, Henrik Janzen, and Dirk Matten (Hrgs.), *Die gesellschaftliche Verantwortung des Unternehmens* (Stuttgart: Schäffer-Poeschel, 2012). Gerd's own thinking on the responsibilities of business has exercised a considerable influence on my own views about the justice of property.

A turning point in my thinking followed an invitation from Susan Dimock to present a paper at a conference held in York University Toronto in May 2011 to mark the twenty-fifth anniversary of David Gauthier's *Morals by Agreement*. Re-engaging with Gauthier's work after a number of years made me realize how much subtlety of thinking in his work I had missed first time round. Although it will be clear that I disagree with a number of his particular arguments, I hope it will be equally clear how much I owe in general to Gauthier's thinking.

My other leading influence was at the other end of the contractarian–contractualist spectrum, namely the late Brian Barry. His death, tragically followed a few months later by that of his wife Anni, has deprived political theory of one of its towering figures of the last few decades. I doubt I could ever have persuaded him to see the justice in mutual advantage, although as an admirer of John Stuart Mill he might have come to see that republics, founded on a contract of equal strength, could be a model to reflect upon.

As I moved through successive drafts, Dominic Byatt at Oxford University Press combined warm support and an ability to manage the process of publication efficiently and to effect. I am extremely grateful to him for keeping me cool-headed at all the right times.

My final and most important acknowledgement is to the dedicatee, Jan Harris. There is so much that I should say but that would make this Preface double its length. I shall just note that, in a book that explores the importance of interdependence in human activities, she has understood more than anyone else the implications of what this means for the two of us at a practical level. She will know what I mean when I say that this book is part of the fruits of our joint labour.

CHAPTER 1

Justice, social contracts, and democracy

1.1. The contest of justice

Within all modern democracies political controversy arises over questions of property and justice. Some argue that the economically productive should be able to garner the full fruits of their labour, whilst others believe that those who are most productive should be required to share their good fortune with their fellow citizens or humanity at large. Amongst those who favour redistribution, some think that it should be consistent with the highest average level of well-being possible, whereas others urge priority to be given to the worst off, even if that involves a drop in the average standard of living. Still others urge complete equality of income so far as that is possible. Some hold that people should not only be allowed to amass wealth through savings during their lifetime but also that they should be entitled to dispose of it freely upon whomever they choose through gift or inheritance. Others propose strict limits both on the amount of wealth that any one individual can hold and on the legacy anyone can bestow. Some maintain that the community at large has a responsibility for the financial costs of health care for all citizens, even when that care is extremely expensive, whereas others think that individuals should take responsibility for providing for the financial risks of ill health, as well as making provision for other risks to well-being. Some see an important role for collective consumption in a civilized society in the form of fine city buildings, well maintained national parks and a flourishing life for the arts. Others believe that collective consumption presupposes an agreement on the common good that is implausible in a diverse society, and therefore that public expenditure should be limited to the minimum necessary to maintain internal law and order and protection from external threat. Some are economic individualists, only favouring intervention and control by the political authorities when no other remedy for a social ill is available. Others hold that only the organized power of the community wisely and widely deployed can create the conditions in which individuals and families can grow and flourish.

Political controversy over property and justice is not new. Discussing the source of political factions in constitutions, Aristotle remarked that economic inequality was a source of political controversy, for those 'that desire equality enter on party strife if they think that they have too little although they are the equals of those that have more, while those that desire inequality or superiority do so if they suppose that although they are unequal they have not got more but an equal amount or less'.[1] Rousseau famously said that the 'first man who, having enclosed a piece of ground, to whom it occurred to say *this is mine* and found people sufficiently simple to believe him, was the true founder of civil society', going on to lament that no one had challenged the impostor and so no one had saved numerous crimes, wars, murders, miseries, and horrors.[2] Madison noted that 'the most common and durable sources of factions, has been the various and unequal distribution of property' such that those 'who hold, and those who are without property, have ever formed distinct interests in society'.[3] Sidgwick, having accepted that private ownership and thereby the right to exclude others from use was essential to the productive value of land, wrestled with the problem of the extent to which uncultivated land ought to be allowed to be taken into private ownership and in what ways the determination of the limits of private and common ownership should be settled.[4]

What these controversies, both ancient and modern, reveal is that disputes about the justice of property and economic advantage cannot be detached from questions about the scope and reach of political authority. Economic differences turn into political controversies because those differences raise issues of justice, and justice is a political principle. Controversy over the justice of property and economic advantage inevitably involves the question of how individuals relate to one another in a political association and what should be the powers of the political association of which they are members. Perhaps deep and long-standing inequalities in wealth and income undermine the common citizenship that is an essential element of a democratic political system; perhaps economic inequalities are a spur to effort, so that there can be no political interest in limiting them. Differences in the assessment of economic relationships spill over into competing evaluations of the political system. Moreover, given differences of view about justice and property, there is a political question about how to deal with and reconcile such disputes. How can political decision making be best constituted so as to resolve these disagreements fairly and to the best advantage of all? Behind questions of economic justice, then, are questions of the character of political association and the constitution of political authority.

One tradition of political thought with a long lineage addresses these joint questions by appeal to the idea of a social contract. According to this tradition, social and political associations should be regarded as embodying a social contract in which the norms and principles of justice are a set of conventions adopted as the outcome of an agreement that all individuals in society have reason to accept. In *The Republic* Plato has Glaucon set out this theory as follows:

> What people say is that to do wrong is, in itself, a desirable thing; on the other hand, it is not at all desirable to suffer wrong, and the harm to the sufferer outweighs the advantage to the doer. Consequently, when men have a taste of both, those who have not the power to seize the advantage and escape the harm decide that they would be better off if they made a compact [*συνθήκη*] neither to do wrong nor to suffer it.[5]

Glaucon is made to present this view as though it were a commonplace of classical Athens. It is 'what people say'. On this account, justice is to be understood as a compact or contract, the term '*συνθήκη*' being the standard Greek word for 'contract'. The contract arises because each individual seeks to exercise power over others. If people could practise injustice without penalty, they would do so. Hence, the virtue of justice is practised reluctantly. Glaucon illustrates this reluctance by reference to the myth of the ring of Gyges, which turns its wearer invisible. With such a ring, Glaucon suggests, no one would have such strength of mind and resolution to do right by refraining from stealing from or killing others when convenient to do so. Without the ring, however, there is a balance of threat and retaliation that prevails in society, rendering the unconstrained exercise of power self-defeating. Although persons could advance their own good if they could be possessive without constraint, they suffer an 'excess of evil' when they are wronged rather than when they commit wrong. So 'those who lack the power to avoid the one and take the other determine that it is for their profit to make a compact with one another neither to commit nor to suffer injustice'. Justice rests on the collective regulation of power, where power is understood as the ability of individuals to effect or bring about their desired ends.[6]

Denyer has shown that Glaucon's account of justice should be interpreted according to the logic of mutual advantage in a prisoner's dilemma.[7] In a prisoner's dilemma each agent would do best by securing the cooperation of others without complying with the rules that others accept. However, if all agents try to secure this individual advantage, the collective outcome is worse for all than it would be if all abided by the common rules. Given equality of power, in which each agent is capable of seeking to free ride on the restraint of others, it is better for everyone to come to a cooperative agreement than to seek to secure relative advantage. Denyer points out that social contract theory of this sort was a persistent feature of the Sophistic and Epicurean traditions in classical thought from the fifth through to the first century BCE.[8] Thus, in the *Protagoras*, Plato has Protagoras say that when humans first came together in cities they originally injured one another 'for want of political skill' that threatened the destruction of humanity.[9] In the *Politics* Aristotle criticizes Lycophron (probably a pupil of the Sophist Gorgias) for holding the view that 'the law is a covenant [συνθήκη] or, in the phrase of the sophist Lycophron, a guarantee of men's just claims on one another, but it is not designed to make the citizens virtuous or just'.[10] Similar views on the contractual basis of political association are to be found in Antiphon the Sophist, the Anonymous Iamblichi, a text generally assumed to be by a follower of Protagoras, as well as, most importantly, Epicurus. Within this tradition, although justice is seen as the result of a human compact, it is nonetheless regarded as morally important and there were persistent discussions as to the extent to which a person of virtue should follow just terms of social agreement even if punishment was not anticipated for breach (as would be the case with a wearer of the ring of Gyges). As Denyer puts it, 'Epicurus may see justice as a human creation, not as something existing φύσει [by nature]; but it would for him be also an error to see it as something that exists merely νόμωι [by convention].'[11]

The logic of mutual advantage requires the assumption of a rough equality of power among those who are parties to the social contract. Denyer finds no equivalent tradition of social-contract thinking after Epicurus, presumably because the institutional context of political thought is no longer that of the city-state in which political membership is seen as a partnership among equal citizens. The link between the relation of political equals in the city-state and the idea of a social contract was remarked upon by John Stuart Mill, who wrote that 'the ancient republics, being grounded in some kind of mutual compact, or at any rate formed by an union of persons of not very unequal strength, afforded, in consequence, the first instance of a portion of human relations fenced around, and placed under the dominion of another law than that of force'.[12] Mill here is reflecting the fact that a number of the Greek colonies were founded on an explicit agreement among the settlers, akin to the *Mayflower* compact in the seventeenth century. His insight is that the practice of collective self-government on the basis of the equality of members has a strong intellectual affinity with the idea that society should be seen as a social contract in which relations of force are replaced by bonds of principled agreement. Within this tradition of thinking, issues of justice are not simply a topic of controversy within democracies; the practice of democratic government, so constructed as to secure a balance of power among its members, enables us to understand what principles of justice emerge from a social contract.

In a number of democratic cultures of the second half of the twentieth century, social contract theory underwent a striking revival, becoming an essential reference point for the intellectual and ideological discussion of social justice. In its modern versions, social contract theory takes many forms.[13] However, the various accounts are united by the thought that justifiable terms of social cooperation are to be understood on a model of a contract that each individual would have reason to make with other individuals, all taking due regard for their own prudential interests. From this perspective, the fundamental question individuals have to face when confronting questions of social organization is not 'What arrangements conduce to my interests?', since no one person can plausibly assume that others will concur with his or her desires. Rather the question each individual has to pose is: 'What arrangements would I have reason to propose as the terms of social and political association that others also have reason to accept?' The differing forms of social contract theory can be seen as addressing the conceptual and logical issues implicit in rendering this question meaningful and significant. With what do we identify the relevant terms of association—morality in general, justice, constitutional arrangements, or principles of political obligation? What is involved in agents having a reason for proposing and accepting a particular set of contractual terms? How much information about their own personal circumstances and abilities is it theoretically plausible to ascribe to the contracting parties consistent with our being able to say that an agreement among agents was one that was just? Is the contract to be construed as the upshot of a rational choice, the result of a bargain or the outcome of negotiations under conditions of reasonable agreement? What is the currency of justice in terms of which contracting parties are supposed to conduct their discussions: is it individual welfare, objective interests, or 'primary goods', understood as those goods it would be rational to want if one wanted anything at all?

One of the intellectual attractions of contract theory is that it is proceduralist. That is to say it renders questions about the content of justice—questions about whether particular rules or practices are just—into questions about decision procedures, asking under what conditions individuals would have reason to make certain types of agreement. Typically, questions about the content of justice seem interminable, with different people pitting competing intuitions against one another—hence the contest of justice. In a situation in which everyone recognizes the endless nature of such conflicts, and where a practical decision is necessary, people can agree on a procedure to make decisions even when they continue to hold different substantive views.

Social contract theory draws upon this possibility of procedural resolution, displacing first-order conflicts about what is just onto a decision procedure about what people have reason to agree to. If we think that we have a better understanding of rationality and decision procedures than we do of the content of justice, so that we think we understand what people would decide under certain conditions, then it is attractive to recast the problem of the content of justice in a procedural form, enabling us to read off from our account of decision making what the content of justice is. Moreover, if our theory takes the form of saying what rules and practices everyone would have reason to accept, then we also seem to provide an answer to the question of why people have obligations, to which they could reasonably assent, to accept rules and practices, even when this was contrary to their short-term interests. For example, they may find it reasonable, within a social contract, to be asked to bear the burdens of taxation or military conscription as the condition for others bearing their share of similar obligations. So, if a practice is one which each person has a reason to agree to in a social contract, then it would seem that each has reason to abide by the terms of the social contract when his or her turn comes to bear its burdens. In these ways, a contract theory of justice offers us an account both of the content and of the practical rationality of social justice.

This procedural element of contract theory provides an obvious link to democratic practice. Whatever else it is, a political democracy comprises procedures for making public decisions. To the extent to which such practices resolve political contests about what should be done, they give content to public decisions. Public purposes are defined by the results of a democratic procedure, even when the details of implementation have to be filled out in more detail by administrative or private action. Moreover, if one participates in a democratic procedure to advance one's conception of the public good or to protect one's legitimate interests, then the only condition on which one could reasonably expect others to accept a decision that goes in your favour and against them is for you to be willing to accept a decision in their favour that goes against you. The procedure provides a way of balancing interests, and exists because interests need to be balanced by the nature of the collective character of the issues involved.

The aim of the present work is to formulate a theory of the social contract that models such a contract on the practice of democratic self-government by political equals. It takes up John Stuart Mill's insight that the practice of the ancient republics provided the foundations of political community on a basis other than force by virtue of the compact or equality of power upon which they were founded. It thus provides an account of what we may call 'democratic justice'. Democratic justice is a theory in which requirements of justice for the members of a community are derivable from the democratic procedures of that community. Provided collective decision making respects basic conditions of democracy and takes place under appropriate circumstances, the theory of democratic justice holds that democratic procedures will generate principles of just obligation. Under certain conditions, in particular conditions in which the power of individuals and groups is approximately equal, well-functioning democratic modes of decision making can provide us with a model of how deliberating individuals would form a social contract and give us evidence of the principles upon which it would be based. Such evidence is derived by considering empirical examples of collective negotiation to common advantage in circumstances of equality of power. One set of institutions exemplifying these conditions is to be found in successful common property resource regimes, which provide us with one paradigm of such relations and so yield evidence about what a partnership of equals entails.

1.2. Conceptions of contract theory

A political theory counts as a social contract theory if it offers an understanding of justifiable principles of political association by reference to agents who join together under agreed terms, those agreed terms constituting the principles of association. Thus the general concept of social contract theory has a logical form in which agents negotiate the terms of their association with one another. Political associations are to be evaluated in terms of the principles to which such agents would agree. The agents are assumed to be rational in senses that different theorists specify in various ways, but as rational agents they are not only capable of entering into commitments with one another but also capable of having reasons for entering into those commitments consistent with a prudent concern for their own interests. Justifiable bonds of political agreement among those agents are to be derived from the process of contractual negotiation. In general, then, social contract theories are defined as accounts of political morality in which justifiable forms of social and political cooperation are to be understood on the model of a social contract that each individual would have reason to make with other individuals, assuming that each was appropriately prudential.

Different conceptions of social contract theory are distinguished by the way in which they specify these common conceptual elements in detail. Among the various theories, one major distinction arises from the different ways of specifying the conditions under which it is assumed that the negotiation over the social contract takes place. In one conception, the negotiation is assumed to be one in which individuals are seeking to promote their interests over a baseline of non-cooperation, and for this reason they are looking to establish a social contract that is to their mutual advantage. In the contrasting conception, the negotiation is conceived of as an exchange of reasons that are to be considered from an impartial point of view by participants in the contract. The distinction between the two conceptions is thus one between a social contract as a form of mutual advantage and a social contract as a form of impartial discussion.[14] A convenient way of marking this distinction, common in the social contract literature, is to distinguish between 'contractarian' and 'contractualist' approaches.[15]

A contractarian theory of justice takes its cue from Glaucon's insight that those who practise and those who suffer injustice come to see in situations where there is an equality of power that it is better to make an agreement with others neither to do wrong nor to suffer it. The theory takes the thought that a society is 'a cooperative venture for mutual advantage' literally,[16] so that justice rests upon a principle of reciprocity among the members of a society. Each associate complies with the demands of justice conditionally upon others similarly complying. The agreement is to be thought of as a joint gain over a baseline situation of non-agreement, where all benefit from the agreement. As Gauthier has put it, for each participant in the social contract, advancing one's own interests is fundamental and agreement is a means both to protect and to advance those interests.[17] Such interests need not be purely selfish in a narrow sense; they can, for example, encompass the interests of family, kith, and kin. However, they are narrower than the set of the interests of all the agents who are associates in the social contract. They are also potentially in conflict. The motive to agreement arises, then, from the need to secure these personal interests, as distinct from the broader public interest, which is why the cooperation over the baseline point of non-agreement has to be advantageous to all. It is this feature that leads Barry to pick out contractarian theories as theories in which only Pareto improvements are allowed above the baseline of non-agreement.[18]

A contractualist theory, by contrast, defines the process of contractual negotiation as one of finding rules for social organization that can be justified to all participants in the contract. From this point of view, it is a conception of justice as impartiality, to use Barry's term, rather than justice as mutual advantage. Instead of beginning with a baseline point of non-agreement from which mutually advantageous gains for all parties can be made, the contractualist says that justifiable rules are those that can be reasonably accepted, or at least not reasonably rejected, by all members of society. This requires us to think of the situation of contractual negotiation as one in which all viewpoints are represented and in which arguments are put forward for joint acceptance rather than particular claims being made upon a social surplus. There is no conception of a baseline above which gains have to be acceptable to all, so that a putative Pareto gain does not define the requirements for socially acceptable solutions. Moreover, the fundamental motive of the contracting parties is the desire to be able to justify their actions to one another, rather than the creation of rules that protect their interests or enable them to advance their good. The desire for agreement—not compromise on a mutual stand-off or concessions to mutual advantage—is what political morality is about.

These contrasting modes of contractual negotiation are associated with the different ways in which the decision-making capacity of the agents who are negotiating with one another are characterized. In a contractarian approach agents are said to be concerned with the rational pursuit of their personal interests, whereas in a contractualist approach agents are concerned with reasonable agreement on the principles of justice that are to govern their joint lives. Freeman, for example, contrasts a Hobbesian contractarian approach, in which moral principles are agreed among rational agents to promote their own ends, with a contractualist approach in which there is unanimous agreement on certain principles without reference to the antecedent desires and interests of the agents.[19] Agents in a contractarian conception can therefore be thought of as rational in their decision-making processes; agents in a contractualist formulation can be thought of as reasonable. The rational is the non-moralized pursuit of self-interest; the reasonable is moralized agreement among agents on joint principles.

As an illustration of the importance of this distinction, consider the role that the principle of equality plays in different forms of social contract theory. Darwall, for example, points out that in a contractarian account the equality of the parties is merely a *de facto* equality, which may constrain the free choice of agents but which does not presuppose a sense of moral equality among the parties, as would be the case in a contractualist account.[20] So, while in a contractarian account agents will rationally need to reflect upon the threat-advantage of those with whom they are contracting, they do not have to weigh the interests of those others in their own deliberations apart from considerations of that threat-advantage.

Whether social theory is specified as contractualist or contractarian, or as being conducted as a reasonable discussion or as a process of bargaining, virtually all modern theorists see the idea of the contract as a purely hypothetical device. It is a thought-experiment undertaken by the theorist, rather than a process related to a functioning set of social and political institutions. Rawls presents this position clearly:

> In justice as fairness the original position of equality corresponds to the state of nature in the traditional theory of the social contract. This original position is not, of course, thought of as an actual historical state of affairs, much less a primitive condition of culture. It is understood as a purely hypothetical situation characterized so as to lead to a certain conception of justice.[21]

A few pages later, the point is reiterated in relation to the nature of the contractual agreement:

> In particular, the content of the relevant agreement is not to enter a given society or to adopt a given form of government, but to accept certain moral principles. Moreover, the undertakings referred to are purely hypothetical: a contract view holds that certain principles would be accepted in a well-defined initial situation.[22]

In short, the dominant and seemingly unambiguous answer in modern social contract theory is that the social contract is to be thought of as a purely hypothetical device of representation (although, as we shall see later in section 2.1, this seemingly unambiguous stance turns out to be more nuanced than it appears at first sight).

One function of social contract theory, according to a number of its proponents, is to provide a means for resolving questions that arise in the contest of justice. In the face of that contest, social contract theory can be regarded as a method of political ethics. That is to say, its function is to provide an intellectual device for determining principles of justice and enabling us to reconcile otherwise conflicting judgements and principles. This is a constructivist project. It involves constructing a theory such that we have a coherent understanding of how principles relate to one another and what the content of a political morality might be. It achieves this by formulating a theoretical decision procedure for ethics. In a canonical way, Rawls characterized this constructivist feature as follows:

> Political constructivism is a view about the structure and content of a political conception. It says that once, if ever, reflective equilibrium is attained, the principle of political justice (content) may be represented as the outcome of a certain procedure of construction (structure). In this procedure, as modeled in the original position (I.4), rational agents, as representatives of citizens and subject to reasonable conditions, select the public principles of justice to regulate the basic structure of society.[23]

Elsewhere Rawls develops the idea that the original position models the requirements of freedom and equality within the theory, and in this respect he has been followed by Barry and Scanlon.[24] Similarly, Gauthier is clear that the contractarian enterprise is constructivist since the normative structure of a society depends upon the deliberation of its members so that for norms to have force they must be ones 'that all members can recognize as ones they would themselves accept given appropriate circumstances'.[25]

Against this background of theorizing, I propose in this work a particular conception of social contract theory that offers an account of democratic justice. The proposed theory is contractarian rather than contractualist. It conceives the problem of forming a democratic contract for justice as one in which political equals have to negotiate common rules to their mutual advantage. The conception of rationality ascribed to the political agents is a non-moralized one. Participants in the democratic contract seek for the advancement of their own interests. The constraints that make the political agreement one of justice are not to be found in the motives of the agents, but in the circumstances in which they negotiate with potential associates.

The main reason for favouring a contractarian over a contractualist conception is methodological. In allowing for moralized reasoning to take place within the processes of contractual discussion and negotiation, the contractualist approach risks logical circularity. For example, in such approaches, contracting parties have to consider whether any particular proposal that they make is acceptable to other contracting parties, where acceptable means something like 'acceptable in the light of their reasonable interests'. The danger of logical circularity in such a case arises because the theorist will naturally want to build into the specification of reasonable claims an idea of what the person concerned is justly owed. But, if one takes a constructivist approach, specifying what persons are justly owed is the purpose of the theory. For this reason Matravers has suggested that contractualist theories are *faux* constructivist: such theories 'do not attempt to construct social or moral norms using non-moral building-blocks', but instead seek to render explicit what is implicit in the ideal of treating people with equal consideration.[26] Some contractualists are willing to accept this criticism. Thus, in response to the claim that his own contracualism was doing little work in justifying his principles of justice, Brian Barry conceded that the contractual device is 'helpful but not essential' and that it constitutes 'an attractive way of setting out a conception of justice of a broadly egalitarian nature', possibly with some degree of deductive rigour.[27] By contrast, within the contractarian view, the idea of a social contract is theoretically appealing to the extent to which it enables us to resolve questions about what justice requires without reference to prior assumptions of a strongly moralized nature. The contract is to be one among parties for their mutual advantage without their having internalized the interests of others in such a way that they are willing to adopt an impartial point of view.

There is, however, one particular way in which the proposed theory will differ from current approaches, whether contractualist or contractarian, namely in rejecting a purely hypothetical or a priori approach to the identification of the terms of political and economic association. Instead it adopts an empirical approach. In place of thought-experiments in which the theorist specifies the key features of the agents together with the conduct and outcomes of their negotiation, the theory will rely on examining a subset of political associations that satisfy, so far as is possible, the circumstances that make it plausible to hold that the upshot of the negotiation is one of justice. The task is to see whether the procedural constructivism implicit in modern contract theory can be vindicated by reference to such an empirical approach. Construing the social contract in empirical terms runs against the overwhelming strand of thinking in modern contract theory, but there are some significant and telling precedents (see section 2.1). It is this placing of a procedural theory of justice in the decision procedures of actual societies that will enable us to link the theory of the social contract with an understanding of democratic practice.

1.3. Social contract and democratic practice

Political democracy can be thought of as a set of institutions by which important issues of public concern depend in some systematic way upon the opinions of the associates within a political community, the vast majority of whom have equal political rights.[28] Political democracy can take a wide variety of forms depending, for example, on the scale of political organization at which it occurs (commune, city, or national level), and the historic traditions of the society in which democratic institutions are found. It can be direct, as when the members of a community determine their own rules through face to face discussion or voting, or indirect, as when political representatives agree legislation on behalf of their constituents. A democracy may involve a separation of powers between legislature and executive or a fusion. It may be federal or unitary. The definition of democracy as a set of institutions in which important issues of public concern depend in some systematic way upon the opinions of political associates is intended to be neutral between these various forms of democracy, as well as between the different ways in which the influence of political associates is exercised upon public choice, for example whether by discussion or voting, as well as the strength of association between public choices and expressed opinion at any one time.

The considerations that lie behind the justification of democracy in this broad sense involve a concern for common interests, the principle of political equality and a recognition of the fallibility of human decision making.[29] Common interests cannot be addressed without the exercise of collective authority. That collective authority should satisfy the principle of political equality. And, in coming to a conclusion as to how public choice is to be determined, there should be a recognition that human decision making is fallible, so that democratic procedures need to contain some error-correction mechanisms. It is this need for error-correction that highlights the importance of deliberation in a democracy. Deliberation is a way of securing public choices in the face of human fallibility; so its role is central to the way in which political democracy should function.

Just as social contract theory flourished in the late twentieth century, so have those theories of democracy that have stressed the role of political deliberation. According to this deliberative conception of democracy, the legitimacy and value of political decision making will be enhanced if citizens and political representatives take advantage of opportunities to engage in dialogue and discussion about matters of public concern. Deliberative democracy sees democratic institutions as dependent upon processes of discussion.[30] Political outcomes are legitimate if they are the outcome of deliberative participation by those subject to them.[31] From the point of view of citizens, deliberative democracy has been usefully formulated by Richardson as the claim that the political process should address each citizen as someone capable of joining in a discussion and that each can be a potential agent of political decision.[32] A number of virtues are claimed for deliberated political decisions. They are said to secure political legitimacy by their being more inclusive and representative, to be based on impartial rather than sectional perspectives, to express the value of public reason among free and equal citizens, and to institutionalize the idea that problems of collective choice should be resolved by argument rather than force or manipulation. Having these qualities, decisions that meet a suitable deliberative standard provide a reason for those subject to political authority to accept those decisions as legitimate, even when there is deep political disagreement within a society.

In seeking to link democratic practice to social contract theory, an inevitable question is how to construe the terms of that relationship, particularly if deliberation is made central to political decision making. One important strand of modern political theory links deliberative democratic theory with hypothetical contractualist theory. From this point of view, democracies can be understood as political systems in which citizens join together in discussions about their common interests seeking to approach problems in an impartial way on terms of equality. Negotiations in a hypothetical social contract can be thought of as a limiting case of democratic deliberation in which the distortions of impartiality induced by the circumstances of the real world are abstracted away, so that we are left with discussions based purely upon public reason as the consensus of the community. Conversely, it might be supposed that only a deliberative democracy in a strong sense, founded on the idea of reciprocity in offering public reasons for action, could provide a setting in which the sense of justice could be satisfied. In this context, it is not surprising, as Dryzek has noted, that Rawls concluded that his form of constitutional democracy should be understood as a deliberative democracy.[33] Taken in this way, democratic practice is a counterpart to reasonable contractual negotiations hypothetically conceived.

If we reject hypothetical contractualism, it follows that we cannot seek theoretically to link democratic practice and the social contract by reference to reasonable agreement for which a hypothetical contract is a limiting case. Deliberative democracy cannot be built upon a *faux* constructivism. Moreover, to the extent to which the results of hypothetical contractual reasoning are indeterminate, this will affect the confidence that we can have in our appraisal of the role of deliberation in a democracy. There are a number of incompatible ways of defining the setting of negotiation for the contracting parties, what the reasoning of the parties is in their negotiations and what assumptions they are presumed to make about the way in which the world operates. What might seem to be the limiting case of democratic practice turns out to have a number of indeterminate and incompatible theoretical specifications.[34]

There is a further reason for supposing that a concern with deliberative democracy is at odds with hypothetical contractualism. A contractualist theory abstracts from the imperfect circumstances in which public reasoning about common action takes place. In positing decision making under ideal conditions, a contractualist interpretation of social contract theory ignores the need to compare alternative policy regimes as they are found in the world of politics. For this reason, Sen has argued that, in framing a theory of justice in terms of a hypothetical contract, a Rawlsian approach focuses too much on the conception of an ideally just society and not sufficiently on the comparative analysis of how far justice is realized in different societies. Moreover, the ideal contractualist also ignores the possibility of disagreement in the original position, where people could equally reasonably take different views and propose different and incompatible principles of justice.[35] Hence, 'the demands of justice can be assessed only with the help of public reasoning' and, though 'there is an intimate connection between justice and democracy',[36] we should make the practice of democracy the basis for our account of justice, rather than seek to design political and economic institutions from an original position. In this view, the higher degree of abstraction to be found in hypothetical social contract theory, by contrast with the real world of deliberative democracy, is a hindrance in formulating a satisfactory account of justice. We do not need the concept of a social contract to understand justice; we need instead the practices of deliberative democracy. On this account, hypothetical contractualism adds nothing to deliberative accounts of democracy.

However, although Sen may be right about the disadvantages that attend a hypothetical version of social contract theory, it does not follow that we can simply substitute the perspective of public reasoning and political deliberation for a social contract. Democratic deliberation takes place under varying conditions, some of which will be conducive to justice and some not. There will be circumstances under which political negotiation and deliberation exemplify forms of justice and circumstances under which they do not. The crucial distinction is not that between those theories of justice that make political deliberation and negotiation foundational and those that do not. Rather, it is between those theories in which deliberation and negotiation take place in circumstances of equal power and advantage on the one hand and those that take place in circumstances of unequal power and advantage on the other.

An approach to justice in terms of equal bargaining advantage is sometimes looked upon sceptically by theorists of deliberative democracy. Deliberative democratic theory is often associated with a critique of what is taken to be the orthodox liberal democratic account of democracy in terms of preference aggregation—the view that politics is about who gets what, when, where, and how and in which the pulling and hauling of contesting forces decides the outcome. As Joshua Cohen has put it, echoing Rawls, even 'an ideal pluralist scheme, with equal bargaining power and no barriers to entry, cannot be reasonably expected to advance the common good as defined by the difference principle'.[37] On this understanding, politics may involve the aggregation of preferences but only insofar as those preferences are not taken as given and fixed but are instead seen to be a product of the political process itself arising through reflection and argument. However, in reply to this objection, it is possible to concede that preferences are not fixed and immutable within a political process without conceding that bargaining to mutual advantage is irrelevant to our theory of justice. We can separate the question of the extent to which political negotiation—whether in the form of bargaining, mutually accommodative discussion, or something in between—leads to preference change (it clearly does) from the question of whether we should model democratic deliberation under the circumstances of justice either as one of impartial reasoning among those who share an agreement motive or as negotiation among those who have a prudent concern for their own interests in a situation in which there is the possibility of mutual gain. Once we make this distinction, it is an open question whether equal bargaining power can deliver justice and the common good or not. To what extent can we understand justice by reference to a model that takes as its assumptions the common features of democratic politics, including the existence of permanent conflicts of interest among the members of a political association, even when they share other interests in common? It is this question that the theory of democratic justice seeks to answer.

1.4. The conception of society

One reason for exploring social contract theory conceived in empirical terms is that we can consider a social contract as a representation of the implicit logic in the normative order of a society. The claim that a social order is to be understood *as though* it were a social contract has been noted by Kenneth Arrow among others. Writing on the emergence of non-market systems of allocation, Arrow notes that:

> The price system is not, and perhaps in some basic sense cannot be, universal. To the extent that it is incomplete, it must be supplemented by an implicit or explicit social contract.[38]

On this account, any set of functioning markets will be embedded in a wider set of social institutions and practices, including the legal recognition of property titles and the moral practices of fair dealing and honesty in commercial transactions. Economic institutions do not arise simply as the outcome of the interactions of individuals within a market, but occur within a broader context of social organization. In a similar vein, Putnam's study of the variation of the performance of regional government within Italian democracy explains that variation in terms of a background civic culture of different regions, where civic culture derives from an implicit contractual logic:

> In the civic community associations proliferate, memberships overlap, and participation spills into areas of community life. The social contract that sustains such collaborations in the civic community is not legal but moral.[39]

As with Kenneth Arrow's observations on the embedding of the price system in a wider set of social relations, Putman is concerned with the way in which potentially competitive, and so mutually destructive, behaviour can be constrained by being embedded in a functioning cultural context that fosters and sustains the contribution that individuals make to the common good. In both accounts the idea is that competitive practices will work to the common advantage when they are embedded in a wider set of social relations that provide the conditions under which purely self-interested behaviour is discouraged.

Implicit social contracts do not always embody just relationships, however. In his discussion of the social bases of injustice, Moore uses the idea of an implicit social contract to reveal what is involved in the idea of outrage against a social order. On this account, underlying all forms of authority are tacit bargains: political rulers provide 'security against foreign and domestic depredation' in return for obedience and material contributions from subjects; the division of labour can be understood in terms of implicit contractual forms ranging from compulsion to persuasion; and a violation of the principle of reciprocity is the common element in the conception of 'a raw deal'.[40] All that is meant by understanding society as an implicit social contract is that the political legitimacy that any social order requires has to be built upon substantial agreement about the social bases of authority and property. Agreed social contracts can be hierarchical, so long as there is a legitimating set of beliefs that are widely accepted. Indeed, on Moore's account, societies are typified by injustices normally brought about because participants cannot envisage an alternative. Conversely, pressure to renegotiate the social contract suggests that dominant institutions are not serving the general interest to a sufficient degree. The contract may be one of political legitimacy but not of justice.

To say that the basic logic of social organization can be understood as if it were a social contract is to say that individuals have to accept certain collective practices and norms if their individual interests are to be secured. In this sense the basic institutions of a society may be regarded as the product of a social contract. Institutions are sets of rules, roles and relations forming 'identifiable practices consisting of recognized roles linked by clusters of rules or conventions governing relations among the occupants of those roles'.[41] In any society, individuals occupy different roles within these practices over the course of their lives, the rules defining their entitlements, duties, powers, and freedoms. An independent society is one whose members have significant control over the shaping of its basic institutions without external determination. This does not mean that a society has to be wholly self-sufficient to be independent. Its members may travel, trade, marry, and in various ways communicate with members of other societies. However, if it is to be independent, control of the institutions defining the structure of rules, roles, and relations within that society must depend to a significant degree on choices that are made by members of that society. To give sense to this conception, it is convenient to have in mind the model of a domestic legal order, the secondary rules of which are subject to change either by domestic institutions alone or by those non-domestic institutions, for example international covenants and agreements, into which the political authorities of the legal order have freely entered, on the model of Hart's account of a legal system.[42]

To be viable, a society must possess institutions that enable social cooperation to produce goods and services valued by its members. Through their command over these goods and services, individuals acquire interests, which can be defined in terms of such command. Individuals also have an interest in command over their person, including such things as secure freedom of movement; freedom of expression and communication; freedom to form households and enterprises with other individuals; and the freedom from invasion of their personality through protection of freedom of thought, conscience, and immunity from propaganda and brainwashing.

However, since social cooperation is a necessary condition for these individual interests, individuals also have a stake in the public interest, which is made up of the interests that they share in common with other members of society. To serve such interests, certain public goods need to be provided, including, at a minimum, a functioning system of law and order, defence from external armed threats, methods of adjudicating conflicts that arise between private interests, general literacy and education, protection from environmental hazards, management of common land and resources, sanitation and provision against communicable disease, a system of transport, agreed weights and measures, maps and geographical information systems and instruments of public communication together with a system of news reporting and recording that ensures that the use of political power is tested for its purpose and justification. Such public interests may be regarded by some members of society merely as the means necessary to protect and promote private interests. For example, a functioning system of private dispute adjudication and resolution may be regarded by some as only instrumentally valuable. An important question in social contract theory—and one to which we shall return in Chapter 8—is the extent to which participants in a social contract also acquire an interest in public institutions as a direct element in their own good, as when the members of a society take pride in the public buildings, thoroughfares, and cultural achievements of their own community, such pride being one element in their sense of democratic justice. To the extent to which these shared or common goods are important, the good of each depends upon the good of all.

The requirement for social cooperation does not eliminate conflict and competition, however. Indeed, in producing a surplus of goods and services greater than individuals could have secured in isolation, social cooperation increases some forms of competition and conflict by creating the conditions for conspicuous consumption, status competition, and the monopolization of power that may exist at any level of social and economic development. Such competition is positional in the sense that the enjoyment of a good on the part of one person is intrinsically and inversely related to the number of other people enjoying the same good. In any society where there is a sense of relative deprivation, or in which conspicuous consumption by some creates an incentive for others to engage in mutually frustrating competitive behaviour, such positional effects are pervasive. For example, some may want larger houses than others, but if all want larger houses, then building densities fall, towns expand and commuting times are longer, with investments made in property with low real returns in improvements in welfare.[43] If these competitive elements are not to become socially counter-productive, then institutions will be necessary to regulate and control their forms and effects, and the existence of these institutions will also be an element in the public interest that individuals share with one another.

Because the regulation of conflict and competition involves constraint, social institutions reduce the freedom of some individuals. However, as long as constraints on freedom can be rationalized in terms of the interests of the individuals to whom those constraints are applied in such a way that it can validly be said that it is protecting those persons' own share of the public interest, then they are justified from a social contract point of view. In an early exposition of contract theory, Grice captured this feature well by saying that to claim that an action was *prima facie* obligatory in a society was to claim that in that society it would be in everyone's interest to make a contract with everyone else to perform that action (when appropriate).[44] Thus, for Grice, it would not be true to say of someone for whom it was burdensome to keep a particular promise that it was in that person's interest to do so. However, it would be in their interests to make a contract with everyone else in which promise keeping was *prima facie* obligatory. In an analogous way, Gauthier frames the social contract enterprise as one in which society is seen as a cooperative venture to mutual advantage such that 'in certain situations involving interactions with others, an individual chooses rationally only in so far as he constrains his pursuit of his own interest or advantage to conform to principles expressing the impartiality characteristic of morality'.[45] Thus, in these approaches there is a reason—understood as valid by virtue of the extent to which it secures individuals' interests by protecting their share in the common good or public interest—for individuals to accept irksome social obligations. In this sense, the good of each is made to depend upon the good of all, but only because the good of all is made to depend upon the good of each.

The unjust social contracts of Barrington Moore can arise in various ways. The division of labour in households or in society at large may create conditions in which some individuals occupying particular roles have considerably more power than others, with them using that power for their own advantage in ways inconsistent with the common interest. For some, perhaps for many, labour may be hard, unremitting, or carried out under conditions of slavery, indenture, or exploitation. Those in positions of power in political or economic organization may abuse their authority. Whole social classes may be excluded from political influence or status. What would make for a just social contract? In answer to this question, we need to introduce Mill's idea that it is in a union of persons of not very unequal strength that the dominion of one over another can be avoided.[46] The idea of a just social contract is one in which the common rules that protect the public interests of a society reflect the approximate equality of power of its members. Of course, under such conditions, work undertaken by members of society could still be hard or unremitting, depending on the material circumstances their society faced, but it will be so in the form of a common enterprise (if only for limited purposes) rather than a structure of exploitation or oppression.

Equality in this context is an expression of equality of status or standing within the political system, rather than an entitlement to any particular share on the part of individuals to available goods and services.[47] The ideal involved is one that has sometimes been termed 'social equality'. This is a conception of equality in which, despite differences in material well-being or praise for personal achievements, there is no hierarchy of political status for different social classes and respect is accorded to individuals as partners in a social enterprise. Initially these egalitarian forms of relationship may only emerge through political struggle and the contest for access by different social groups to political power. Equality of democratic status is the power to help shape the social contract through the political relations of the institutions of governance in a society. That contract may comprise a regime under which returns to productive economic activity are unequal, so that during the course of their working lives individuals end up with different shares of resources. Of course, if individuals have to be offered reasons that credibly motivate their participation within the social contract, it is unlikely that inequalities in the command over resources can be allowed to become extreme. To ensure that the good of each is a condition of the good of all requires limits on the accumulation of property, but within a contractarian account there is no *a priori* commitment as to what those limits will be and no requirement that they conform to a specific principle of distribution.

The fundamental conception of society that lies behind social contract theory, then, is one in which the members of society share certain common interests and equality of status, but in which they also have competing and sometimes incompatible interests. The corresponding conception of the person requires a theory of rational human action. The key element in such a theory is the ability of persons to have a sense of their own interests on the one hand and the ability to make commitments to others to maintain common interests on the other. It follows from these twin requirements that rationality must be more than consistency of rank-ordered choice exhibited by agents at any particular time in the face of given alternatives. It must at least require that individuals be able to see enough of the consequences of their choice to make some present sacrifice in order to achieve some future good. This is compatible with saying that individuals always act from reasons thought of as their present desires, including their present desires for their future good. It is not to say that all action from present desires is effective in securing future good.

In practice, individuals may be prevented from achieving their own future good, because, although they are rational, their rationality is a bounded rationality. Herbert Simon, whose notion this is, characterized the idea in contradistinction to synoptic or Olympian rationality according to which individuals can identify all the feasible alternatives involved in a decision and can also identify all the relevant consequences of each of these alternatives.[48] By contrast, boundedly rational individuals have limited attention spans, can focus on only a limited range of relevant information at any one time, factor the world in which they have to act into discrete segments, and cannot foresee all the consequences of their actions.[49] One implication of taking persons as boundedly rational is that asymmetries of information among different individuals interacting in a common world are pervasive and a source of political difference. Even in public bureaucracies, which are supposed to share a common governmental orientation and where there are strong pressures to conformity, 'where you stand depends on where you sit'.[50] Another consequence is that, although individuals need to be able to make credible commitments to one another, if they are to protect and advance their common interests, the commitments into which they enter are necessarily incomplete contracts, in which important eventualities are not anticipated, since no party can foresee all the contingencies that may occur. Flexibility and the monitoring of performance thereby become essential.

Bounded rationality contrasts with standard game-theoretic accounts of rationality built upon models of games of poker or chess in which, in principle, all logically possible consequences of any move can be foreseen. In such models rational individuals are logically omniscient, even when they face uncertainty. They can foresee all logically possible moves, even if they cannot tell in advance which ones will actually occur. As Shackle put the matter in an early critique of game-theoretic notions of rationality, in 'the *games of chance* universe of ideas is the notion of the existence and the attainability of a list, complete and known to be complete, of all the possible outcomes of an action'.[51] One reason for holding that individuals *cannot* be logically omniscient is that they are capable of innovation and creativity in thought. Innovation and creativity require individuals to have inventive capacities, from which it in turn follows that no individual can foresee all the consequences of their or others' actions, let alone all the logically possible consequences of those actions. Insofar as creative innovation enables societies to move from suboptimal situations, in which best use is not being made of available resources, to better arrangements, any account of collective improvement must allow for the possibility of unanticipatable thought. Open texture in the description of the future limits the ability of agents to specify in advance a contingent course of action. In consequence, bounded rationality also means that individual and collective reasoning is defeasible. Reasoning is defeasible when its premisses are prone to revision in the light of new information. In the face of innovative or unforeseen choices by others, individuals will find that they need to revise their decision premisses since assumptions that they made when they deliberated about the course of action they should choose turn out to be partial or mistaken. Defeasibility is thus a recognition of fallibility and requires a conception of rationality in which there is a built-in correction mechanism, such that decision premisses can be revised in the light of new and unanticipatable information.

The conception of individuals and society presupposed in the theory of the contract for democratic justice includes the ideas of society as a system of rules, roles, and relations requiring both norms of cooperation to mutual advantage and institutions for the regulation of competition. Individuals living in a society are only boundedly rational and so their individual and collective reasoning is defeasible, being liable to revision in the face of experience and the particularity of circumstance. Since social cooperation involves reasoning, we have to take this element of boundedness into account in our theory. A satisfactory account of obligatory norms in society requires there to be suitably prudential reasons for individuals to constrain their otherwise free action. That contract will be just when it is made under conditions of a rough equality of power among participants. We thus have the ideas of common interests (the focus of the cooperative element), approximate equality (the constraining element on competition) and reasoning towards common collective action (which is nonetheless bounded and defeasible).

How does such a conception of society, particularly one stated in a highly abstract way, contribute to a theory that will bring together an account both of justice in property and of democratic deliberation? One answer is that it serves to highlight the significant elements of society that will form models for such a theory. Actual societies vary in their regimes for property and political control. However, there is an empirically observable subset that meets the conditions of common interest, approximate equality, and rational collective action, such that we can use their workings as a model, and therefore evidence, of what are the requirements for just and democratic design. The chief example to which I shall appeal are successful common property resource regimes (see section 2.3). In accounts of successful common property regimes, we can understand how the parties will reason about public purposes and what concessions and burdens they will accept as fair. To the extent to which this is done democratically, such models also supply us with an account of what legitimate political action requires.

None of this means that institutions present in the circumstances of justice can be transposed in a straightforward way into other settings. A model in this sense is not a source of institutional prescription, but a device for thinking through the logical connections of a theory. The contractarian logic of well-functioning common property resource regimes provides some indication of what the requirements of justice and democracy are. Such regimes define norms, rules, and conventions that govern the basic terms of cooperation among actors. Regimes that meet the conditions of protecting and advancing common interests under conditions of approximate equality where participating agents are reflective and innovative provide a model for what we should understand as a just and democratic society.

Our approach aims to bring together considerations of the good and considerations of the right in a complementary way. The Kantian turn in modern political theory has led to the dominance of the claim that 'the right is prior to the good' in a theory of justice. What this means is that it is inconsistent with a theory of justice to sacrifice individuals to the calculus of some social good.[52] Yet, as Hart argued, we cannot simply assume that the right is prior to the good in all cases: there is an unresolved tension between a concern for rights in political theory, taken as a way of protecting individuals from the unrestrained consequences of aggregative reasoning, and the justifiable concerns of utilitarianism, which involve both common interests and the balancing of claims to rights when they are incompatible.[53] Since any democratic form of government requires the notion of a public purpose, which may impose burdens upon individuals, reconciling justice and democracy will require a teleological element in our theory of justice. A contractarian conception of society secures that teleological component by ensuring that the social good is conceived as the shared interest of individuals taken severally.

However, the conception of deliberative rationality also enables us to see the democratic component of just regimes. The public purposes that are pursued within regimes are formulated under conditions of bounded rationality, in which the revision of those purposes in the light of unanticipated information is an integral part. One advantage of focusing upon empirical examples of social contract regimes is that we do not wish away the defeasible deliberative rationality of agents via some assumption about deductive rationality. Agents face the world, especially the collective world, not only unsure of the outcomes of their actions but often unsure about the ways in which they are to pursue their own goals and purposes. In this space there is much room for collective deliberative rationality.

1.5. The ideological context

The conflict between a deontological and a teleological view of justice is replicated in the conflict between individualism and collectivism that has dominated ideological controversy since the industrial revolution.[54] Those on the individualist side have stressed the connection between freedom of contract and a weak state, well exemplified in an address given in 1884 to the Liberty and Property Defence League in which freedom is said to be 'the true solution for many of our troubles—the utmost freedom that can be given to industry—the utmost freedom for a man to contract, or to bestow his labour upon any subject that he chooses, without State interference'.[55] By contrast, those on the collectivist side stressed the advantages of cooperative arrangements in which communal activities predominated over private ones and in which, in the words of Graham Wallas, there would need 'to be owned by the community the land in the widest sense of the word, and the materials of those forms of production, distribution, and consumption, which can conveniently be carried on by associations larger than the family group'.[56] Wallas even thought that in a socialist society family meals would eventually become a communal matter in which the 'waste and discomfort' of separate family preparation would be overcome.[57] In short, individualists have favoured commercial contract, private property, and the price mechanism together with a minimal state as the organizing economic principles of society, whereas collectivists have favoured the coordination of production, distribution, and exchange through the instrument of democratic public political authority.

Although the contrast between individualism and collectivism provides a broad orientation towards ideological conflict, it needs to be qualified in many respects. For example, the search for a 'middle way' between thoroughgoing individualism and unabashed collectivism has been a persistent feature of ideological thought since at least the end of the nineteenth century.[58] The links between such ideological discussions and competing interpretations of social contract theory are equally wide and complex. Social contract theory has been deployed by various theorists to justify such collectivism as is implicit in the institutions and practices of the welfare state, where the welfare state is understood as a means by which the state takes responsibility for the provision of social and economic security as well as goods such as education and health care.[59] Although he never fully developed this aspect of his theory himself, this would also be an implication of Barry's social contract theory.[60] By contrast, other versions of social contract theory have been interpreted as endorsing a strong form of economic individualism. Though recognizing that in many ways it would be too simple a reading, Braybrooke noted that those on the libertarian right would rejoice at Gauthier's broad commitment to property rights, the enthusiasm for the market, and its denunciation of 'free riders' and 'parasites' in *Morals by Agreement*.[61] In yet another contrast, in the Preface to the revised edition of *A Theory of Justice* Rawls famously says that one of the two main changes he would want to make from the first edition would be to distinguish more sharply the idea of a property-owning democracy from the idea of a welfare state, suggesting that a fundamental principle of a property-owning democracy is that all citizens should be placed in a position where they can interact with one another from a position of independence and equality rather than their being the recipients of transfers determined by a political elite exercising political and economic control.[62] O'Neill and Williamson wonder whether Rawls's account might not serve as a vision of a society that would constitute an alternative both to the welfare state and what they term 'the predominant neoliberal paradigm'.[63]

With its fundamental intellectual focus upon the terms of social cooperation that individuals could rationally accept, social contract theory should offer an account of how to reconcile individualism and collectivism. It should also have implications for our understanding of markets, private property, democratic authority, and the way in which these practices are related. In what follows, I suggest that a strong individualism also requires collective provision for common interests. The choice is not between a political economy in which all citizens should be placed in a position where they can interact with one another from a position of independence and equality as against a political economy in which they are the recipients of transfers determined by a political elite. Democratic contractarianism endorses a welfare state making provision for social savings with policy determined by a broadly representative legislature. Liberal and individualist freedoms of trade and movement combined with the protection of civil liberties may be married to collectivist protection against economic and social insecurity where that is necessary. Although such a set of institutional implications cannot be established deductively, their justifiability is a plausible implication of a prudent social contract. To establish such plausibility, we first need to consider what an empirical model of the social contract might look like.

CHAPTER 2

The democratic social contract

2.1. Social contracts and democracy

According to social contract theory the institutions of a society may be thought of as though they embodied the terms of a social contract. A theory of social contract, from this point of view, models social relations and so makes explicit the implicit rules of social order. The rules, roles, and relations of social and political practices may be understood as if they had been agreed by individuals. Behind this line of analysis is the insight that some institutions and practices, most notably markets and other economic relations that rest on a generalized egoism, also presuppose a broader set of rules, conventions, institutions, and practices maintaining the normative conditions that support their working. Thus, in order to function well, markets require of their participants a disposition towards fair and honest dealing so that trade takes place in ways that are mutually beneficial. Markets themselves, however, cannot supply such dispositions. Without broader institutional and cultural constraints, generalized egoism leads to a breakdown in social cooperation to everyone's disadvantage. If we think of the logic of social organization as one in which individuals need to cooperate with one another, restraining the short-term pursuit of their own ends for longer term advantage, then one way of modelling this logic is in terms of an implicit social contract. Where social institutions, including institutions of competition, rely upon a background set of institutions and norms that constrain behaviour within the competition, they can be said to have a social contract.[1]

To say that a social contract is necessary to avoid the breakdown associated with lack of social cooperation is not to say that all cases in which social cooperation is achieved rely upon fair or just social contracts. Social contracts, implicit or explicit, may secure a minimum of order and security but still embody unjustifiable patterns of social and economic relations. The conditions of political legitimacy are logically distinct from those of social justice.[2] Moore, for example, was able to speak of the implicit social contract for societies that were not only highly unequal, but also obscured from its disadvantaged members the objective possibilities of advance that were latently present.[3] In those societies the implicit social contract was asymmetric, its terms arising from the imposition of the more powerful on the less powerful. If stability marks an implicit social contract that binds the members of a society, the contract to which the members are bound may be stable but unjust. It is stable because its weaker members have no alternative but to accept the terms that are imposed upon them. It is unjust because, had they been stronger, they could have negotiated better terms.

The impulse towards the hypothetical *a priori* approach in modern contract theory arose in part from an attempt to abstract away from unequal power relations in the definition of social justice, by placing the imaginary individuals who were to people society in a situation of negotiation and choice that secured their freedom and equality. As Rawls put it, 'the conditions for a fair agreement on the principles of political justice between free and equal persons must eliminate the bargaining advantages that inevitably arise within the background institutions of any society from cumulative social, historical, and natural tendencies'.[4] It is this impulse that motivates the use of the veil of ignorance in hypothetical contract theory. Behind a veil of ignorance no party is in a position to tailor specific institutional proposals to his or her advantage. In pursuit of this programme, the dominant analysis of social contracts among modern theorists has been to take the contract as an idea of reason, one offering a thought-experiment for thinking about issues of economic justice and political constitutions. Actual social contracts may be unjust; hypothetical social contracts will be just because the terms and conditions under which they are negotiated are fair. Yet, with conflicting ways of characterizing fair terms and conditions, as well as different ways of specifying the rationality of the agents in a social contract, first-order disputes about justice and property become displaced onto second-order disputes about how to construct a theoretically defensible model.[5]

However, we need not be caught between a world of actual implicit social contracts, contracts that reflect the balance of power and class advantage in society, and a world of purely hypothetical social contracts, contracts that are free of power by construction. There is a third way. Some empirically realized implicit social contracts emerge in conditions of a balance of power such that their outcome can be interpreted as being just. In particular, if agents, prudent about their own resources and future, negotiate about matters of common interest, each having similar bargaining advantages, then we have reason to think that the agreements to which they come will embody rules and principles that are just. (We certainly have as much *prima facie* reason to conclude this as to think that hypothetical social contracts will yield a plausible account of justice.) It was the possibility of finding circumstances in which political union was premissed on relations of equal power that led to John Stuart Mill's speculation about the ancient republics. According to Mill, being founded by compact among persons of approximately equal strength, the arrangements that they made for the political union of citizens ensured the subordination of force to common judgement. Even if relations with slaves remained ones of domination, as they did, the republics still provided the context in which a full doctrine of human equality could emerge among the Stoics.[6] If we are looking for a third way between actual, but unjust, social contracts and hypothetical, but indeterminate, just contracts, we can find it by examining the variation among societies in respect of the balance of power among their members. The theory of democratic justice seeks to exploit this empirical variation to identify instances of actual societies that embody such sufficient equality of power that their social contracts can be thought just, in the same way that, on Mill's analysis, the social contracts of the ancient republics provided the first examples of political relations built on principles and not force.

This approach addresses the concerns raised by Sen.[7] For Sen, the framing of questions of justice in terms of hypothetical contract theory focused insufficiently on the analysis of the comparative justice of societies and ignored the possibility that agents in the hypothetical original position could reasonably disagree with one another. For these reasons, according to Sen, we should make the practice of democracy the basis for our theory of justice. Yet this cannot be the whole story, given the variations in performance among democracies. We can sort political systems into democracies and non-democracies by reference to suitably defined criteria. Democratic societies differ from non-democratic or authoritarian societies. However, they also differ in themselves with respect to their structures of power and advantage. As a consequence, the concept of democracy can be understood not only as a sortal term but also as a scalar one.[8] That is to say, above the line that separates democracies from authoritarian regimes, there is significant variation. To the extent to which we can appraise their performance and institutions, some democratic political systems will perform better than others. For example, some democracies manage a wide representation of legitimate interests together with relatively uncorrupt public administration, whereas others marginalize less powerful groups or have to cope with inefficient and corrupt officials. Naturally, there are disputes about the criteria by reference to which we define the scale of achievement of different democracies. (Should we assume, for example, that political societies with a higher level of direct citizen participation in decision making, say through devices like referendums on public policy issues, are necessarily 'more democratic' than societies that make such decisions through elected representatives?) Yet, however complex the issues about the suitability of particular criteria, some democracies perform better in their workings than others, as assessed by democratic values. Those that perform better on these democratic criteria have a greater claim to making political decisions that are justifiable than those that perform less well.

This is particularly so in the case of political deliberation, which is of special interest in the light of Sen's critique. In the original work on deliberative democracy Bessette made a descriptive claim, to the effect that the United States was in practice a deliberative democracy.[9] By this he meant that decisions were arrived at not simply by a process of preference aggregation, with the hauling and pulling of different political forces determining the outcome, but also involved discussion and reasoning. However, even if one accepts this assessment, it still leaves open the question of how well the deliberation is performed. In a notable comparative contribution Jürg Steiner and his colleagues have subjected different democracies to evaluation in terms of the deliberative quality of their principal legislative institutions.[10] The analysis suggests that, even if we accept that the US is a deliberative democracy, the quality of its legislative deliberation is lower than in other mature democracies such as Germany and Switzerland. Since the quality of deliberative reasoning is an essential element in any account of the practical rationality of collective decision making, this finding, if it can be substantiated, has clear implications for the comparative appraisal of political institutions and regimes within actually functioning democracies. If we are looking to the practice of democracy to define criteria of justice, then we need to focus on those democracies that perform well by reference to appropriate criteria.

All theories of social justice, whether grounded in democratic deliberation or in an appeal to a social contract, make reference to contrary-to-fact claims. Identifying the respects in which a society is unjust, and so identifying what changes would improve it, involves a contrary-to-fact subjunctive conditional. A theory that appeals to the results of a democratic deliberative procedure adds a second contrary-to-fact conditional, namely specifying a procedure according to which persons could agree on principles of justice, including comparative principles. In this respect, democratic deliberation as a criterion of justice is no different from social contract theory. The distinction between the two does not depend on whether there is a reference to contrary-to-fact conditionals or not. The difference lies in the grounds upon which a claim of justice is made. Whereas contractualism projects principles of justice from a purely hypothetical situation of choice, deriving standards from an *a priori* thought-experiment to determine what hypothetical contracting parties would agree, democratic contractarianism looks to deliberation made under conditions in which power is balanced among social groups.

There is a further reason for looking at particular cases of democratic deliberation. Brian Barry once noted that the *a priori* method of purely hypothetical contract theory will not take us very far as a method of political ethics. If our aim it to resolve disagreements over the content of justifiable political principles, the *a priori* method may simply end up displacing those first-order disagreements onto second-order disagreements as to how best the hypothetical contract is to be modeled. However, this does not mean that we should give up on the constructivist ambitions of social contract theory. By contrast with the *a priori* method, Barry suggests that we might adopt the empirical method to determine what parties to a social contract would agree, a method which he described in a passage worth quoting at length:

> The empirical method starts from observation rather than pure thought. It is animated by the consideration that actual societies approximate more or less closely the conditions . . . that I shall refer to for convenience as 'the circumstances of impartiality'. Thus, a society in which each section of the population has its own organizations and organs of communication to articulate its interests and aspirations is closer to the circumstances of impartiality than one in which, say, business is well organized but labor is not, and in which almost all the organs of mass communication are owned and controlled by the rich. Similarly, a political system in which parties represent the distinctive interests and aspirations of different groups is closer to the circumstances of impartiality than one in which all successful candidates have either to have money or to be acceptable to those who have it. Again, a society in which there is a good deal of fellow feeling for other citizens will be closer to the circumstances of impartiality than one in which many people are unmoved by the lot of sections of the population with which they do not identify. And, finally, a culture in which politics is widely regarded as a matter of debate rather than as a game–where arguments are thought of as more than the window-dressing for self-interest–will obviously be closer to the circumstances of impartiality.[11]

On Barry's account, the circumstances of impartiality resemble, so far as the world allows, the conditions of a hypothetical impartial social contract, but they differ from an *a priori* approach in providing a source of observable evidence about what political associates would determine as the conditions of their collective life.

The same idea is picked up by Barry in a more extended discussion in section 16 of *Justice as Impartiality* where he develops the notion of the circumstances of impartiality as an empirical counterpart to the Scanlonian original position and where the guiding idea is 'that just laws and policies are more likely to arise in actual societies the closer they come to instantiating these hypothetical conditions'.[12] What, on this view, characterizes a political culture of impartiality and reasonableness? For Barry the answer is that policy making needs to be transparent and open so that measures are consulted on widely and with a real chance that the consultation will make a difference. Citizens need to be well informed and educated, with no monopoly of the means of communication and with public funding of political parties. Policy makers need to respect expert opinion. Committees in the legislature need to be strong relative to the executive, with weakly disciplined political parties so that legislators can follow the logic of the argument, a pattern that will be facilitated by multi-member constituencies using PR with a low threshold of representation. Empirically, the conditions under which political decision making is governed by a norm of reasonableness are to be found 'in some of the smaller Western European countries such as the Netherlands and Scandinavia'.[13]

In Barry's approach, those societies that approximate the circumstances of impartiality are empirical counterparts to a purely hypothetical social contract defined in an *a priori* way. Because we cannot be certain in the hypothetical model how the contracting parties would reason, we use the counterpart as a control on our *a priori* theorizing. For Barry, this is not to say that the societies that are the empirical counterparts to a hypothetical model have a contractual basis, for example that their origin can be traced back to a particular constitutional moment. Neither the Netherlands nor any of the Scandinavian societies was historically founded on a social contract negotiated in conditions of impartiality. Rather the argument is that, whatever their history, their political practices resemble the conditions that we would want to specify in a social contract for justice.

However, if we are prepared to go this far, why not go further and simply substitute for hypothetical thought-experiments suitably specified political systems in appropriate empirical circumstances? Going the extra mile requires the assumption that there is a structural affinity between the social relations that make for justice among persons and the political relations that defines a democratic society of equals. There are significant, if not frequent, flashes of this approach visible at various times in political theory, quite apart from Mill's example of the ancient republics as founded on a mutual compact. When, in the Putney Debates on the Agreement of the People, Rainborough said that 'the poorest he' that lived in England had a life to lead as 'the greatest he' and explicitly linked this claim to the principle of political equality, he was expressing this affinity.[14] Hannah Arendt saw the creation of the American republic as the establishment of a new political order that embodied, if not a social contract explicitly, the 'few elementary truths on which this theory rests'.[15] Meiklejohn used the experience of the New England town meeting to illustrate the meaning of freedom of speech in a community of political equals whose founding goes back to the Pilgrim Compact in *The Mayflower*.[16]

However, perhaps the most striking example of the use of an historical example to model the principles of justice is to be found in Rawls's account of how the US Supreme Court can be regarded as an instrument of deliberative democracy. Rawls characterized the establishment of the US constitution as an exercise of the constituent power of a body of citizens to establish a new regime which fixed 'once and for all certain constitutional essentials', especially equal civil and political rights and the rule of law. Once this original contract was established, the task of the Supreme Court was to apply and extend the relevant constitutional principles to matters of public policy and concern, whilst still embodying the 'political ideal of a people to govern itself in a certain way'. In short, the founding of the American republic involved a commitment to a continuing constitutional contract.[17] For someone like Rawls whose official account of social contract theory made it purely hypothetical, this is a remarkable line of argument. Be that as it may, and putting this example alongside those of Arendt and Meiklejohn and the broader current of ideas in which they can be located, there are certainly precedents for identifying an intellectual affinity between the idea of political communities that function as self-governing republics with the idea that such communities rest upon a social contract the terms of which define a just political order. Barry's proposal for an empirical method of social contract analysis can therefore be located in broader strands of political thinking about political organization and the idea of a social contract.

Within this broad approach it obviously makes a difference as to which societies we take as our selected examples. Barry's own examples prompt the question as to how far the circumstances of justice, specified by Barry in terms of impartiality, require a certain level of economic development or a certain historically specific political culture. Consider, for example, the statistically significant association between political democracy and the historical legacy of protestantism.[18] It is not difficult to imagine how the protestant ethic of the smaller countries of north-western Europe could have shaped societies in such a way that political equality, a rationalistic problem-solving frame of mind, and a culture of debate rather than the imposition of authority became dominant elements in their political practices and arrangements. If we add to this the imperative of making social peace in order to avoid mutually destructive conflict, as in the Dutch Pacification of 1917 or the Crisis Agreement in Sweden between the Social Democrats and the Farmers League in 1933, we can see how political power could be institutionalized in such a way that all significant social groups felt that their views and opinions were reflected in collective political decision making. By the same token, however, the examples also raise the question of how far they can provide a more general model for societies that have had very different histories. The circumstances that make these societies what they are cannot be replicated elsewhere. If the empirical method is really to be of use, we have to think about how it is to be specified and what conditions any putative contract that uses the empirical method ought to meet.

Moreover, we need to detach the empirical method from Barry's own contractualist theoretical commitments. Barry rejected justice as mutual advantage for his own reasons, arguing that the value of human equality could only be recognized in an impartialist analysis. We do not have to follow him in this regard. Indeed, one can argue that, rather than embed the concern for equality in the putative motivations of the contracting parties, it is better to represent the concern for equality in the way in which the social contract is constructed, in particular in finding societies in which there is roughly equal power among participants. This approach has some claim, at least, to being a form of authentic constructivism, as opposed to the *faux* constructivism identified by Matravers.[19] Obviously such an approach imposes an extra constraint upon the selection of suitable empirical models, but if that constraint can be met, it would anchor our reasoning about justice more firmly in empirical evidence. It is also arguably the approach we should take if we wish for a theory of democratic justice, since democratic political institutions quintessentially enable different social groups to bargain and negotiate to mutual advantage over their legitimate but conflicting interests.

2.2. Procedural democracy

If we are going to reason according to the proceduralist ambitions of social contract theory, and we are going to use political democracies as empirical models of just social contracts, we need to formulate our concept of democracy in procedural terms. In this mode, to say that a political society is democratic is to say that it meets at least four conditions: firstly, it is self-governing (to a significant degree) in the sense that it has final control over its own political agenda; secondly, its collective choices determine key elements of the basic structure of social and economic organization; thirdly, it operates according to a principle of political equality; and fourthly, its members are capable of reasoning their way to solutions for collective action problems.[20]

For a polity to be democratic, it should, firstly, be self-governing in the sense that it has the final say over its own political agenda, at least to a significant degree. This means that no other association shapes its agenda, a condition that would not obtain, for example, if the polity were merely the province of a higher political authority and the higher authority determined significant issues on the political agenda. To be sure, maintaining final control over a polity's political agenda faces practical difficulties of realization in conditions of economic and environmental interdependence. No political community can completely escape some form of interdependence and many small countries with open economies have very restricted room for manoeuvre in terms of their policy choices, just as formally independent communities that suffer cross-border environmental damage may also have very limited choices. Nonetheless, even in situations of interdependence, there is a significant difference between a situation in which a polity has formal authority to decide on important matters of public policy and situations in which it does not. The study of corporatist policy making in small countries with open economies shows how much room for manoeuvre may be secured in one important class of cases.[21] In legal terms, the condition of self-government does not mean that a polity refuses to enter into international agreements, but it does mean that the authority of those agreements derives from the agreement of the polity. *Pacta sunt servanda* makes sense as a principle of international obligation because such pacts have been deliberately entered into by those who are free to determine their choices.

The condition of collective self-legislation requires that the political system be able to determine the key elements of the basic structure of the economic and social organization within which its members live. This means that the polity should be able to determine its own criminal law and other forms of legislation that control and limit the actions of associates. It also means that the polity should be able to determine those secondary rules that facilitate the transaction of business and civil relationships more generally, including such matters as the provisions for marriage and divorce, the age of majority and thus the conditions under which people can enter into independent legally enforceable relationships with others, the ownership and transfer of property, corporate personality, and the legal liability of corporations. An important set of items under this heading include the determination of the political constitution, covering such matters as the specification of the legislative procedures by which rules and laws are made, the conditions for holding public office, the limits of political authority as exemplified in such instruments as bills of rights and the institutions and processes by which constitutional revisions can be made.

It may be argued that the requirement that a polity should be in a position to determine the basis structure of its social and economic organization rests upon a controversial political ideal. Influential strands of modern political thought have questioned the role of collective self-legislation in the determination of the basic structure of social and economic organization, proposing instead a more individualistic view. In place of such collective self-legislation, they have suggested that social relations be viewed as the outcome of the sum of choices that particular individuals make in respect of their relations with others. Thus Hayek criticized the idea of parliamentary sovereignty and contrasted a planned society with a society viewed as a matter of spontaneous order. Oakeshott distinguished civil association and enterprise association as rival accounts of the state, the former being more favourably viewed than the latter. Nozick's hypothetical reconstruction of the emergence of a minimal state saw political authority as the result of a series of bilateral trades between individuals and protective associations, one of which became dominant.[22] In all these accounts, the principle of equality is understood as one of equality before the law. According to Oakeshott, for example, the members of the civil condition relate to one another 'as suitors to a judicial court'.[23] In Nozick, individuals are protected, in a quasi-legal way, by private protective associations, who mutate over time into a dominant protective association and then transform into the state. For Hayek, the fundamental principle of constitutional liberty is that individuals be allowed to pursue their own purposes, limited only by rules of general application. In all cases, the equality of persons is understood as being subject to common rules, but not subject to collective self-legislation.

One way of thinking about these theories is to see them as giving theoretical priority to the idea of government by the rule of law in a purely judicialized form that makes collective deliberation and determination of the basic structure marginal to policy making.[24] In the ideal form of such a theory, judges derive legal authority either from a doctrine of natural rights or from pre-existing and traditional codes, but not from legislated statute. Collective deliberation and legislation is attenuated because society is seen as a collection of separate individuals rather than members of a body for whom some issues are matters of common concern.

Sidgwick noted a major problem with any system of government in which there is no legislative body, and consequently in which there are no explicitly formulated legislative rules, namely that it leaves a large penumbra of uncertainty surrounding individual legal obligations.[25] Courts proceed by making decisions on the individual cases that are brought before them. Although their decisions are binding as precedents within a common law system, they do not seek to anticipate the future judgements of courts on related matters by making rules that clearly demarcate the class of cases that are covered. In the absence of legislation, members of a society may be left in doubt as to what their rights and liabilities are. In addition to Sidgwick's concern, we can also note that such a system of government can only react, and not anticipate, certain classes of policy problem. It has no way of dealing with the cumulatively undesirable consequences of individual interactions that taken on their own are quite legitimate. Social problems such as environmental pollution, traffic congestion, and urban sprawl arise as the cumulative effect of a series of individual actions. In the absence of any legislative capacity to regulate the whole series of actions, and not simply particular instances, individuals in a society may find themselves worse off than they otherwise need be.

However, in the present context, the issues raised by the individualist account of collective self-legislation are conceptual rather than substantive. It is a feature of such accounts that democratic political authority has no special standing. Governments do not have a formal relationship of accountability to the governed and this is built into the structure of the theory. Consider the emergence of the minimal state in Nozick through processes of bilateral negotiation between individuals and protective associations and the emergence of a dominant protective association by virtue of its relative power. Leave aside any doubts about the plausibility of the story. Even were a state to emerge in the way Nozick supposed, such a process of state formation would not imply that the resulting polity would be democratic. It would have whatever constitutional form resulted from the choices that had been made between individuals and the protective associations with whom they had contracted. In short, if we wish for a definition of democracy, we have to include the condition of collective self-legislation, and the particular form of individualist theory that is sceptical of the justification of collective self-legislation establishes that point by virtue of the lacuna in its own account of political authority.[26] Rather than showing that the condition of collective self-determination is unnecessary to an account of democracy, strongly individualist theories of political authority show the contrary.

The third defining feature of a democratic polity is that it is a system whose associates enjoy equal political standing. There are two dimensions to equal standing: the first is the degree of inclusiveness within a political association and the second is the relative influence that anyone included can have in the making of collective decisions. It is possible to regard inclusiveness as a separate condition from that of other aspects of political equality, as does Dahl.[27] In some cases there can be good reasons for treating the idea of inclusiveness in this way, but if we wish to treat the idea of political equality in a general way, distinct for example from the idea of equal voting, then it makes sense to regard inclusiveness as one aspect of political equality.

The key requirement of inclusiveness is that all those who fall within the authority of the collective self-determination of the polity should have the same standing as to how that collective self-determination is exercised. This requirement can be rationalized in various ways. One is simply by reference to an argument of self-protection: if there are some groups who are subject to the collective self-determination of the polity but not able to influence the way in which that self-determination is exercised, then they would obviously be liable to exploitation or oppression. Another way of rationalizing inclusion is based upon the idea of individuals or groups being members of the polity, where the idea of membership is taken in a rich sense to mean not only being part of but also to fulfilling all the roles that members are expected to play. Where there are exceptions made to the principle of inclusion, those exceptions should rely upon reasons that can be justified. For example, even in the most inclusive political system children below a certain age are precluded from the exercise of power, as are short-term residents, tourists, and those lacking the requisite mental capacity. Insofar as such exceptions can be justified, it is by reference to the requirement of each included individual having either sufficient competence or a requisite stake in society.

Taken on its own, the principle of inclusion does not specify the unit of standing. In modern democracies, the usual assumption is that the unit is the individual. However, the principle of inclusion does not have to be read in this way. On some theories of interest, one could say that the principle was satisfied if households were the unit of representation, so long as all affected households were given political standing. In other contexts, work groups might be the unit of representation. By itself, the principle of inclusion can be understood to cover all of these cases, and an independent theory of interests is required to say why it is individuals rather than any other unit to which the principle of inclusion applies.

The second dimension of political equality concerns the relative influence that associates have in the exercise of collective decisions. One way of thinking about relative degrees of influence is in terms of voting. One could think about voting purely in formal terms, on the model of 'one person, one vote', or one could think about it in terms of actual influence, say the probability that one's vote or votes will make a difference to the same degree as anyone else's vote. These two ideas are not the same. In a committee of three voters where two voters have five votes each and one voter has one vote, the power to decide is still equal provided that decisions are made by a majority and there is no sinister interest coalition among those voters who have five votes. There is, in fact, no easy way of ensuring an allocation of votes that ensures that all voters have an equal probability of being decisive. More importantly, equal voting is a derivative idea from that of political equality. If a political community makes its decisions through discussion rather than voting, then equal voting rights are unnecessary for equality of political standing so long as members have equal rights to participate in the discussion. Equal voting rights may not even be sufficient if we allow, no doubt contentiously, any plausibility to John Stuart Mill's claim that we can have equality of political inclusion without equality of voting rights.[28]

A stronger version of equal standing arises from the case where each associate has the power to block a collective agreement. Instead of the model of equal voting, in which each associate is given an equal chance of securing an outcome that they favour, and so an equal chance of having an outcome that they do not favour imposed upon them, it is possible for a political community to operate on the rule that each has a right to block any decision other associates favour. If the community uses a system of voting, this gives each participant a right of veto over any move from the status quo. If the community operates by discussion, then the norm is that no decision is taken unless there is consensus. Such a rule is likely to make sense only where the status quo is reasonably tolerable to all associates, or where no one can gain a disproportionate advantage by holding out against a collective decision until they secure a disproportionate share of the joint benefits.

That there should be different ways of institutionalizing the idea of equal political standing should not be surprising. Collective choices need to be made in many different circumstances and for many different reasons. One important element in any choice as to which particular scheme to implement turns on the extent to which associates are prone to engage in strategic behaviour, using their political power to manipulate the process to their own advantage.

For example, veto power poses less danger of misuse among the members of a community linked by strong bonds of ideological or religious sentiment, than among those who merely have commercial relations with one another. What is important is that, however the principle is institutionalized, political equality is defined in procedural terms, rather than moralized ones. We do not start with a strong principle of equality understood, for example, in terms of human dignity.[29] If we are hoping to use the construction of the democratic contract to capture the sense of justice, we need instead to relate the idea of political equality to the practice of democracy understood as a set of procedures.

The fourth condition for a polity to be democratic is that its associates be able to reason their way to solutions for collective action problems. It might seem that this was a redundant condition in defining a procedural democracy. Why can we not just rest content with defining democracy as a political system whose members have final control of the political agenda determining the collective conditions of their lives together in circumstances of political equality? After all, we can imagine a political system oriented towards common interests on the basis of a strong equality of standing, but without much attention to deliberation. When Rousseau says that in democratic assemblies the first persons to speak merely says what all have felt when arriving at the general will, he is articulating an account of democracy in which common interests and equality are central but in which there is little or no deliberation.[30] Making deliberation constitutive of procedural democracy might look as though it risks making the definition look merely persuasive.

However, there are at least three reasons for building a deliberative requirement into our conception of democracy. The first is that collective agency should meet the conditions that any rational agency must meet; namely, a capacity to deliberate. Practical rationality involves voluntary action preceded by deliberation (see section 3.2). Secondly, even if one wishes to construct an aggregative system of democracy, in which democracy is understood as a functional relation between individual preference and social choice, the conditions that the social choice function needs to satisfy have themselves to be deliberatively agreed by members of the polity or their representatives, otherwise an external authority will be determining what those conditions are, so negating the final control of the agenda condition of democracy. The third reason is that if we allow any scope to creativity in dealing with collective action problems, then we have to have a conception of practical rationality that is rich enough to allow deliberation to inform action.

The conditions of purposive rationality oriented towards common interests under conditions of political equality and deliberative rationality spell out what it means for a polity to be procedurally democratic. The conditions of control over the final agenda and responsiveness through collective choice stipulate that significant choices should depend upon the body of those who are citizens of the polity and not upon an external agent or a limited caste within. Equality of political standing is in some sense definitive of democracy. And collective deliberation is required by the conditions of practical reasoning. To say that such a polity models a social contract that has a claim to be just is to say that when these conditions are met, there are grounds for holding that the principles by which democratic communities are governed provide evidence about what justice requires. The empirical approach requires that we find examples of such communities. Can we do so?

2.3. Common property resource regimes

Consider communities in which natural resources have to be managed in common for the purposes of production, for example communities in which, as a condition for sustainable agricultural practice, forests have to be collectively managed for logging, open meadows for grazing, water resources for irrigation, or waters for fishing. Such communities have been called 'common property resource regimes'.[31] Ostrom identified the underlying organizational logic of such management in terms of the governance of common pool resources.[32] Common pool resources are a variant of pure public goods. Pure public goods (in the economist's sense) are characterized by non-rivalness and non-excludability in their use or consumption. When goods are non-rival, then the consumption of one person does not deplete the availability of the resource to others. One person's use of clean air or the benefits that anyone derives from living in a tolerant society are non-rival in consumption. Non-excludability in consumption means that if one person in a society is able to gain access to the good, then anyone in the society can gain access. Again, clean air within an air shed or the practices and institutions of a tolerant society are non-excludable in this sense. With common pool resources, by contrast, there is some rivalness in use, since appropriation by a sufficiently large number of people will deplete the value of the resource for any particular individual. If wood cutting is unrestrained, forests will reduce in size. If animals are grazed without restraint, meadows will be exhausted. If water is abstracted without control, then irrigation will dry up. If fishing grounds are over-exploited, fish stocks will decline. Unless the activities of individual agricultural enterprises can be constrained, the cumulative effect of individual use is collectively self-defeating to the disadvantage of all. With common pool resources, open access implies rivalness in use or consumption.

Problems of public goods, including common pool resources, are often treated by social scientists as instances of the prisoner's dilemma, the classic example being Hardin's discussion of the 'tragedy of the commons', by which the rational use by each individual of a common grazing area results in that area being depleted in value.[33] Each herder has an incentive to graze, independently of what others do. Either others will graze or not. If they graze, then there is no individual advantage in not grazing (for the resource will be depleted in any case); if they do not graze, then there is an individual advantage in grazing (for there will be more of the resource available). If we think about these problems in terms of a game-theoretic model of the prisoner's dilemma, then resource depletion is built into the structure of the game, since it is unconditionally better for each to use the resource to the point where *individual* benefit equals *individual* cost, whatever the overall consequences. Moreover, if each individual makes a cost-benefit calculation in choosing whether or not to use a resource on the assumption that everyone else will restrain their use for the purposes of conservation, each agent is in effect hoping to secure a positional advantage over others, gaining from their restraint whilst at the same time making an individually rational calculation. However, if everyone thinks in this positional way, none will gain and all will be worse off through resource depletion than they would had they been able to make a collective agreement to stay within sustainable limits.

Applied to questions of resource use, the prisoner's dilemma model is of course *a priori* and hypothetical. As Berkes nicely puts it, 'the usefulness of the paradigm lies in its insolubility—the fact that it is a tautology'.[34] A one-off prisoner's dilemma game is written so as to ensure mutual defection, since the pay-offs simply record the rank-orderings over possible outcomes of all individuals.[35] Within this theoretical framework, the only ways of avoiding self-defeating individual competition are either through repeated plays of the game, where it can be shown that cooperation can emerge by trial and error, or by the imposition of suitable incentives by a hegemon, such as a Hobbesian Leviathan, who is thereby able to secure cooperation.

However, instead of looking at these issues in an a priori and hypothetical way, it is possible to examine empirically cases in which such common pool resource problems have been successfully managed (sometimes over centuries) by contrast with those cases in which they have not been managed successfully. One of Ostrom's examples will give the flavour of what successful management involves.[36] In Alanya in southern Turkey, coastal waters were being overfished as a result of the over-capitalization of the fleet and the competition for increased yields. In the early 1970s the local cooperative in Alanya began experimenting with allocating fish sites to local fishers, which consisted of the following system:

1. Each September a list of eligible fishers was prepared.
2. Within the area normally used, all fishers and all usable fishing locations were named and listed. The sites were so spaced that the nets in one site would not block the fish in an adjacent site.
3. These named locations were in effect from September to May.
4. In September the named fishers drew lots and were assigned to the named fishing locations.
5. From September to January each day each fisher moved east to the next location; after January each fisher moved west one place.

These rules form an institution in Young's sense consisting of 'identifiable practices consisting of recognized roles linked by clusters of rules or conventions governing relations among the occupants of those roles'.[37] Institutional practices of this sort operate by providing norms that individuals take to govern their actions, thus enabling coordinated human activity to take place in ways that avoid collective self-damage. Theorists of common property resource regimes argue that institutions, of the sort of which Alanya provides an example, solve the collective action problems associated with the management of common-pool resources in ways that could not be achieved by uncoordinated individual action. In essence, the institution is providing norms of behaviour for individuals, and action in accordance with those norms is necessary, and sometimes sufficient, to secure the common good on which the interest of each participant depends.

Common pool resource regimes emerge in situations where the physical environment and mode of production create the interdependence in which short-term individual maximizing behaviour will create adverse effects for others and ultimately redound to the disadvantage of all. The examples of successful regimes cited by Ostrom include mountain grazing and crop harvesting in Switzerland and Japan and water management in Spain and the Philippines. These are cases where agreement on common rules is necessary if the underlying resource is to be conserved for the future. The success of regimes is evidenced by the length of time that they have performed the function of conserving resources. Among the oldest are the regime that governs grazing and foraging rights in Törbel in Switzerland, where the articles of association were signed in 1483, the management of common lands in Japan during the Tokugawa period (1600–1867) and beyond as well as the water irrigation regime in Valencia, Spain going back to 1435.[38] These and other regimes have survived fluctuating pressures in fragile environments. A particularly striking example of the important role of ecological pressures on common property regimes is given by Wade's discussion of such regimes in the Kurnool district of Andhra Pradesh.[39] Villages in the district share a common culture and are economically inter-related through market transactions, but only some—in particular those in which spillover risks associated with both common grazing and irrigation water drawn from a common canal—have strong institutions of collective governance. In short, the material situation in which agriculture is practised creates the conditions under which a logic of cooperative choice emerges. It is an empirical matter to establish the conditions under which cooperation will arise, not a consequence from a tautology of hypothetical choice. The point is reinforced by noticing how similar institutions emerge at different periods of history and against diverse cultural backgrounds. This suggests that successful common property resource regimes are an expression of an underlying logic of rational interaction under certain conditions rather than their reflecting the specific values of any particular culture.

Inductively summarizing from the successful cases, and contrasting with cases of regime failure, Ostrom offers an account of the conditions that enable successful common-pool resources to survive.[40] They include:

1 Clearly defined boundaries: those entitled to use the resource must be identifiable.
2 A fit between appropriation rules and local conditions.
3 Individuals affected can participate in changing or modifying the rules.
4 There is an ability to monitor compliance.
5 There is a system of graduated sanctions in place.
6 There are conflict resolution mechanisms.
7 External authorities do not challenge the right to organize.

Institutions embodying these conditions may be regarded as models of implicit, and sometimes explicit, social contracts. They represent an enforceable agreement (5) among identified parties (1) that allows for continuing participation (3) and (4) in which feasible solutions to common problems have to be identified through deliberation (e.g. the scheme for sharing out the use of the waters in Alanya) and in which conflicts about the application of the rules can be discussed (6) and which represents a form of self-government (7). Of course, such institutions do not have the scope of authority that social contracts in the full sense would enjoy. They may not possess, for example, authority in respect of important matters of criminal law and they may sit alongside other institutions established by the state or other political authorities. However, within their limits, they can serve as models of a social contract and they embody to a significant degree the conditions that we should require of an empirical democratic social contract on which we can model an account of justice.

All the successful common pool resource regimes require joint action by agents in order that such agents can achieve their individual good. Each participant has a reason to subscribe to the rules as a condition of securing the general restraint that is necessary for resources to be conserved. This does not mean that participants are purely self-interested. For example, since the household is the principal unit of production in many such communities, members of each household will care about other members of the household. However, though not wholly self-interested, altruism is limited because solidarity within a household is compatible with competition for resources between households. Each participant may value social constraint not for itself but for the advantages that it brings in raising returns to effort over a non-agreement baseline with its accompanying over-exploitation of resources. In this context, Ostrom highlights the extent to which we need to distinguish between the act of appropriation of a resource, for example catching fish or abstracting water from a river basin, where producers are in competition with one another, from the act of maintaining the resource system, for example stocks of fish or river basin management, where producers have an interest in common in maintaining the integrity and well-functioning of the system.[41] Producers are in a situation of scarcity not abundance, and so they are in competition with one another for the harvest that comes from the joint resource system, but they need to cooperate with one another to maintain that system in being. Given this situation they cannot avoid questions over the terms of their cooperation.

Common property resource regimes exhibit some elements of a democratic social contract. The conditions of procedural democracy require that associates be participants in forms of collective control and legislation. In common property regimes collective control is required because in all cases common property resources sit side by side with private property.[42] Thus the world of such regimes is not one of wholly privatized property in which transactions can be limited to processes of market exchange. There is an essential task to be performed in the collective management of common property resources. Common property resource regimes, then, must have the capacity for self-government. Netting expressed this nicely in relation to Törbel by saying that under its earliest articles of association we may see 'an association of free peasant landholders with a tradition of village-level self-determination rooted in the political forms of early tribal society'.[43] Wade characterizes Kottapalle and those villages in Kurnool that have high levels of collective governance as 'village republics' to capture the idea that the regime of management involves self-determination by producers of common interests independently of outside determination.[44]

Successful regimes of common property resource management require some autonomy over their use of resources. If external political authorities were to set the rules of resource use, then participants could not set the principles upon which they could determine principles that it was reasonable for each of them to follow. The key element in regime autonomy is the knowledge of local circumstances contained within a community, which it is impossible or highly costly for an external authority to replicate.[45] Where rules meeting a condition of common acceptability have to be crafted, local autonomy is a necessary condition of success. This is not to say that all the regimes rely wholly upon local self-determination. For example, the authority of the Alanya cooperative depends upon national legislation, providing the legal power for the cooperation to make rules.[46] Significantly, however, the legislation is of an enabling kind rather than one setting the substance of the policy to be followed. From the point of view of a normative theory of social contract, this condition is also an important one, since it guarantees that the results of collective deliberation will emerge from a contractual, rather than imposed, process.

The idea of collective control among equals, all of whom share a stake in the common interest, is integral to the contractarian logic of common property resource regimes. Since the decision calculus operates in very different cultural contexts, it reflects the underlying logic of an egalitarian social contract and the decision calculus to which resource pressures give rise. However, the definition of who is entitled to participate as an equal in the regime is not independent of cultural and historical context. Not all of the communities that manage common property resources are egalitarian in the sense that they fulfil the condition of political inclusiveness. Wade's village republics in Andhra Pradesh rest upon caste differentiation in which, for example, Harijans ('untouchables') lead marginalized lives and there is a dominant landowning caste (the Reddy caste) who employ labourers and who form the group that participates in resource-use rule formation.[47] From this point of view, they resemble the early modern republics of Florence and Venice, in which collective autonomy was combined with the dominance in political institutions of merchant classes and leading families who set their policies.[48]

How far does this elite element in some common property regimes limit the extent to which we can use them as a model of a democratic contract? In part, the answer to this question is contingent upon upon whether there are different results depending upon whether we are dealing with fully democratic or qualified republican versions of common property resource regimes. If the principles are the same, at least as they affect those who are entitled to participate in the making of the rules of the regime, then there is no difference. The principles and norms that emerge from the agreement are ones that govern relations among equals. Of course, if we are thinking in terms of modern democratic theory, we should want to impose a condition of inclusiveness upon any political system that was a candidate to be called a democracy. The democratic principle is that those who are subject to common rules should have a part in the making of those rules. However, of itself, this does not mean that, for the purposes of theory construction, we need ignore any evidence that emerges from regimes that are less than fully inclusive in their workings, provided that the principles that they determine would be compatible with an inclusive political system. A similar issue arises when considering the extent to which common property resource regimes ought to be taken as indicative or prescriptive given that the household, rather than all adult individuals, is typically the unit of account (see section 4.4).

2.4. The circumstances of justice?

Even if we take successful common property resource regimes as modelling a democratic contract, do their workings tell us anything about justice? The main reason for saying that they do is that their collective decision making takes place under such conditions of approximate equality of power so that no group can exercise a privileged influence upon the outcome. To understand the significance of this claim, we need to place it in the context of the circumstances of justice, the standard account of which derives from Hume, as elaborated in particular by Hart, Lucas, and Rawls.[49]

The first circumstance of justice is that of moderate scarcity. Human societies enjoy neither superabundance nor generally suffer extreme scarcity. In a situation of superabundance, there would be no point in a theory that allocated goods to some people rather than others, since all could have as much as they wanted. Extreme scarcity, by contrast, will generate unrestrained competition for resources. Because justice involves mutual self-restraint, it would be an unnecessary virtue in a situation of superabundance but an impossible virtue, except for saints and heroes, in situations of extreme scarcity. We have no evidence of societies, as distinct from groups within some societies, who live in a situation of superabundance. We are familiar with extreme scarcity, and it is clear that many social conventions break down in such situations. However, most societies most of the time are situated in a position of moderate scarcity. Even if the society is poor, it is not so poor that there are not adequate resources for everyone, though rations may be modest. In a situation of superabundance, as Hume points out, there is no 'laborious occupation required: No tillage; No navigation'.[50] But with moderate scarcity, goods do not come into the world without human work and effort. Common property resource regimes model this feature well. Production cannot be detached from incentives to work. What is available to consume results from human effort.

Marx rightly insisted that a theory of economic production should presuppose social forms rather than taking place in a Robinson Crusoe economy in which one solitary person produces goods of value to that person.[51] Common property resource regimes satisfy this condition. Such regimes arise as a result of spillovers of production from one agent to others, and the common rules of management show the central role of collective decision making. Such spillovers would not occur were each associate to internalize the well-being of all others in making decisions. Provided that they could undertake the calculation correctly, each associate would only use resources to the point where social marginal advantage equalled social cost. However, limited altruism, the second circumstance of justice, means that people are willing to press their claims against one another, so that they consume resources to the point where individual marginal gain equals individual marginal cost. Limited altruism does not mean that people are never willing to show unrequited support for others. It is possible in a society characterized by limited altruism that there were a good number of purely altruistic acts performed by a large number of individuals. Individuals might give blood freely, support favoured charities, help those in emergency situations and take in strangers. However, a society of limited altruism would be a society in which altruistic motives could not be relied upon as a central force in motivating the members of society to production and work activity. Those supplying labour, for example, would expect an economic return and those consuming resources would expect to have to pay for them. When speaking to the butcher or the baker in a society of limited altruism, we would not address ourselves to their humanity by speaking of our needs but to their self-love by speaking of their advantages, as Adam Smith pointed out.[52]

The collective effects of limited altruism are augmented by bounded rationality. Bounded rationality means that, even if individuals were willing to take up an impartial point of view, to the point where they acted in such a way that the marginal social gain of their actions equalled the marginal social cost, they could never be sure what the point of equilibrium would be. Moreover, with each individual acting in isolation, there would be insufficient coordination to reach the equilibrium reliably.

Common property resource regimes thus exhibit moderate scarcity, entailing the necessity of work, and limited altruism among agents whose productive activities have spillover effects on other agents. Participants in such regimes do not enjoy such economic abundance that there is no competition between the different members of society. However, if the resource system is well maintained, neither are they in a position of such intense scarcity that time horizons become very short and rules of controlled behaviour break down. Hence none of these societies are in the words of Hume in 'such want of all common necessaries, that the utmost frugality and industry cannot preserve the greater number from perishing, and the whole from extreme misery'.[53] In fact, Hume's summary of the conditions of justice could well serve as a general summary of the circumstances that we find in common pool resource regimes:

> The common situation of society is a medium amidst all these extremes. We are naturally partial to ourselves, and to our friends: but we are capable of learning the advantage resulting from more

> equitable conduct. Few enjoyments are given us from the open and liberal hand of nature; but by art, labour, and industry, we can extract them in great abundance. Hence the ideas of property become necessary in all civil society.[54]

But how do we know that the ideas of property that are learnt in such situations are ideas of justice?

The answer to this question is that the regimes arise in situations of rough equality of power of the sort that Mill had in mind in respect of the ancient republics. Under such circumstances all participants have some ability to impose harm on others, perhaps even triggering a return to the default non-agreement point.[55] Thus, in Törbel, Netting notes that highly terraced agriculture means that control of water use and maintenance of walls are important, because an unrepaired wall could wash out years of planting and threaten lower terraces.[56] In Alanya, Berkes points out that without regulation, fishing boats could easily interfere with one another by placing their nets too close and crowding out the best sites.[57] In Kottapalle, Wade notes how the absence of local households who have disproportionate control of resources means that collective governance is made more likely.[58] If the circumstances of justice require equality of power in a strong sense, then the interdependence of agents created by the fragility of the environment or the prevailing technology of production provides the conditions within which a rough but substantial equality of political power is realized.

This does not mean that there are no inequalities of power or asymmetries of advantage. For example, those upstream in a water source have an intrinsic advantage of those downstream, since they are able to over-abstract without private loss, at the risk of tail-enders having insufficient supply. Even so, it may be that the construction of the governance regime does not simply reflect these underlying differences of advantage but can actually offset them in its operation. In Kottapalle, tail-enders in water supply press for action through the regime to seek to ensure themselves adequate supply for their rice paddies, since yields on rice are highly sensitive to water.[59] Thus, the general situation with successful common pool resource regimes is that each participant has some ability to impose harm on the rest, as when there is interdependence in production, or other means can be brought to bear to even out inequalities of power. As Glaucon noted, these are the circumstances in which those who have not the power to seize the advantage or escape the harm have an incentive to form a contract of justice for mutual advantage.[60]

Brian Barry denied that it was possible to use the condition of equality of power to explicate a principle of justice.[61] Discussing Hume's version of the condition in the *Enquiry*, he noted that Hume himself thought that if an approximate equality of power was required for justice, then the commitment to justice depends upon that condition obtaining in practice. Barry cites Hume's supposition to the effect that if humans intermingled with less powerful creatures, those creatures would have no claim of justice on humans, just as European settlers would be beyond justice in relation to those whom they colonized. The lesson, Barry thought, is not that equal power is the ground of justice but that justice needs to be exercised in just those situations in which unequal power relations are found.

However, it is one thing to note the circumstances in which the virtue of justice is particularly called for and another thing to assert that circumstances of equality of power tell us nothing about what justice requires. One way in which people come to the virtue of justice is to ask whether their actions would be prudent were those suffering the effects able to retaliate in kind. Thus, even in highly stratified societies in which there is great injustice between social classes, the members of each class are likely to behave more justly to one another than they are to those with less power precisely for fear of retaliation for doing otherwise. This is one of the reasons why it is difficult, if not impossible, to have social justice—as distinct from individuals practising justice at the level of everyday interaction—outside of a democratic society, because it is only in democracies that power is allocated on an inclusive basis.

Taking one's cue from Hume, rather than Mill, is a mistake on this question. Hume's moral theory was tied to a naturalist programme, the concern of which was to explain how ideas arise as a result of the impressions that people receive. Given this programme, it would of course be true for Hume that, in the absence of a crucial circumstance of justice, sentiments of justice would no longer motivate. However, justice is a free-standing idea. It is not merely a function of the circumstances in which people are placed, but plays an independent role in their practical reasoning. As an idea of practical reason it may have its origins in the experience of relations of equal power, but that does not imply that its scope is limited to relations of equal power. Indeed, the extension of the scope of practical reasoning beyond the circumstances of it origin is an important feature of practical rationality generally, applying just as much to the principle of prudence as it does to justice. Although the norms of common property regimes enable participants to overcome the collective action problem, not all communities who are confronted with the collective action problem act on the practically rational motive. Ideas, as well as circumstance, are needed to move people to action.

2.5. Model in what sense?

At different times political thinkers have looked to self-sufficient farming communities in which households existed on a roughly equal footing as a political ideal, usually a lost ideal. This was a persistent theme of the theory of the Norman Yoke in English political thought from the seventeenth to the nineteenth centuries, in which egalitarian Anglo-Saxon society and institutions were said to have provided justice and democracy before the Norman invasion.[62] In his *Notes on the State of Virginia* Jefferson identified widespread landholding as a source of republican virtue, and was himself influenced by the theory of Norman Yoke, so that he 'painstakingly collected every scrap of evidence to reconstruct the history of his "Saxon ancestors"'. The Narodniks in nineteenth century Russia idealized the simpler peasant societies that they thought feudalism and imperial Russia had destroyed.[63] In all cases the characteristics identified with these communities were presented as ideals, but they were mythical ideals. As examples of simple and egalitarian social orders, they could be presented as a model for political and social reorganization. Their mythical status ensured that they could never be realized in practice.

Barry sometimes writes of the societies he takes to approximate the circumstances of justice to be ideals or blueprints, rather than merely logical devices. Taking the smaller Western European countries as his models, he was prepared to advocate that citizens of larger societies should consider their country being broken up into several independent countries (or at least strengthen the autonomy of their regional governments), in order to realize the circumstances of impartiality.[64] Yet, to suppose any type of regime to be a model in this prescriptive sense takes the empirical method off in the wrong direction.[65] To regard certain societies as usefully modelling a social contract is not to regard those societies as paradigms to be followed literally in their institutional details. The term 'model' can be used in this sense and applied in the context of social and political reform. Thus the village of Saltaire near Bradford in West Yorkshire in England was built by Sir Titus Salt as a 'model village' with the intention of creating a form of enterprise and production that would advance public health and education for others to follow. In the same spirit Rowntree built the garden village of New Earswick near York to embody the principles of Ebenezer Howard's garden city movement, principles that were later followed in such garden cities as Letchworth and Welwyn Garden City in Hertfordshire.[66] In these cases and others, the original is intended to provide an exemplar for others to follow. However, the empirical models of justice in modern social contract theory need to be interpreted in another sense of the term.

A second sense of the model is what Mary Hesse has called an analogue machine.[67] This is the sense in which one system models another when it stands as a replica or miniature of the system that is being modelled. Although such analogue machines may resemble in many respects the things they are supposed to be modelling, as when a scale model of an airplane in a wind tunnel resembles the design of a plane that is being tested, this is not strictly necessary for analogue machines. Phillip's hydraulic model of the economy, in which a system of pipes containing fluid modelled the performance of the economy, might be used to assess the implications of a greater pressure of demand in the economy through an increase in fluid pressure, but there is no sense that increased economic demand resembles the increase of pressure in the pipes. It is that one is just a convenient machine displaying relevant analogies to the other.

There is a sense in which common property resource regimes provide a model of just social orders in this analogue machine sense. For example, if it is important to the success of common property resource regimes that the individuals affected by common rules can participate in the modification of those rules, then this would suggest a requirement for an analogous institutional feature in any democratically just society, rather in the way in which if a scale model of an airplane needs a tail fin in a certain proportion to the rest of the body to attain maximum performance, then any real airplane will have to meet the same condition. Similar considerations apply in the case of other crucial features of successful common property resource regimes, for example clearly defined boundaries, the ability to monitor compliance, and the absence of external authorities challenging the right to organize. However, precisely what satisfying these conditions might mean in practice in different societies can remain obscure. It may be hard to know, for example, what participation in modifying rules to which one is subject means in a large-scale society in which rule-making is not a matter of face-to-face decision making among those subject to the rules.

Given the difficulty of understanding these institutional implications, it is also possible to adopt an account of models different to that of the analogue sense, and to think of the common property resource regimes as embodying or realizing the features that any regimes of common management is going to need if it is to be successful. We may think about these features as in some sense undefined until they are embodied in particular sets of institutions. This would mean that the common property resource regimes model social contract theory rather in the same way that logicians think about a model as being one way of representing a set of axioms within a formalized system. Formalized systems in mathematics are built upon axioms that have no definition independently of their use within the system. Thus, in a formalized system of geometry, for example, the axiom 'Any two points lie on one and only one straight line' will not take its sense from observable points on lines in the world. Instead, the notions will be defined implicitly, that is to say in terms of the implications to which the axioms give rise within the formal system. It follows from the notion of implicit definition that we cannot check directly whether any set of axioms is consistent or not, but we can construct an interpretation of the axiomatized system to test for the consistency of the axioms. If to the counterparts of the formal system there exists in the model a set of true statements, we can at least say that the axioms are consistent, since inconsistent statements within the model will indicate that at least one axiom is false.[68]

When we use common property resource regimes as models of a social contract, we are using them as constructs to identify the relevant logic of social cooperation that underlies a just social order. In successful social cooperation, there must be institutions and practices of commitment, reciprocity, and collective authority, as required by the model but the model itself is only suggestive of what these institutions and practices might be under very different conditions, of which spatial and population scale are most important. This answers one line of objection to using democratic practices as models of just social contracts. Estlund, for example, rejects the analogy between democracy and a social contract (although it is primarily the contractualist version of the social contract that he has in mind) because he holds that each contracting party must have their own personal point of view in mind, but that this in turn requires each having a veto power and this is inappropriate in 'real and large democratic choice procedures'.[69] In fact, even in large-scale democracies there may be a high degree of unanimity among political representatives who validly represent their constituencies, as the example of representational democracies goes to show (see Chapter 6). Nonetheless, the general point is a good one: pure veto power is inappropriate in large-scale societies. However, the examples of common property resource regimes exhibit a general logic in which high levels of agreement are generated to the benefit of joint gains for all. It is an open theoretical question what the counterpart to this logic might be in large-scale societies.

Common property resource regimes provide us with evidence about what principles would come into play under the circumstances of justice, but is this enough? Rawls defined political constructivism as a view about the relation between the structure of a political conception of justice and the content of a theory of justice such that 'the principle of political justice (content) may be represented as the outcome of a certain procedure of construction (structure)'.[70] The idea is that the original position models this relationship and the consequence of this is that the procedure of the original becomes criterial for the democratic conception of justice. Justice means what would be determined by contracting parties in the original position. Method defines substance. Can we make an equivalent assumption about decisions made in an empirical social contract? Do the terms and conditions of political and economic association defined by such associations define justice?

There is one important reason why we cannot move from the observation of agreements in common property resource regimes to a conclusion about what the content of justice requires, and this relates to the units of economic activity. In many of those regimes, it is the household that is the principal unit of production. The resource regimes govern agricultural production and, as Peter Wiles noted, in agriculture, family members are involved in processes of production, because the internal distances of production are all important. It is crucial to be near the place of harvesting, and so the potential for economies of scale is limited.[71] One could think that this is unproblematic. After all, as a way of dealing with the problem of intergenerational justice, in *A Theory of Justice*, Rawls conceived of the parties to the contract 'as representing a continuing line of claims. For example, we can assume that they are heads of families and therefore have a desire to further the well-being of at least their more immediate descendants.'[72] Rawls thus made heads of continuing households the agents in the contractual construction. However, Rawls has been strongly (and to my way of thinking rightly) criticized for making this assumption, since power relations within households will give rise to questions of justice.[73] One could thus argue that taking common pool resource regimes as models of social contracts simply replicates the Rawlsian mistake. This is an important topic to which we return in Chapter 5. However, for the present, I shall assume that the core of the answer is to distinguish between the common pool resource regime as a model from which we can infer reliably what terms of agreement might emerge from contracting parties, treating the model as a source of evidence rather than a criterion of justice, and the ability to abstract from that model so that it can be applied to other sets of social relations. Households themselves are typically units of production and reproduction in which there is a division of labour and in which inequalities of power will lead to unjust allocations. If we can use an observable situation of rough equality of power to understand reasonable terms of cooperation, then we should be able to apply the analysis more widely. One particularly important sphere in which to apply the model concerns the principles upon which produced resources are to be allocated. We turn to that task in the next chapter.

CHAPTER 3

Economic justice and the democratic contract

3.1. Individualism, collectivism, and economic justice

'[T]he first man who, having enclosed a piece of ground, to whom it occurred to say *this is mine* and found people sufficiently simple to believe him, was the true founder of civil society', wrote Rousseau. Was he right? Reflection on common property resource regimes suggest that the answer is 'yes'. Without a demarcation of the spheres in which individuals and groups can appropriate resources to themselves and those in which they cannot, there is no civil society and there can be no governance, democratic or otherwise. Social conventions and systems of governance are necessary if property is to exist. Rousseau was wrong, however, to believe that 'the imposter' who persuaded others to believe his claim to the rightful ownership of material objects as property was the source of 'numerous crimes, wars, murders, miseries and horrors'.[1] The same social conventions and systems of governance that define and protect property are also necessary to avoid the tragedy of the commons. That is the lesson from the analysis of common property resource regimes. Without the demarcation of property rights provided by convention and governance, there is simply a collectively self-defeating struggle ending in resource depletion and at the limit there is, as Hobbes noted, 'no place for industry; because the fruit thereof is uncertain; and consequently no culture of the earth; no navigation, nor use of the commodities that may be imported by sea; no commodious building; no instruments of moving, and removing, such things as require much force; no knowledge of the face of the earth; no account of time; no arts; no letters; no society'.[2] Where there is no place for industry, because the fruit thereof is uncertain, people will not labour in vain solely for the benefit of others, and there is no justice.

Of course, claims to property rights can be a source of war and conflict. Yet property rights founded in justice cannot provide a reason for people to study war or engage in conflict. There is no chain of reasoning, by definition, in which just property entitlements are made vulnerable to delegitimation by political associates. But what is it that makes for just property entitlements? On what principles of property allocation is there no reason for anyone to contest the right of others to the resources over which they lay claim? To answer these questions is the task for a democratic theory of economic justice.

Democratic contractarianism requires that the test of legitimating or justifying property rights over resources has to be grounded in the logic of contractual association among political equals. In other words, it is a matter of identifying the principles upon which the members of a democratic association would determine economic entitlements. The empirical approach requires in addition that evidence of the negotiated outcome of social contracts be derived from functioning examples. Common property resource regimes combine individual rights to appropriate resources, for example trees from a forest or water to irrigation, with the collective management of the natural resources systems, the forest, or the waterways, that are a necessary condition of individual appropriation. These two sets of rights, the individual and the collective, correspond to the two interests that participants in common property resource regimes have, namely the individual right to appropriate, where participants in the regime are in conflict with one another, and the collective right to manage, where participants have a joint and shared interest in ensuring that the resource base is managed prudently. The linking of these two sets of interests suggests that what is required is an adequate balancing between the collective interests that individuals have on the one hand, and their separate and conflicting interests on the other. Property rights cannot be so collectivized that there is no individual right of appropriation, use, or consumption; equally they cannot be so individualized that no collective control is possible.

One implication of these twin requirements is that property acquisition and ownership cannot be derived from a Lockean right to appropriate the natural world through work or possession in a world in which the act of appropriation leaves no others worse off than they were before. Such a world would be a Robinson Crusoe world. So, from a democratic contractarian perspective, a Lockean right of initial appropriation is problematic. Were it to exist, it would be a moral entitlement prior to the social contract and the strong contractarian programme aims to make claims of justice the outcome of the contract, not one of its presuppositions. Moreover, if we formulate our theory of property acquisition on the basis of individuals appropriating parts of the natural world without prejudice to the rights or interests of others, there is an immediate puzzle as to how there is any right of collective ownership or control at all. Those who have followed Locke in his theory have been willing to embrace this implication. Thus, the Ricardian socialist Thomas Hodgskin explicitly contrasts the natural right to property with the Benthamite position that all property is a consequence of law-made rights, a position which if it were accepted would give the community operating through the law no right to determine individual ownership. In a different but complementary mode, Nozick assumes that individual appropriation will absorb all the natural world, possibly leaving nothing for which collective control is suitable.[3]

A converse position is that all resources are in principle under collective control. Many modern discussions of economic justice take for granted John Stuart Mill's claim that, whereas the production of wealth is subject to natural laws partaking of the character of physical truths, the same is not true of the principles of distribution, which are matters for human institutions only. So, for Mill, it is a matter of natural law that a doubling in the quantity of labour on a piece of land will not produce a doubling in the quantity of food produced without some other improvement taking place. However, once the produce is there, it can be disposed of by the choice of the collective, so that in any state but one of complete solitude, even 'what a person has produced by his individual toil, unaided by any one else, he cannot keep, unless by the permission of society'.[4] The assumption that principles of distribution can be detached from consideration of the way that goods and services are produced leads to the utilitarian tradition of modern welfare economics, in which the task of government is seen to be that of determining maximum social welfare as though it were a benevolent social planner. The Rawlsian theory of justice shares with utilitarianism this same collectivist assumption, since the difference principle 'represents, in effect, an agreement to regard the distribution of natural talents as in some respects a common asset and to share in the greater social and economic benefits made possible by the complementarities of this distribution'.[5]

In the Lockean and Rawlsian positions there are two distinct and opposite logics of appropriation. In one, pre-social appropriation gives producers a right to the fruits of their labour. In the other, contractual association makes the fruits of labour part of the common pool to be distributed according to socially agreed norms. By contrast, and true to his contractarian spirit, Gauthier offers an account of how one might combine the individualist and collectivist elements needed in any theory of the social contract.[6] In his account, prior to the formation of the social contract, individuals are able to appropriate resources through their labour, subject to a Lockean proviso according to which they cannot worsen the situation of another. The pre-contractual state is individualistic. However, once the logic of externalities leads to the formation of a social contract, that portion of an individual's return on work that constitutes economic rent will be part of a shared pool, subject to rules contractually agreeable. Gauthier's theory thus combines a strong individualism prior to the formation of the contract with an equally strong collectivism after its establishment.

None of these ways of bringing together collective control and a right of individual appropriation fits the logic of democratic social contracts, in which in common property resource regimes there is a right to appropriate the fruits of one's labour provided that there is equal access to the means of production as common property. If contractual association is brought about through the need to control the spillover effects of each appropriator upon the other, then the grounding of property rights and the control of economic goods must arise through the social contract that resolves the collective action problem those spillover effects create. This means that the right of individual appropriation cannot rest upon a Lockean pre-contractual right, since that would take determination of the scope of the right out of the hands of the collective political authority. On the other hand, since producers have a right to appropriate the fruits of their own labour without an obligation to pool those fruits with others (except in special circumstances dealt with below), the logic of contractual association must find a way of generating such a socially recognized right as an implication of the collective agreement that is embedded in the social contract. How might these twin requirements be satisfied?

3.2. Labour and the means of production

In common property resource regimes, a general principle is that participants receive the full fruits of their labour within the constraints of socially agreed rules on rights of access. The fish participants catch, the wood and plants they harvest, or the cows they graze belong to them. Often work is organized around the household, as it is in Törbel, where kin live together and undertake the basic work including the provision of food and shelter.[7] In the Turkish fishing communities, the boats need not be household-based but involve a number of different individuals.[8] These different arrangements presumably reflect the different technologies of production, as does the employment of wage labour in Kottapalle.[9] However, within those variations, the general rule is that the product of labour is owned by those who undertake the work involved in securing that product. It is not shared across the community at large or any designated subset not involved in its production. (That it is frequently households that are the unit of production is an important fact to be taken up in Chapters 5 and 7.)

The logic of the full fruits principle seems inegalitarian. It allows those who enjoy better luck, greater skill, or more productive power to harvest and keep more than those without those advantages. Yet the communities in which common pool resource regimes operate are egalitarian in the sense that producers enjoy an equality of status and power in determining the functioning of the regime. Indeed, the very strong notion of equality of power presupposed in characterizing the democratic contract underpins the idea of the political equality and equality of standing that participants possess. So, if the operative principle of common pool resource regimes is that producing units enjoy the full fruits of their labour, political equality co-exists with economic inequality. How is it possible that democratic justice understood as a social contract leads to a seemingly unequal distribution of resources?

Although the basic principle of economic justice in common property resource regimes is that producers are entitled to the full fruits of their labour, this is an incomplete description in a number of ways. Firstly, although households have their own private property, all have access to the common resources and so to the central means of production within the economy. In theory it would be possible in many forms of agriculture for there to be private ownership of those means of production, with the owners leasing or selling access to producers in exchange for rent. In the limit, one owner within a community could control the means of production, leasing it to those who wished to use them. Yet a significant feature of common property resource regimes is that the commons remain under collective control, with communal rules determining the conditions of their use. Having such resources in common thus plays a role in limiting the extent to which individuals can accumulate advantages over others through their control of the means of production. The full fruits principle is applied in a situation in which it is labour, rather than a return to ownership as such, that provides the basis of appropriation.

This feature is reinforced by there being a random, and therefore equalizing, element in the assignment of rights to harvest or to use the common resources. In Törbel, for example, the trees used for heating and construction are marked to be felled, and assigned by lot to a group of households. In Hirano, Nagaike, and Yamanoka each *kumi* (collection of households) is assigned a zone by rotation for harvesting winter fodder, and the crop is harvested collectively for technical reasons to do with the minimization of accidents. In Valencia a rotation scheme is used for access to water via the communal canals, from which each farmer can extract as much as possible in turn; in Murcia each farmer is assigned a fixed time period for water use. In the *zanjera* communities in The Philippines, when water is scarce, rotation systems are established. To be sure, randomization (and therefore equalization over time) is not the only rule that is used for allocating rights to harvest. In Törbel, a proportionality rule is used for grazing rights, with each farmer allowed rights in proportion to the number of cows owned and a proportionality rule is used in the lower *zanjera* communities for the allocation of water. However, such proportionality, whilst a modification to a strict egalitarianism, is not a gross departure from an egalitarian arrangement given its limited extent.[10]

There are some forms of redistribution from productive effort to be found in the common property resource regimes. Sometimes it involves provision for the poor, as has been true in Törbel since the original terms of the social agreement in 1473.[11] However, such provision appears to be a matter of charity rather than a matter of enforceable right. A more serious departure from the fruits of labour principle is noted in some fishing communities by Berkes, citing previous literature.[12] In the Cornish oyster fishery at Fal River, a boat with a catch considerably higher than the average would be a source of adverse comment; in the New York Gull Haven fishery, the cooperative manager set a quota that could be sold at an acceptable price and the proceeds of sale were shares among all the crews; and in the fisheries of eastern Lake Erie in Canada, those who landed more than their share were forced to average out their catches with others. However, these forms of enforced sharing across work units seem to have as their rationale the controlling of collective over-exploitation rather than the imposition of a redistributive scheme for sharing the product of labour among those with equal entitlements.

Complementing the egalitarian elements in the institutional arrangement of common property regimes are features of the mode of production that constrain the degree of inequality arising from the operation of the full fruits principle. In particular, the mode of production is such that variation in the ability to harvest reflects primarily skill differences and luck rather than position within an organization with control of the coordinated resources that such an organization allows. Members of the community are harvesting from nature and therefore have a limited capacity to increase their returns above a certain level. What is more, where skill acquisition is through custom and practice, the span of taught ability in productive activities will be low, as skills and techniques are diffused throughout the community. In short, differences in productivity are not related to the emergence of a separate class of persons who can control the means of production, the scale, and the pace at which others work.

From one point of view, the fundamental principle of appropriation can be regarded as one of equality of opportunity to pursue one's productive activities to the best of one's ability, where the relevant opportunities are made up of access to the means of production with a suitably randomized allocation of appropriation rights. Yet the system does allow the opportunity to become unequal. Nevertheless, the property regime is such that there is no ability on the part of any of the participants to accumulate so much property that they would fall into a different economic class from their peers. The unequal outcomes that arise as a result of the equal opportunities are thereby limited in scope and extent. Even so, the rule of appropriation from labour is not one that is based upon a substantive conception of what participants are entitled to; for example, a rule that they are entitled either to a minimum or an equal share of product or even to a share that, though unequal, maximizes their expectations of gain. The implicit rule is free appropriation subject to the collectively determined conditions of appropriation. How might such a rule be rationalized within a democratic contractarian framework?

3.3. The logic of the full fruits principle

A contractarian theory of economic justice requires a non-agreement baseline from which the contracting parties negotiate to mutual advantage. One way of specifying such a baseline is Hobbesian, allowing unrestrained predation in the state of nature of anyone upon anyone else. As Hobbes put it:

> [I]f one plant, sow, build, or possess a convenient seat, others may probably be expected to come prepared with forces united, to dispossess, and deprive him, not only of the fruits of his labour, but also of his life, or liberty.[13]

In such a state of nature, each agent is assumed to have 'a right to everything; even to one another's body'.[14] However, this is an extreme example of a productive system without governance. Indeed, such is its capacity for self-destruction that it is probably not correct to call it a productive system at all, since it is hard to see how any extensive production could take place under such circumstances. So severe would be the disincentive to work that it would be rare to observe any persons living within a state of nature, since their lives would be so brutish and short that their society would escape observation. Hume's empiricism served him well on this point, when he remarked whether 'such a condition of human nature could ever exist, or if it did, could contrive for so long to merit the appellation of a state, may justly be doubted'.[15]

Suppose, in place of the Hobbesian state of nature with its right of all to everything, we consider the situation before the establishment of a common property resource regime—before a social contract—as one in which each producer enjoys Hohfeldian liberty-rights. A Hohfeldian liberty-right allows each person the freedom to be the first to appropriate resources, with no one having the right to interfere with that appropriation, but with no one under any obligation to allow others to be the first to appropriate.[16] For example, under a regime of liberty-rights, two vessels may compete with one another to be first to fish a school of fish. When one vessel arrives first, the second is under an obligation to allow the first to fish. However, prior to such occupancy, the second was under no obligation to allow the other to be first. Such a situation contrasts with the Hobbesian state of nature in which freedom of action is unconstrained (so that the second boat could attack the first) and it resembles a Lockean state of nature governed by respect for the appropriation of others through labour of others. However, there is no guarantee that the Lockean proviso will be met under which each has to leave enough and as good for others, even if those appropriating do so within the limits of their own use.[17] The unintended cumulative effect of each person exercising their Hohfeldian liberty-right is to deplete or destroy the natural resource for all. Even if each person intends to leave enough and as good for others, the cumulative effect of their appropriation is to leave too little for anyone. The operation of such a logic would in principle be observable, at least where systems of production begin to push up against the limits of available natural resources or other pressures. Indeed, Michael Lipton has argued that many traditional forms of land tenure in the modern world are drifting towards the prisoner's dilemma through population growth, developmental change, and risk-aversion, all leading to an erosion of trust.[18] In short, the relevant pre-contractual state of nature is not hypothetical but the product of social processes that are clearly observable.

Suppose that a social contract taking the form of a common property resource regime is a contract to replace a regime of Hohfeldian liberty-rights, giving participants claim-rights to access to be respected by others. In such a context, the full fruits principle represents an agreement on the part of each producer to allow every other producer to appropriate according to their labour within the collectively determined right of access. Within common property resource regimes, there are duties to refrain from interfering with others' appropriation, for example by waiting one's turn in a rotation system. However, once those constraints are respected, the participants secure the full fruits of their labour and are under no obligation of justice to share their product with others. Why should this be? A conjectural answer runs as follows. The contract abridging the Hohfeldian liberty is intended to be one to mutual advantage. That is to say, each participant intends to be better off as a result of the contract than is possible without the mutual restraint, the contract promising an end to the mutually destructive exercise of Hohfeldian liberties. Yet no one would rationally agree to give up their Hohfeldian liberty unless it was advantageous to do so. In this situation, those who can anticipate being more productive or luckier in respect of their labours will not accept a contract that gives them less than the anticipated product they would obtain by working to the point where marginal return was equal to the marginal effort involved in securing that return. Those who anticipate being less fortunate cannot force the more productive to do so. The full fruits principle can be seen as the best that the most productive can do in exchange for giving up their Hohfeldian liberties.

Is this line of argument adequate, however? All it establishes is that without some gain, it would not make sense of an appropriator to sign a contract requiring a restriction upon the freedom to appropriate. It does not show that in a contract from which each gains, some gainers might have to share the reward of their work with others. After all, one can gain and still share some of the fruits of that gain with others. Indeed, the principle that, in gaining, one is under an obligation to share the fruits of one's labour with others is a central part of Rawls's rationale for the difference principle, which is 'an agreement to regard the distribution of natural talents as in some respects a common asset and to share in the greater social and economic benefits made possible by the complementarities of this distribution.'[19] Moreover, it can be argued, those who anticipate being less productive cannot be forced into an arrangement in which there is no sharing at all, since they could always threaten to continue acting under the regime of Hohfeldian liberty-rights appropriating what they can, and so undermining the basis of the social agreement. Of course, this threat could mean that there is less available for all, since over-harvesting of a resource will lead to the depletion of that resource, but that would simply be a consequence of the threat-advantage that the less productive have.

In this situation there is no formal model of bargaining that we can use, even if we thought it suitable given a deliberative account of practical rationality (see section 4.2). Existing formal models of bargaining are built upon bilateral negotiation, and complications over potential coalition formation suggest an empty core to multilateral agreements.[20] An alternative is to look at informal arguments in which focal point solutions are important. In this context, in particular, we need to look at the notion of equal threat-advantage assumed in the democratic contract. Any equal threat-advantage precludes our regarding the distribution of natural talents as a common asset. To be sure, from the point of view of the less productive, it would clearly be advantageous to move from a regime of Hohfeldian liberties to a regime in which they could make a claim upon the resources produced by the most advantaged, say in line with the difference principle. However, the same power that they could exercise in transferring some portion of output from others to themselves could be used by those others to transfer resources from them to those others. Symmetry of threat-advantage cannot translate into asymmetry of reward advantage. By the same token that we could assume that the less productive would want to transfer resources from the more advantaged, so a social contract in which the more productive could transfer some of the output of the less productive to themselves would be more advantageous than a regime of Hohfeldian liberties. Compulsory labour generally tends to be the lot of the less advantaged, not the more advantaged.

Is there really is symmetry of threat-advantage, however? Those who stand to gain less from an arrangement may thereby gain a bargaining advantage, since the cost to them of not securing an agreement is smaller than the cost to those who have much to gain. Those who have less to gain have less to lose if the agreement is not made. In making a contractual agreement, the less advantaged may be supposed to be willing to hold out longer until the agreement contains an arrangement to transfer some resources from the more productive. Yet the gain to participants in a well-functioning common property resource regime is so significant that relative gains are likely to be small by comparison. In exchange for secure gains through labour, any hold-outs would be exchanging insecure relative gains that would be lower than the level of return they secured through agreement to the full fruits principle. A social contract, allowing each to keep their own, can be seen as a focal point of agreement, just as refraining from using gas was a focal point for adversaries in the Second World War.[21] The right to keep one's own product emerges as a mutual stand-off in a situation in which exercising one's power is constrained for fear that others may exercise a similar power, in circumstances in which any exercise of power is potentially highly destructive.

The principle that emerges is that of being willing to give up one's freedom to appropriate at will in exchange for an agreed system of appropriation securing protection against the mischief that the cumulative effects of unconstrained appropriation would lead to, provided that others are prepared to do likewise. Hohfeldian liberties are exchanged for claim-rights. That is to say, unconstrained free appropriation is given up in exchange for rule-bound appropriation, but the original concept of a liberty underlies the character of the exchange. Each is constraining only his or her own freedom to appropriate. Each retains the freedom to keep what has been successfully appropriated under that agreed set of mutually advantageous rules. There is fairness embodied in the full fruits principle, but it is the fairness of mutual restraint, according to which 'when a number of persons conduct any joint enterprise according to rules and thus restrict their liberty, those who have submitted to these restrictions when required have a right to a similar submission to these restrictions from those who have benefited by their submission'.[22] The similar submission is a willingness to keep to the agreed rules, not the willingness to share the benefits that those rules allow.

Considerations of freedom and fairness can thus be said to shape the terms of the contract.

Some might argue that the form of the agreement was simply reflected in the transaction costs associated with the redistribution of income. John Stuart Mill may have been right, in principle, to suppose that individuals cannot keep what they have produced themselves without the permission of society, but the setting up and maintenance of institutions to grant and enforce such permission may be costly, and the gains of control outweighed by the expense of its organization. In a world of asymmetric information and opportunistic behaviour, it is not possible to monitor the performance of producers in many crucial respects, so that the full fruits principle can be simply regarded as making a concession to the practicalities of implementation. Support for this proposition might come from the example of those fisheries regimes in which those who land more fish than their allocated share are forced to average out their catches with others, since it is clearly easier to organize the compulsory sharing of landed fish than to organize the sharing of many other forms of agricultural product. Yet, without being entirely able to rule out such an explanation, one striking aspect of the fisheries case is how rare the practices of compulsory sharing are, suggesting that their principal rationale is resource conservation rather than allocation according to a collectively agreed principle of distribution.

The argument so far has been that the social contract typical of common property resource regimes can be rationalized by reference to the balance that it strikes between collective control and individual freedom. Collective control is justified because the conditions that would enable individuals to appropriate resources privately and without damage to their own interests do not exist. Individual freedom is justified because the rationale of a jointly agreeable contract transfers to the common property regime as much freedom of appropriation as possible from the pre-contractual state. Three alterative positions are possible. The first is the individualist line of argument to be found in Locke and the tradition that he inspired, according to which the permission of society is not needed for appropriation. The second is to be found in collectivist Rawlsian principle that one should regard the distribution of natural talents as in some respect a common asset. The third is Gauthier's contractarian balancing of the rights of individuals with the permission of the collective. We look at each in turn.

3.4. The Lockean alternative

Consider accounts inspired by Locke's theory of primary acquisition. Locke formulated a right to property as a result of the effects of labouring on the natural world:

> He that is nourished by the Acorns he pickt up under an Oak, or the Apples he gathered from the Trees in the Wood, has certainly appropriated them to himself. No Body can deny but the nourishment is his. I ask then, When did they begin to be his? When he digested? Or when he eat? Or when he boiled? Or when he bought them home? Or when he pickt them up? And 'tis plain, if the first gathering made them not his, nothing else could. That *labour* put a distinction between them and common.[23]

The argument here appears to be a form of backward induction. Suppose we have a chain of necessary conditions from A to D, such that: only if A, then B; and only if B, then C; and only if C, then D. Then if D is permissible, so must be A, B, and C by the principle of those who will the end, also will the means. If we believe that it is right for people to have appropriated, then we are committed to thinking that the sequence of acts that led to the appropriation was permissible.

Locke construed the right to property as a natural right. That is why he thought that when individuals appropriated resources from the commons, they were free to do so without the consent of others.[24] On this account, people may labour for the same acorns without either infringing the property rights of the others. Of course, when some are successful and others are not, then the losers have not been able to exercise their rights to advantage. However, for Locke this is no injustice since all, winners and losers, are in a situation in which there is enough and as good left for others by those who have successfully appropriated. Locke intended his argument to be a refutation of Filmer's claim that God gave the earth to Adam, and so to his successors in common, so that any individual appropriation would require the consent of the community. In other words, his argument is intended to be a refutation of collectivism. Locke hoped to show by appeal to the labour theory of property that the consent of the community is not necessary.[25]

Locke thought that there would always be as much and as good for others, because the same law of nature that allowed the appropriation of the fruits of the earth also forbade appropriators to take more than they could enjoy by themselves: 'Nothing was made by God for Man to spoil or destroy.'[26] By the same token, people are entitled to acquire land, so long as there is enough and as good for others: 'For he that leaves as much as another can make use of, does as good as take nothing at all.'[27]

The Ricardian socialist, Thomas Hodgskin, in *The Natural and Artificial Right of Property Contrasted*, pursued the individualism implicit in the Lockean approach. He endorsed the right to property through labour as a claim of natural right. Appealing to Locke's passage on the right to acquisition cited above, he denied that capitalists and landlords had any right to the product of those who laboured.[28] Hodgskin contrasted this natural rights position explicitly with the Benthamite doctrine that all property is a consequence of the law and that the law-maker establishes the rules of property. Positive law is a form of collective control that infringes the right of workers to the full fruits of their labour. Laws may give landlords and capitalists a legal right to a return on their assets, but in doing so they are establishing an artificial, rather than a natural, system. It would be possible to overturn the artificial system, not least because rising productivity, the result of the application of human skill and ingenuity, enables workers to live on smaller and smaller plots of land.[29] Although a regime based on the natural right to the fruits of one's labour would permit inequalities in the returns that people earned, it would deny a share in the product of labour to those who were not involved in producing it.[30] Anton Menger pointed out that the right to the full product of one's labour was a central claim of the socialist movement in the nineteenth century.[31]

Hodgskin's position seems to be the correct one for someone who is persuaded by Locke's labour theory of property as a natural right arising as a result of mixing one's labour with nature. Yet that natural right is hard to defend. To be sure, Locke's backward induction is correct if one is concerned with a theory of possession. Once you have eaten the acorn, there is no doubt that you possess it. But why should possession in this sense be construed as a right to property, rather than a mere appropriation? Moreover, once we move beyond the realm of immediate consumption to the ownership of more permanent goods, the claims that others may make upon one's possessions are not limited by the physical fact of possession. If I borrow your coat without permission to go out on a cold night when I know that you are staying at home, I have infringed your property right, but I have not deprived you of your possession. Only if we construe the right to property as a matter of 'full liberal ownership' are the two concepts coextensive.[32]

At the root of the problem is Hodgskin's supposition that when property is an artefact of the law, workers are deprived of their right to property. Naturally, this is always a possibility because laws can be unjustly made (although there is no reason to believe that there is a special problem in this regard in respect of Benthamite legislation). However, from the fact that laws can be unjustly made, we have no reason to think that the concept of a natural right to the fruits of one's labour is an idea that can be rendered plausible. To be sure, if there is a natural right to the fruits of one's labour, any law made in accordance with that right will *ipso facto* be just. Yet it does not follow that laws made not using the natural right as a ground or justification are unjust. In the absence of common rules that are legislatively agreed in some way, there is no satisfactory way to define one's right to possess certain objects. Neither Locke nor Hodgskin give reason for thinking that there is a natural right to the full fruits of one's labour. Both rely on a concept of an original appropriation that is free from political control and governance. However, absence of governance can only arise if we assume that the Lockean proviso can be satisfied. If the proviso is not satisfied, then collective control is required. Does this mean that individuals lose their right to the fruits of their own labour? This seems to be the alternative logic.

3.5. Natural talents and the difference principle

Within social contract theory broadly conceived, the single most famous argument about economic justice is that of Rawls to the effect that participants in a social contract would favour the difference principle to govern the terms of their economic association. His canonical statement of the principle runs as follows:

> Social and economic inequalities are to be arranged so that they are both:
> (a) to the greatest benefit of the least advantaged, consistent with the just savings principle, and
> (b) attached to offices and positions open to all under conditions of fair equality of opportunity.[33]

Provided the just savings and equal opportunity principles are satisfied, no inequality is just unless it works to the advantage of the least well-off. Rawls urged that the difference principle was an implication of his general conception of justice, according to which all social values were to be distributed equally unless an unequal distribution of any or all was to everyone's advantage, and this interpretation was a consequence of adopting the idea of democratic equality.[34]

The difference principle is often interpreted as an 'end-state' principle of justice, that is to say a principle that judges the justice of a distribution by its correspondence with a particular pattern of resources.[35] An end-state principle places an obligation on those agents for whom the duties of justice are relevant to bring about that end-state. An end-state conception of justice would thus oblige the political authorities to bring about that end-state, or at least establish institutions the general tendency of which was to produce that end-state. Any collective authority emerging from a social contract would be obliged to operate in accordance with this principle.

Although the difference principle is often interpreted as an end-state principle, this is only one possible reading and one that is arguably incompatible with Rawls's mature formulation. In the mature version, the principle is not understood as placing a duty on members of a society to ensure that the position of the least well-off is as high as it can be. Rather, it says that when individuals seek advantages for themselves, they can only do so in justice so long as this is consistent with maximum benefits to the least advantaged. Thus, in the revised version of *A Theory of Justice*, Rawls says:

> [T]he more advantaged have *a right to their natural assets, as does everyone else; this right is covered by the first principle under the basic liberty protecting the integrity of the person.* And so the more

> advantaged are entitled to whatever they can acquire in accordance with the rules of a fair system of social cooperation.[36]

In this formulation, the right to one's natural assets is prior to any obligations one may have to promote the well-being of the least advantaged. That this is an important element in Rawls's mature formulation is highlighted by the fact that the italicized words are added to the corresponding passage in the first edition, which simply reads:

> [T]he more advantaged representative man cannot say that he deserves and therefore has a right to a scheme of cooperation in which he is permitted to acquire benefits in ways that do not contribute to the welfare of others.[37]

There is thus a move in Rawls's rationale for the difference principle from the earlier claim that one has no liberty to acquire advantages unless one thereby benefits others to the later claim that one has a liberty to acquire advantages provided that others are benefited. Although people do not deserve their natural talents, principles of freedom and the basic integrity of the person mean that people do have a right to their natural assets.

The revised formulation undermines an interpretation of the difference principle as an end-state principle requiring members of society to bring about a particular pattern in economic possessions. The end-state interpretation is misleading because it requires members of a society, as a matter of justice, to act so as to maximise the well-being of the least well-off. However, if we see the difference principle as a condition on individual appropriation rather than a goal implying a duty on individuals to undertake appropriation, then the difference principle does not impose an obligation upon any group to raise the well-being of the least well-off to the highest level possible. Rather, when the more productive use assets that are rightfully theirs, they should also accept an obligation to pool the benefits of those assets. The difference principle says that when seeking to advantage themselves, all members of society may only take those benefits that arise from a system in which the well-being of the least well-off is maximized. There is no general obligation on anyone to raise the well-being of the least well-off.

The distinction has implications for the extent to which the more productive are required to exercise their abilities.[38] Taken as a goal of public policy, a goal to be internalized by the more productive, the difference principle would require those who were more productive to work beyond any level of effort they might freely chose in order to raise the well-being of the least well-off, an obligation inconsistent with a right to one's natural assets grounded in ideas of basic liberty and personal integrity. To illustrate the issue, consider how the balance between work and leisure might be structured. Suppose a society in which the more productive chose to work only three days a week. In such a society, the least well-off might be better off were the more productive to work for five days a week. Yet, if working the extra two days is not valued by the more productive, the situation of the worst-off is not improved. The more productive might not work the extra two days because they did not value the gain they receive in material goods as highly as they value the loss of leisure they incur from the extra days of work. Under a scheme in which the combination of work and leisure were freely chosen by the more productive, the least well-off may not be as well-off as they could be.

We can strengthen the contrast even further by noting that the lot of the least well-off could be improved, without any loss of economic efficiency, by tilting the incentives of the better off toward longer working hours by imposing a lump-sum tax on ability that the well-off were required to pay. In these circumstances, the better off would work longer hours and a portion of the material benefits they produced would be available to the least well-off to improve their position in accordance with the difference principle interpreted as a social goal. Standard economic theory shows that a lump-sum tax does not distort incentives at the margin and so will not reduce work effort below that which is maximally attainable. Were such lump-sum taxes to be imposed, then there would be grounds for Nozick's otherwise implausible claim that taxation is 'on a par with forced labour'.[39] Another way of putting the point is to say that lump-sum taxation is inconsistent with recognizing the separateness of persons.[40] If we look at the issues from this point of view, it is possible to see why Rawls revised his earlier formulation of the difference principle to make it clear that the freedom and integrity of the person needed to be preserved in any account of a just distribution. The fruits of the labour of the better off are to be redistributed to the least well-off, so far as possible, but conditional upon a free choice about work effort made by the better off.

Yet, if we accept this interpretation of the difference principle, there is no rationale for a principle that requires redistribution more extensive than the full fruits principle, constrained by equal access to the means of production. This difficulty stems from the difference principle being an expression of a conception of society that is at odds with an understanding of the social contract as a means of securing the benefits of cooperation to mutual advantage in line with the principle of reciprocity. Sharing this conception of society, the democratic contractarian conception starts with the basic freedom of individuals, understood as Hohfeldian liberties, and inquires into the character of a collective agreement that would take individuals beyond their non-agreement point. Social union is not assumed but emerges as a product of an agreement that all individuals, from their different points of view, can accept. By contrast, behind Rawls's understanding of the difference principle in its end-state interpretation, there is a specific conception of society, the economy, and the part that individuals severally and collectively play in production, in which social union is presupposed as the basis for agreement. Here is the crucial passage worth quoting at some length (differences from the first edition are stylistic rather than substantive):

> The difference principle represents, in effect, an agreement to regard the distribution of natural talents as in some respects a common asset and to share in the greater social and economic benefits made possible by the complementarities of this distribution. Those who have been favored by nature, whoever they are, may gain from their good fortune only on terms that improve the situation of those who have lost out. The naturally advantaged are not to gain merely because they are more gifted, but only to cover the costs of training and education and for using their endowments in ways that help the less fortunate as well. No one deserves his greater natural capacity nor merits a more favourable starting place in society. But, of course, this is no reason to ignore, much less to eliminate these distinctions. Instead, the basic structure can be arranged so that these contingencies work for the good of the least fortunate. Thus we are led to the difference principle if we wish to set up the social system so that no one gains or loses from his arbitrary place in the distribution of natural assets or his initial position in society without giving or receiving compensating advantages in return.[41]

It is this commitment to the idea of natural talents as a common asset that formed the moral core of Rawls's proposal for the difference principle.

If we compare the idea in this passage that we are 'to regard the distribution of natural talents as in some respects a common asset' with the idea that 'the more advantaged have a right to their natural assets', then there is an obvious tension. If the distribution of natural talents is to be regarded as a common asset, it would be allowable to require of the most able that they work so as to raise the position of the least well-off, and it is hard to see how one could resist the permissibility of lump-sum taxes on ability if they were required to achieve this aim.

Moreover, if the end-state interpretation were correct, G.A. Cohen would be right to say that Rawls's acceptance of economic inequality—even the limited economic inequality associated with the difference principle—is problematic, because, if the more productive members of society were to affirm the underlying values of the difference principle, they would see that they had no right to secure greater advantages by holding out for incentives when they could make the same contribution for the same final income as everyone else.[42] Apart from the sort of 'incentives' necessary to compensate for the extra expenses involved in training to enhance ability or invest in human capital, there would be no case for higher returns to the more advantaged. By contrast, if the more advantaged have a right to their natural assets, it would be a violation of the integrity of their person to require them to work longer than they would freely choose, no lump-sum taxes would be permitted and differences in returns would be allowed.

A further counter-intuitive implication arises from the assumption that the labour of each is owned by all. Suppose that the well-being of the least well-off could be raised by *their* being made to work longer. The more advantaged might argue that underlying their advantages are superior skills of personal organization by contrast with those trapped in a 'culture of poverty' and the poor could be made better off by being brigaded into teams and provided with productive opportunities. They would gain not only in economic benefit but also in the enhancement of human capital. Indeed, we might suppose that the more advantaged were not being selfish in advancing this argument, since its acceptance would lead to a reduction in their own relative advantage. They could offer their organizational skills for free whereas the poor would be rewarded for their work effort. If there really is an agreement emerging from the social contract to regard the distribution of natural talents as in some respect a common asset, then it is hard to see what could be said against such a proposal. The only counter-argument is that a component of well-being is a freely chosen work-leisure trade-off on the part of individuals. But this reverts to the idea that individuals should be free to exercise their talents or not as they choose, rather than those talents being part of a common pool under collective control.

There is one further implication of the common assets assumption that seems not only counter-intuitive, but also at odds both with the full fruits principle and, on this point, the Locke/Hodgskin position. The common assets assumption makes the exercise of one's labour power a means by which the value of one's labour is lost. Without either a Hohfeldian liberty or a right to one's natural assets, labour power comes to be regarded as part of a common store of capacity under the control of the community. In the Locke/Hodgskin interpretation of the full fruits principle, the exercise of labour power is the means by which goods and products are removed from the common store and reserved entirely to the use of particular individuals. Thus, rather than regarding labour power as a common asset under the control of those who manage common assets, the full fruits principle rests on the assumption *that labour distinguishes what is common from what is private*. In this respect, the Locke/Hodgskin theory and the practice of common property resources regimes rest on the same assumption, namely that no one owns the labour of another. In place of the ownership of each by all, there is the recognition that, in order for individuals to enjoy the returns to their own labour, they must grant a similar right to others. The collectivism of the common assets assumption can thus be contrasted with the individualism in both the mature Rawls's account of the difference principle, with its assumption of individuals having a right to their natural assets, and a contractarian viewpoint built upon the idea of Hohfeldian liberties in the non-agreement point. In this respect the mature Rawlsian account of the difference principle is closer to the constrained full fruits principle than it is to the common assets version of the difference principle.

Supposing this analysis to be right, it does not of itself provide a knock-down argument for deciding either way between collectivism and individualism. There is no easy way of arbitrating between the collectivism of the common assets viewpoint by contrast with the individualism of the basic right/Hohfeldian liberty account of the grounds of distribution. One might take on the implications of the collectivist interpretation of the difference principle (or Cohen's egalitarian gloss) as part of a broader conception of society. However, in choosing between different conceptions of society, there is one relevant consideration. The strongly collectivist viewpoint really only makes sense for the members of a tightly knit ideological or religious community who see themselves solely as the instruments of a common purpose and where the labour of each is seen as a contribution to the whole. There is a sense in which the members of such a community are beyond what Hume called the 'cautious jealous virtue' of justice which presupposes a distinction between 'mine and thine'. From this point of view, Marx was right to think of justice as a principle of bourgeois right. Yet, whereas a number of the common property resource regimes have lasted many centuries, egalitarian communities have been relatively short-lived, even when they have been founded on strong ideological or religious convictions. Thus the community of Oneida, in central New York, to which Menger referred stressing its sharing of the fruits of labour, lasted in effect less than twenty years, despite the quality of its products being high and the education of its children being progressive.[43] If communities that are strongly motivated to communal ends cannot successfully reproduce themselves over time (and Oneida was the opposite of a sect burdened by the principle of celibacy), it is unlikely that other types of community can successfully implement the collectivism that the full sharing of the fruits of labour requires. It is possible to think of social organization on the model of a camping trip among friends; but life is not a camping trip.[44]

3.6. Full fruits and economic rent

Gauthier offers an explicitly contractarian account of economic justice that balances in a distinctive way the individualism of the full fruits principle with the collectivism of a social contract.[45] According to Gauthier, the full fruits principle makes sense within a Crusoe-type economy in which people only have such resources as they have been able to produce by their own labour. On a negative definition of freedom, there is no abridgement of freedom in such an economy, even if people cannot secure all that they want, since no one is forcing anyone to work more or less than they individually choose to do. By analogy, the same is true in a perfectly competitive market in which workers are price-takers for their labour and in which the sum of others people's willingness to pay for their product is akin to the natural constraints of a Crusoe-type economy. In the perfect market, equilibrium and optimality are combined. In effect, this is to assume that all productive entities in a perfectly competitive market are Crusoe-like beings, in which productive effort is entirely a consequence of their own internal constitution with no spillover effects, either positive or negative, on the productivity of others.

However, when externalities occur, the market is no longer perfect: equilibrium and optimality come apart. Hence, there are joint gains to be made by some form of cooperation. In order to be fair, such cooperation must take, as its initial starting-point, Gauthier's version of the Lockean proviso, by which individuals are not entitled to improve their own situation by worsening the situation of others. However, the terms of cooperation have to go beyond the right to the full fruits of one's labour secured by the Lockean proviso to a socially agreed basis of allocation, since the existence of cooperation yields a social surplus over which participants are free to bargain. The sequence in Gauthier's analysis thus runs from Robinson Crusoe, through the perfectly competitive market to the externalities that call for some collective intervention.

Economic rent is the positive difference between the return that a person earns in a market for doing a job and the lower return that would induce them to do that job compared to their next best alternative. According to Gauthier, rent does not occur in a Crusoe-type economy, and so it cannot be said that not receiving rent interferes with one's freedom.[46] Rent 'is no part of the freedom of a solitary being; the surplus represented by rent arises only through interaction'.[47] By analogy, the same logic carries over to a perfectly competitive market in which workers are price-takers for their labour and in which the sum of others people's willingness to pay for one's product is akin to the natural constraints of a Crusoe-type economy. However, when externalities occur, because social cooperation is required, the factor rent to labour arising from that cooperation should be included in the shareable social surplus. To derive this conclusion, Gauthier offers a conceptual argument to the effect that persons are still free in their occupational choices if they do not receive rent, since they are free to secure an alternative line of employment, which is the opportunity cost of remaining in their present job. The rental return to market transactions is thus available for sharing on the basis of the bargain that is struck over the terms of cooperation.[48] This will result in a situation in which individuals are entitled to an income sufficient to induce them to take up a particular line of economic activity, and to a per capita share of the surplus derivable from the factor rent that is generated by social cooperation. The normative authority collectively to control returns to economic activity does not occur until there are externalities in the market, but, once it occurs, it covers the whole of the increased returns.

There are problems about the internal consistency of Gauthier's argument, but these can be put to one side in the present context.[49] A serious problem, however, with any prohibition upon economic rent is that rent is earned by all intra-marginal workers, that is to say all workers who would continue to do the same job for less pay.[50] As such, it is a pervasive feature of an economy, and should be regarded as one of the benefits of economic growth. Without rent, individuals are always poised on the cusp of a choice between their present occupation and their next best alternative, with all the associated anxiety of decision making. With rent there is some opportunity to exercise discretionary power over the pace and intensity with which a job is done. To transfer rent is to regard skills and talents as belonging to the common ownership of society, part of a pool of skills and talent subject to collective control. As argued in the previous section, this assumption is incompatible with a contractarian conception of society according to which the contract arises from individuals having good reason for giving up their freedom in order to secure the gains of cooperation. Whereas it is right to forbid individuals worsening the situation of others in order to benefit themselves, it is hard to see how it is right to prevent individuals improving their own situation when it does not harm others. Rent is just one of the ways in which that improvement is taken.

Gauthier's contractarianism shares with democratic contractarianism the recognition that the individualism of the full fruits principle needs to be balanced by the governance of collective control. However, whereas democratic contractarianism imposes governance so as to secure for each producer access to the means of production the fruits of which can be gathered consistently with the maintenance of the natural resource, the appropriation of rent in Gauthier's scheme imposes collective control over the outcome of social cooperation. What looked initially like a rugged individualism turns out to be the assertion of a strong collectivism. If there were any libertarians who thought that Gauthier's theory justified their ideological stance, as David Braybrooke suggested, they were wrong.[51]

3.7. Luck and needs

Contractarian reasoning in the empirical mode suggests that at the core of economic justice is the idea that those who work are entitled to the full fruits of their labour provided that the labour takes place in conditions that are suitably constrained, both with respect to the aggregate burden that is imposed on productive resources and with respect to the ability to secure equal access to the means of production. Such a position will allow inequalities of return to productive effort, skill, and luck, where effort and skill may themselves be dependent upon prior luck.

Luck egalitarianism is the principle that inequalities in economic circumstance are justifiable if they result from the choices that responsible individuals made (for example to work harder or to invest in one's talents by extra study), but not if they are the result of circumstances over which they have no control.[52] In La Fontaine's fable of the ant and the grasshopper, the grasshopper does not have a right to the ant's winter food, because while the ant was working to store up supplies, the grasshopper was merely singing. To the extent to which equivalent differences of behaviour in human beings reflect choice rather than genes or other unchosen determinants of behaviour, it follows that an equivalent difference in economic returns should be allowed. Choices can turn out well or badly, so a useful distinction for luck egalitarians is that between option luck and brute luck.[53] The standard case of option luck is that of a gamble that is voluntarily entered into. Before the event, the gambler does not know whether the backed horse will win or lose. Those who backed the losers should not complain by saying that they are now less well-off than those who backed the winners, since they knew the range of outcomes that confronted them. Brute luck, by contrast, covers all those cases of advantage or disadvantage that are outside the control of individuals, including such things as the skill and talents that one was born with or the windfall gains that come one's way. So the luck egalitarian position leaves people with the rewards of their chosen lucky choices, with the losses of their unlucky choices and with no claim on the returns to brute luck.

The principle of luck egalitarianism does not impose an obligation upon individuals to contribute towards the collective. Rather, it says that no gains are permissible if they are the product of brute luck. One way of putting this is to say that inequalities of good or bad fortune are to be evened out, but not the economic inequalities arising from the effort that people put into their work. To implement the principle would require more collective control than the full fruits principle under collective management of common pool resources, since the regulation that luck egalitarianism requires applies to the gains that people can make from productive activity, and not just to the conditions under which people enter into productive activity. Under the full fruits principle, someone who is lucky in harvesting resources, even someone who enjoys cumulative good luck in harvesting resources over a period of time, is entitled to keep the value of what they produce. By contrast, under a principle of luck egalitarianism, circumstantial advantages secured even when access to the means of production is equal are to be ironed out.

In common property resource regimes, both brute and option luck are involved in determining the returns that producers secure for their efforts. In such systems there is both a set of rules that by and large allows people to keep the value of what they produce and a set of rules that randomizes access to the resources by which they can exercise their productive skills. Brute luck is involved because the randomization in question is not like a gamble undertaken by individuals. Rather, it is a collectively imposed device to conserve natural resources and share out opportunities. Similarly, brute luck is also involved in determining the skills and abilities that people bring to their productive tasks. Where the household is the main unit of production, there is a large amount of brute luck involved in being born to one family rather than another, even though the lottery of marriage seems a paradigm case of option luck. To the extent to which people have a choice as to how long or how hard they work, as well as how much advantage they take of opportunities to improve their skills, it is also a matter of option luck. However, brute luck may be involved in determining one's ability to take advantage of the options. One may work harder or more efficiently through having been well trained when young by parents or teachers, or perhaps one just has more strength. Under a common property social contract, the full fruits principle will entitle one to keep the product of one's labour, however it arose through the combination of luck, skill, and choice.

It is possible to challenge the conceptual distinction between brute luck and option luck. Dowding offers examples in which brute luck can be transferred into option luck. Contestants in sporting competitions will have a history of plays between them, and it can well be the case that an initial piece of brute luck gives one the edge over the other, so that there is an arbitrary path-dependence of outcomes. The choices that each makes about the way to play, whether for example to play aggressively or defensively, will reflect this history, but the choices are ones that are made in a fully responsible way.[54] In other words, unless we regard every little twist and turn of fate as transforming option luck into brute luck, whenever it has measurable effects on subsequent performance, the significance of the distinction is difficult to uphold. However, it is not simply a question of how hard it is to operationalize the distinction between brute luck and option luck. Social science may one day advance to the point where it can, for example, identify the influence that good parenting has on the ability of children to make prudent choices, and will find some way of extending the practices of good parenting to as many children as possible, compensating the others where this is not possible. Rather it is a question of whether the distinction between brute and option luck is one that is meaningful within a theory of social justice.

The principle embodied in the practices of common property resource regimes is that inequalities that derive from differences that are arbitrary from the moral point of view are justifiable provided that they are not too great and are consistent with individuals enjoying political equality and equality of status as partners in a common enterprise protecting collectively important interests. Although some people benefit more than others as a result of good fortune, no one is in a position to benefit to the extent that their resources provide the means to dominate others. Equality of social relations is preserved.

There is one obvious problem with this approach. An important element in our thinking about justice is that goods—or at least some goods—should be distributed according to need.[55] The point is not simply that a good society is one that ensures that the needs of its members are met. Rather, to claim that distribution according to need embodies justice is to say that those in need have claims that they can assert as a matter of right against fellow members of their society. Where the relief of poverty or destitution is not associated with claims based on right, then we may have a regime of humanity or compassion, but we do not have a regime of justice. Yet redistribution according to need seems incompatible with the principle that those who work are entitled to the full fruits of their labour, even in its socially constrained form.

This dilemma was put very well by Cohen from within his own socialist theory of justice, although he notes that the same point was made by Anton Menger who, nearly a hundred years before, identified the conflict between a right to the full fruits of one's own labour and a right to subsistence.[56] Cohen begins by noting that the traditional communist theory of the working class was that it combined four distinct elements: it constituted the majority of society; it produced the wealth of society; its members were the exploited in society; and its members were the needy people in society. For Cohen, a significant problem facing any theory of justice is the way in which, under contemporary class conditions, these elements come apart:

> Particularly problematic, from the point of view of a socialist political philosopher, is the coming apart of the exploitation and need features. It forces a choice between the principle of a right to the product of

> one's labor embedded in the doctrine of exploitation and a principle of an equality of benefits and burdens which negates the right to the product of one's labor and which is required to defend support for very needy people who are not producers and who are, *a fortiori*, not exploited.[57]

Thus the right to the fruits of one's labour is at odds with the satisfaction of basic needs. The implication of this disjuncture of circumstances is that a theory of justice can no longer be based upon a claim by workers to the full fruits of their labour. How can one respond to this difficulty?

At this point we are brought to the limit of what we can directly infer from the example of common property resource regimes. The merit of looking at such regimes was that they provided empirical evidence about the agreements that would be made in a democratic contract for justice, because they exemplified relations of approximate equality of power. They could thus provide a model social contract in a situation of political equality, practical reason in the face of fallibility and concern for common interests. The circumstances of justice in collective decision making were met. However, the practices of common property resource regimes cannot be applied without modification to the circumstances of other societies. In particular, the societies in question are small-scale and the needs of individuals are primarily met within the household. To answer the question about the role of needs in a theory of justice, we need to consider both the abstract features of common property resource regimes regarded as models of democratic social contracts (Chapter 4) and the transformation that comes over societies when they cease to be face-to-face communities and become great societies (Chapter 5). This will provide the background for looking at the grounds of redistribution in those great societies, an examination that will also requires us to develop principles of justice for reproduction as well as production (Chapter 7).

CHAPTER 4

The theory of democratic social contracts

4.1. The democratic social contract

If the democratic procedures of the sort represented by common property resource regimes model a social contract, what type of social contract is it that they model? Any contract theory, whether hypothetical or empirical, works by incorporating into its description of the contractual situation—in particular its description of the agents in that situation and their mode of negotiation and agreement—conditions and constraints such that the upshot of the contractual agreement can be plausibly regarded as justifiable. The contractarian approach involves agents located in a suboptimal baseline, who have a common interest in improving collectively on their situation. They are required to deploy their practical reasoning to overcome the dilemma in which they are located. If they have similar levels of bargaining power, then the conjecture of democratic contractarianism is that the agreements that they make will incorporate principles of justice, of which one example is a willingness to allow producers to keep the fruits of their own labour, provided that access to the means of production remains open to all on roughly equal terms. In this way, a suitably constructed theory of the social contract provides us with a decision procedure by reference to which a plausible conception of justice can be determined (within feasible limits of specificity). In terms of democratic theory, such contracts can be interpreted as the operation of collective self-governance. That is to say, the social contract is democratic in character if it is formed among self-governing persons, under conditions of equality, capable of deliberating about their common interests and willing to legislate for their collective life in a way that is responsive to the preferences and opinions of political associates. The logical structure—rational agents negotiating to mutual advantage over matters of common interests where each participant has equal standing—is isomorphic between the two interpretations.

A theory of democratic contractarianism should offer an account of the key elements of this conception, including the rationality of the parties, the form of equality they enjoy, and the common interests around which contractual agreement converges. Since common property resource regimes model the democratic social contract, the theory of that contract can draw its evidence about what is required of a democratic social contract from the features and working of those regimes, although the theory itself will need to be stated in more abstract terms. Since a fundamental element of the democratic social contract is the collective determination of the circumstances of common life—in the case of common property resource regimes, rules determining such matters as extraction and harvesting rates or access to the use of specific resources—a theory of the social contract must also offer an account of the public reasoning that underlies such rules. The purpose of this chapter is to address these theoretical issues. In particular, its purpose is to state in a conceptually general way the key features that are empirically observable in the common property resource regimes that model the requirements of social justice. One important implication is that, in order to move beyond the particular circumstances of common property resource regimes, we need to understand the central theoretical concepts in terms of which they can be characterized. These theoretical concepts will also be important when we consider the circumstances and conditions of 'great societies' in Chapters 6 and 7 to which principles of democratic justice have to be applied.

A democratic social contract is a contract among a plurality of actors. This fact of plurality captures an essential feature of politics, namely that a common course of action is required in circumstances in which individuals and groups have different interests and opinions.[1] Such differences are, in part, a consequence of bounded rationality, the result of which is that the attention spans of political agents are limited, as is their ability to identify the full implications of their decision premisses. The outlook of political actors is necessarily partial. These features of rationality would exist even if, *per impossibile*, all individuals were similarly placed in terms of their personal attributes, social standing, and economic productivity. If there is variation among persons in certain key respects of their lives, political organization will reflect the differences arising from that variation.

It follows from this fact of plurality that the social contract for democratic justice cannot be one in which contracting parties are located behind a thick veil of ignorance with respect to their own position in society. Yet they have to negotiate to a common solution in the face of plurality. Of course, the same bounded rationality that will lead the contracting parties to have different opinions and interests will also create uncertainty for each participating agent about his or her future role and place in society, even if that uncertainty falls short of a complete veil of ignorance. At the very least this will lead to some convergence of practical judgement about such matters as providing for economic and social security in the face of common risks, just as uncertainty creates the conditions under which insurance markets arise. However, even a high degree of bounded rationality is unlikely to lead to complete convergence of judgement and view, which is why political procedures are necessary in order to reconcile differences.

Mere plurality does not require the collective determination of rules if the preferred actions of individual agents are compossible.[2] A group of Robinson Crusoes on separate islands could cultivate their own gardens to their hearts' content without having to worry about the need to coordinate with others. In such a situation there is no call for justice, since as a virtue it plays no practical role in the deliberations of any of the agents. However, in managing a common resource, the need for coordination arises. With the conservation of resources as central to production as woodlands, fishing waters, irrigation water, and grazing rights, the requirement of common action goes beyond mere coordination and extends to the interest that each participant has in the continuing viability of those resources, whatever their other differences might be. Just as some degree of bounded rationality induces some commonality of interest and opinion, so does the fact that justice arises on the occasion of the need to conserve a common resource.

The common property resource regimes taken to model social justice impose a rough equality of power upon participants. Within democratic contractarianism the assumption of equality of power ensures that the principles of justice do not reflect mere imbalances of advantage of a morally arbitrary kind. Contracting parties are precluded from appealing to an asymmetric threat-advantage in a coercive way to impose a particular solution as the collective outcome. In this respect, the equality of power assumption resembles the assumption of a thick veil of ignorance in hypothetical contract theory. Both assumptions are made to eliminate morally arbitrary advantages among the contracting parties, but they function in different ways within their respective theories. In hypothetical theories with a thick veil of ignorance, the parties know that they will have to make rules for societies in which there will be a plurality of different views, although they do not know what their own view will be. In theories that do not employ the device of a veil of ignorance, but endow the contracting agents with knowledge of their own circumstances and abilities, there has to be some other way of ensuring that morally arbitrary differences of circumstance and ability do not distort the negotiation process. The assumption of equality of power, understood as equality of bargaining advantage, captures this requirement.

Any putative solution emerging from negotiation about a social contract must be one in which the good of each is a requirement for the good of all. If each person is to find it advantageous to sign a social contract rather than put up with the disadvantages associated with the lack of social cooperation, then each person must find the proffered terms of cooperation more advantageous than a non-agreement point. This condition of individual advantage is at the core of contract theory, providing a counterpart, in the construct of the contract, to the requirement in the theory of justice that not only is each person's interests to be counted as one and no more than one (as would be true average utilitarianism) but also that in counting these interests there are certain components of well-being that cannot be sacrificed to the social good. Mill's thought that sentiments of justice gather around the notion that we have a claim 'on our fellow creatures to join in making safe for us the very groundwork of our existence' is to be met in a contractarian way.[3] The gain of everyone over a non-agreement point must be a gain for each. The requirement of agreement is that each person is put in a position in which the groundwork of their existence is not sacrificed to others.

Social deadlocks can be broken in various ways, and in some occasions their resolution will be effected by a small group in society that has hegemonic control over the instruments of political authority, yielding a distribution of benefits from social cooperation that is highly unequal and exploitative. The social contracts discussed by Moore fall into this category.[4] If the baseline point of non-agreement is sufficiently harmful to human interests, many people may be willing to agree to a social contract simply to escape a worse fate. Olson, for example, imagines roving bandits becoming stationary bandits. In becoming stationary, they acquire a long-term interest in the productivity of those over whom they rule, and so are prepared to invest in public goods to improve that productivity. Stationary bandits have an incentive to increase the productivity of those over whom they tyrannize.[5] The contract of rulership is not just, but it may be acceptable to a population if the alternative is a succession of roving bandits. The Normans may have provided the Saxons with protection from the Vikings, but at the cost of feudal service, a contract similar to that of Olson's stationary bandits. Indeed, Thomas Paine, writing in the tradition of theorists of the Norman Yoke, referred to the Conquest as a 'French bastard landing with armed banditti and establishing himself King of England'.[6] A democratic social contract must be more than a contract of mutual advantage, because any approach to social contract theory that takes as its baseline point of non-agreement predatory behaviour cannot respect the equality of power requirement that is an inherent feature of the social contract democratically conceived.

The good that agents pursue in common property resource regimes is access to productive resources. Resources are like primary goods, indeed they can be thought of as a subset of primary goods, the general-purpose means to human well-being. They produce food, fuel, fabrics, house-building materials, and so on. One reason why resources are the focus of any theory of justice is that they are the objects of competition and appropriation among the members of a community. However, it may be thought that a focus upon resources as the object of justice is inadequate, since the ability to use resources also affects human welfare. Resources are a means to an end, not an end in themselves, and we should be interested in the way in which resources combine with the ability of persons to make use of those resources to produce capabilities.[7] Yet a focus on capabilities would be both misleading and premature. It is misleading since it is clearly access to productive resources that are the concern of common property resource regimes. It is premature since we cannot have an account of capabilities without an account of needs, and that part of the theoretical story is to come (see Chapter 7).

The good of individual persons in the social contract need not be equated solely with their personal good. Individuals generally have wider interests than their own personal ones, most obviously the interests of their family or household. What is more, they may have strong motivational attachments to their church, their political party, their region, country, language, or culture. In the practical reasoning of individuals, it is sometimes a sufficient condition for their acting that the interests, well-being, or ideals of a group to which they belong is advanced by their action. So to say that a social contract must advance each individual's good is not to say that it should advance solely their own material interests. However, that individuals have significant attachments beyond their own interests still requires there to be a social contract, because neither personal interests nor different conceptions of the good automatically harmonize with one another. Different individuals, attached to social groups whose ideals are distinct and incompatible with the ideals of other groups, have to find sufficient advantage in a social arrangement if it is to be one that they can find reason to support. The idea is not that each person finds the contract maximally advantageous *tout court*, but that each finds the arrangement the best that he or she can secure given the distinct and potentially conflicting interests and opinions of others.

If the social contract is one amongst agents with an interest in advancing their own good in the context of a plurality of actors in a situation of rough equality of power, what does this imply for the account of rationality? One feature of common property resource regimes is that deliberation is not a consequence or implication of the agreement process but is a characteristic of that process. Agents need to craft solutions to collective action problems that meet the condition of there being a fit between appropriation rules and local conditions. Agents need to participate in changing or modifying the rules so crafted. And agents need to apply sanctions in a graduated way. These were among the conditions identified by Ostrom for the success of common pool resource regimes (see Chapter 2.3). All three features presuppose deliberative capacity on the part of participating agents. That is to say, public deliberation is not a practice on which putatively utility maximizing agents would agree as a way of realizing their goals. Rather it is the means by which agents arrive at and implement the agreed terms of a social contract. Deliberation enters at the ground floor of the social contract. This requirement provides a guide to the requisite theory of rationality, with implications that link that theory to our understanding of democracy. The democratic theory of justice is a contractarian theory of mutual advantage, but it is also a theory that seeks to account for the role of deliberation in democracy.

The method of constructivism requires the construction of the negotiating situation to define just terms of agreement, rather than these terms emerging from the motivation of the parties. The construction has to show how the situation of negotiation secures the agreement of the practical reason of the participating agents where the notion of practical reason is defined independently of moral motivation and in terms of an idea of prudence. Deliberative prudential rationality is taken to characterize the rationality of the parties negotiating the social contract. Given prudential rationality, equality of bargaining advantage models the contractual negotiation. Insofar as the rationality is democratic as well as deliberative, it is the rationality of participant actors, pooling their local knowledge under conditions of approximate equality of power, yielding an account of practical public reasoning. Rather than deriving the justification of democratic self-government from the logic of a contractual bargain, we seek to understand social contracts as the expression of democratic self-government under specifiable conditions.

4.2. Practical rationality

Contractarian theories are typically associated with utility-maximizing accounts of rationality, in which rationality is defined by a set of consistency conditions upon the rank-orderings that agents exhibit over sets of outcomes.[8] In consequence, all the burden of defining the social contract as a contract of justice has to fall upon the way in which the situation of contractual negotiation and choice is characterized by the theorist offering the construction, and this is sometimes the rationale for a thick veil of ignorance.[9] On the other hand, contractualist theories are normally thought of in deliberative terms, in which an assumption is made that each agent is motivated to justify his or her action to others on terms that they can accept.[10] The giving of reasons that all can share is an axiomatic assumption of such approaches. However, mutual advantage theories of justice need not be tied to a utility theory of rationality. A theory of rational choice as the consistent rank-ordering of preferences may be adequate for a number of purposes, as in conventional consumer theory. Often, however, some account of deliberation is needed in theorizing prudent choice, not least to account for phenomena like that of weakness of will or choices in which reasons are detached from desires.[11] Minimally moralized notions of prudence can still be deliberative.

What, then, are the principal features of deliberative rationality? To answer this question, begin from Aristotle's remark in the *Nicomachean Ethics* (1112a, 16–17) that choice is 'voluntary action [ἑκούσιον] preceded by deliberation [προαιρετόν]'.[12] In the modern developments of this notion, the idea of deliberation has been spelt out by an analysis of the practical syllogism, that is to say, of a chain of reasoning that ends in an action or a direction for action.[13] Rational agents act to bring about some end or advance their conception of the good. This is not to say that all the actions of agents are consciously purposive; some actions may be habitual or simply learned routines. It is to say that in respect of those actions related to governance and property rights, purposive action is central. Of course, to say that action is end-oriented in this way is a purely formal characterization. It says nothing as to whether those ends are selfish or altruistic, guided by the local or global, base or noble. In Aristotelian terms it requires that agents act for some good, but it says nothing about what the content of that good might be. However, if the theory is to retain its constructivist features, the pursuit of any good has to be consistent with agents' concern for their own prudent self-interest. Yet such self-interest also has to be an enlightened self-interest, one that recognizes that the pursuit by each of his or her self-interest can frustrate the achievement by all of their interests. The elements of rationality that we specify spell out the capacities upon which such enlightened self-interest can rest. We are seeking to define a deliberative and enlightened prudence.

The first element of such deliberation is that agents should be capable of reflective distance on the situation of choice that they confront. When thinking of common pool resource problems as a prisoner's dilemma, orthodox game theory insists that any commitment to cooperation before the game is played has to be modelled as a move within the game if it is to be credible.[14] In other words, preplay agreements to play cooperatively have no substance unless the rules of the game are altered by that agreement in such a way that it pays to behave cooperatively. However, if there is an agreement to remodel the moves in the game, then this implies that the agents facing a collective action problem can step back from the first-order logic of their decision making and appraise the situation as one that they themselves have to remodel. In standard representations of a prisoner's dilemma, the pay-off matrix specifies the rank order of choices for those playing the game. Transforming the game by remodelling the pay-offs is not to make a move within the game but to seek to institutionalize a different game given the interests of all the parties. By definition, prudent individuals will play defect in an orthodox prisoner's dilemma. By contrast, prudent and reflective individuals negotiating an empirical social contract will seek to construct a different game in which it is no longer prudent to play defect but instead play cooperatively as the condition for realizing joint gains. Reflective distance should enable agents to realize the difference between a prisoner's dilemma and games like the battle of the sexes, in which shared action is preferred by each party to separate action.[15] A social contract involves agents themselves undertaking the remodelling of their everyday decisions, and in order to do this such agents must be able reflectively to appraise the situation they are in.

It is useful here to highlight the distinction between remodelling a collective action problem by means of a social contract and the evolution of cooperation in situations where plays of a prisoner's dilemma are repeated. It is well known that if agents confront one another in repeated plays of a prisoners' dilemma, then under certain conditions a stable pattern of cooperation will emerge.[16]

The crucial conditions concern the relationship between the time discount rates of the players and the ratio of cooperative advantage to the advantage secured by defection. Roughly speaking, if the agents are sufficiently long-sighted and the ratio of cooperative to non-cooperative advantage is relatively high, they will not take the short term advantage if that closes off their being able to attain a higher sum of advantages by cooperation over time. Such cooperation can arise without any reflective appraisal, as is shown by the fact that models of such cooperation operate within the non-human animal world. The practice of 'you scratch my back and I will scratch yours' can emerge within a non-human animal population, and it can be shown that those individuals who behave well towards one another may become a dominant proportion of the population. The evolution of cooperation in this sense is an important element in the biological account of population dynamics, but it rests upon different logical foundations from those of deliberative contract theory.[17] A deliberative social contract is a multi-lateral agreement among prudently reflective individuals; the evolution of cooperation in a population is an unreflective outcome of mutually beneficial interactions between pairs of individuals, the overall effect of which alters the balance of cooperation and defection within that population. This is not to say, of course, that trial and error processes are unimportant in the development of a deliberative social contract, or that the terms of any social contract will not be modified in practice as participants experiment consciously or unconsciously with modifications of the agreed rules.

If reflective capacity is the first feature of deliberative rationality, deliberative competence is the second. Deliberative competence is the ability to follow a chain of reasoning from premisses to practical conclusion. Here again there is a useful contrast with the discovery of mutually beneficial exchange as it might be found in non-human species. Successful mutual back-scratching does not have to be reasoned: it merely requires that both agents find it to their long-term benefit, however they first hit upon its usefulness. By contrast, rotation systems in access to water rights or forest cutting have to be practically constructed through design and agreement. A chain of reasoning has to show how they solve the collective action problem through altering the moves of the game. The chain has to be part of some individuals' calculations and probably, to be stable, must be understood by all participants.

Deliberative competence can be understood in terms of the centrality of the practical syllogism to the explanation of human action and an important account of such practical inferences has been provided by von Wright.[18] Modifying slightly von Wright's scheme, the practical syllogism can be represented as follows:

> *X* now intends to make it true that *E*.
> He thinks that, unless he does *A* now, he will not achieve this.
> Then his conduct is an act of doing *A* or, unsuccessfully, aims at doing *A*.

In this account, the agent has an end to be pursued and understands that there is a necessary condition to be met in order to secure that end, the condition depending upon the action of the agent in question. From this follows the practical character of the syllogism. The chain of practical reasoning ends with the conclusion of the syllogism in an action description that needs to be consistent with what is performed. Any piece of agent's behaviour that is inconsistent with the action description is also logically inconsistent with the premisses.

As von Wright points out, there are a number of qualifications that, in a strict account, need to be added to this core analysis, most importantly that the person is not prevented from doing *A*. For present purposes these qualifications can be left to one side. The value of von Wright's scheme is that it shows one way in which we can understand deliberative competence as the ability to follow a chain of reasoning. However, as it stands, the account is too restrictive, because it requires the inferred action to be a necessary condition of bringing about the end, whereas in many practical situations the only requirement is that the action be sufficient for the end.[19] In formulating this element of sufficiency complications arise, since what is sufficient may also be excessive. No prudent person uses a sledgehammer to crack a walnut, but a practical syllogism in which the means was sufficient but not necessary would seem to license any sledgehammer where a nut was the issue.[20] Either taking the train or taking a taxi may suffice as means for transport to London. On the sufficiency model the imperative for the taxi is just as great as the imperative for the train, even though it may be much more expensive. Whatever the technical ways of coping with this problem, the core idea is that what a deliberatively competent agent would undertake is an action consistent with the conclusion of a practical syllogism.

A third key element of deliberative rationality is the ability of agents to specify what actions count as a contribution to the achievement of a goal. Suppose that someone has the intention of preventing the flowers in his or her garden from wilting. In terms of the practical inference, this is represented in the von Wright's scheme by the person having the thought that the only way of achieving this end is by watering the garden. When someone has the thought that the flowers are wilting combined with the thought that only by watering the garden would this be prevented, then we understand that person's behaviour because we see the action following as a conclusion from the premisses. The intelligibility of the action depends upon our understanding the choice in this way.

There is of course no one way of watering a garden. The same end may be achieved through a bucket, a sprinkler, or a hose pipe. That any particular action is a way of achieving the intended goal is a matter of assessing how far an action counts as one of watering. In particular, it is a matter of determining what counts as fulfilling the minor premiss of a practical syllogism. Of course, in the case of gardening, the problem of specifying a minor premiss is straightforward. Little practical experience is needed to determine what constitutes a suitable act of watering. However, when we come to actions exhibited in the case of common property resources, the task of specification becomes more difficult. To determine that a particular rotation of user rights will conserve fish or forestry stocks is a much more complicated task, and may involve gathering experience over a number of years, quite apart from the difficulty of knowing how far others will cooperate appropriately in the common enterprise. Even assuming the full compliance of others, there is still a problem as to whether an identified pattern of agreed action is in fact likely to serve the purpose that is collectively intended. To assess the answer to this question adequately requires the rational ability to identify a set of actions as meeting the specification that is implied by the practical syllogism.

The task of knowing whether a class of actions meets the relevant specification of a practical syllogism is made complicated by the fact that some specifications will have to be invented. Thus the practice of designating fishing waters and then using a rotation system following the random assignment of fishing locations, as agreed in Alanya, is a good illustration of the ability not only to craft solutions but to craft solutions that have to be invented. Whilst it does not require innovation, deliberative rationality allows for innovation and creativity, for the 'fact that man is capable of action meant that the unexpected can be expected from him', so that choice is not 'a passive response of the chooser to a set of choosables each fully relevantly specified, finitely numerous and thrust upon him without his participation' but the chooser 'is free to originate the choosable entities, the mutually rival acts within reach and their respective skeins of envisageable (practically supposable, not-impossible) sequels'.[21] Rationality includes the capacity to invent new solutions to problems, solutions that in the nature of the case cannot be anticipated before they are invented.

The identification of practices that constitute the content of successful collective action would be a problem even if we allow for full compliance, but the conditions of compliance are also matters of deliberative rationality. One element of being deliberatively rational is that not only does one have reasons for acting in certain ways, but also that one is the sort of creature that can give oneself reasons. As Kenny has put it, 'it is only those beings who have the ability to give reasons who have the ability to act for reasons'.[22] This is not to say that every time individuals act for a reason, they always self-consciously give themselves a reason. Many actions that we have good reason to perform take place on occasions where we do not give ourselves a reason to perform any particular action, for example in carrying out everyday routines of personal hygiene. Nonetheless, unless we could give ourselves a reason for acting in certain ways, we would not say that our actions were deliberatively rational. So, in order to be deliberatively rational, we have to be able to articulate the reasons for our actions.

The giving of a reason to oneself is a form of normative self-determination. Social contracts are devices for the construction of norms of action for individual participants. So they presuppose the capacity for normative self-direction. Without the capacity to give themselves reasons for acting, participants could not be subject to norms that were grounded in a social contract. For example, in a common property regime in which access to resources is allocated in turns, each participant has a reason not to jump their turn or to take more than they are due, a reason that arises from the norms that have been agreed. The ability voluntarily to enter into a social contract requires the ability to give oneself the reason to comply with the norms that emerge from agreement. Without the ability to acknowledge that norms form reasons that one can direct oneself to follow, the social contract would be nugatory. Others would have no reason for finding the commitment credible. Moreover, if one thought that one's own case generalized to others, then one would have no reason for thinking that a social contract was anything other than epiphenomenal. If action is the upshot of practical rationality, then a social contract requires participants to make a particular normative content of practical rationality—namely the norms that arise from agreement—their own.

So far, we have seen that deliberative rationality requires reflective distance, deliberative competence, the ability to understand particular specifications as means towards determined ends, including specifications that are novel, and the ability to give oneself reasons and to reject the temptations associated with compliance in respect of those reasons. One feature that arises in consequence of these characteristics is that practical rationality is defeasible. To say that a pattern of reasoning is defeasible is to say that an otherwise valid chain of reasoning is vulnerable to new information. In this respect defeasible reasoning contrasts with the deductive rationality of classical first-order logic. In classical first-order logic, a valid inference is unaltered by the addition of new premisses. If 'all men are mortal' is true and 'Socrates is a man' is true, then the inference 'Socrates is mortal' is not only valid but immune to the acquisition of new information, for example our observing that Socrates jumped over the Parthenon.[23] This property of validity being immune to new information is known as monotonicity and classical first-order deductive logic is monotonic.[24] Within classical first-order logic, as sentences are added to premisses so the number of conclusions must increase. In a deduction the conclusion is contained within the premiss: the class of men includes Socrates, so that anything that is true of each and every member of the class will be true of Socrates. However, if reasoning is defeasible, then this immunity to new information no longer holds, and the logic of inference is non-monotonic. Consider a familiar example from the writing on non-monotonic logic. Although we would normally infer from 'Tweety is a bird' to 'Tweety flies' (because that is what birds typically do), we would not be entitled to draw that conclusion if we discover that Tweety is an ostrich. The inference is non-monotonic because it is not immune to the addition of such new information.

Over the last thirty years, logicians and researchers into artificial intelligence have produced important insights into the conditions under which non-monotonic inference can be sustained and the characteristic forms that it can take.[25] In particular, they have shown the different ways in which incomplete information gives rise to particular problems of inference. For example, much everyday reasoning may refer to prototypical cases. We are generally right to infer of any bird that it flies, because that is what birds typically do, although we know of a number of cases where the inference would not be valid (where the bird is a penguin or an ostrich, where it has been injured and so on). Moreover, prototypical characteristics may be combined in odd ways. We know that Quakers are usually pacifists and Republicans hawks, so do we infer that Richard Nixon, both Republican and a Quaker, is a pacifist or a hawk? Only new information will resolve the matter. Or we may establish a presumption, deliberately allowing the possibility that evidence will overturn it, as in the standard rule that persons accused of a crime are innocent until proven guilty.[26] In all these cases our reasoning is defeasible.

It has been persuasively argued that theoretical reasoning, as well as practical reasoning, is defeasible.[27] For example, in knowing whether a dry well-made match is liable to light if struck, we need to make assumptions about the initial conditions under which the striking takes place. A match that is struck outside of an electromagnetic field will light, whereas the same or like match struck inside an electromagnetic field will not. The credibility of generalizations that we make about physical relationships is therefore subject to assumptions concerning the initial conditions under which those relationships occur. *Ceteris paribus* clauses are ways of signalling that any generalization has to be relativized to specific initial conditions.

The distinction, then, between theoretical and practical reasoning in respect of defeasibility is one of typical purpose rather than logical kind. In theoretical reasoning we typically focus on ascertaining the truth of generalizations under similar conditions formulated as law-like statements. For example, Gresham's law states that bad money drives out good and it is a plausible hypothesis that this generalization holds across a number of different cases (for example whether we are talking about US dollars, pounds sterling, or euros). In practical reasoning, by contrast, we typically face the dilemma of knowing whether a routine piece of behaviour that works in one context will also work in another, sometimes in a situation in which the choice is serious. We may have good reasons for holding that a particular plant variety will give high yields, but doubt if this is true when planted on certain soils or at times when it is vulnerable to unseasonably hot or cold weather. Theory ascends from the particular to the general; practice only needs as much generality as necessary to make it efficacious. In particular, in practical reasoning the scope of the initial conditions is important. For this reason a rule of some non-monotonic logics is to prefer the more specific over the more general within an hierarchical classification of types.[28] We do better in our inferences if we know that Tweety is an ostrich than if we know that Tweety is a bird, even if we could infer a great deal that was true and important about Tweety from knowing its avian status.

In the collective action theory of common pool resource regimes, this characteristic of deliberative rationality is underlined by the importance of ensuring that appropriation rules are suited to the particular characteristics of the locale in which the regime operates (this was Ostrom's second condition for successful regimes, section 2.3). The notion of appropriate here means suited to the specific conditions under which the regime has to operate rather than conforming to some general directive. For example, in Valencia the rules fix the order in which farmers can receive water and each farmer can use as much water as he decides, provided that water is not wasted. This is the *turno* system. In Murcia and Orihuela, each farmer is assigned a *tanda*, a fixed time period in which he can receive water, but he does not know how much water will be available at that time. Both sets of rules can be understood as different ways of conserving water, with the variation depending upon the specific circumstances of the locality and the contingency of the decision of the local collective decision-making body. Generalizing from one case to the other would have limited relevance.

A conclusion of practical rationality that would specify one and only one of these ways of implementing a rotation system would be defeated by evidence from the other.

4.3. Equality of power

Democratic contractarianism conceives the social contract as a contract among equals. In the model social contracts of common property resource regimes, one respect in which participants are equal is that they each have their own good to protect and advance, in particular the benefit that each derives from the resources that they are able to harvest. The well-being of households depends upon the productive activities of its members, but it also depends upon those members being able to appropriate sufficient resources from the natural and cultivated world to make those productive activities beneficial. Each participant is equal in that each has an interest in securing sufficient resources to survive and flourish. In this respect, participants are in competition with one another. However, each also has an interest in the long-term maintenance of the common pool resource itself, and this is an interest that each has in common with other participants. Thus participants are interested in their own good, but they also have an interest in being able to bargain to mutual advantage with one another over the good they share in common. To say that there is an equality of bargaining advantage is to say that the influence that each can play in those negotiations is approximately equal, or at least that no subset of actors so dominates the negotiation that they can achieve their own goals without compromise.

How are we to conceptualize this equality of bargaining advantage? The key idea is that of a balance of power among the relevant actors. Since the pioneering work of Schelling, it is clear that the idea of a balance of power is best understood as a form of interdependence, in which there is a reciprocal ability of agents to bestow, deny, or deprive other agents of something that they value.[29] In the common property regimes this condition is satisfied by the circumstances of production. In Törbel, for example, highly terraced agriculture meant that all were potentially vulnerable to poor maintenance on one of the terraces. In Alanya, if fishing boats crowded too closely together in search of a school of fish, they risked fouling one another's nets. In Murcia and Valencia, waste of water meant that others could be deprived of a vital resource. These examples suggest that the core notion of a balance of power is that each has sufficient control of natural resources to bestow, deny, or deprive others of something that they value and in which they have an interest.

Power, in the general sense, is the ability to bring about an outcome.[30] There is nothing specifically human in this sense of power. A detergent can have the power to dissolve oil, a computer may have the power to process certain types of data, and the sound of a waterfall may have the power to calm the nerves. In ordinary speech, this general sense of the word 'power' comes close to that of the word 'ability', although there are clearly contexts where it would be strange to replace the second with the first. Thus it seems odd to say that someone has the power to do long-division sums in the head, although it does not seem odd to say that the same person has the ability to do so. However, this may simply be a matter of linguistic convention rather than an issue of meaning or conceptual significance. Certainly the word 'capacity' can often be substituted in cases in which the word 'power' appears, and capacity is close to ability. What all terms have in common is that they are dispositional: having power, ability, or capacity is not the same as exercising power, ability, or capacity, although we often do not know whether something has the power until we can observe its exercise. However, it would simply fall into the fallacy of the verificationist theory of meaning to suppose that the evidence for the power was what was meant by having the power.

The characteristic, though not the only, way in which power is exercised in politics is that one agent uses power in order to bring about an outcome consisting of a second agent's behaviour in conformity with the ends of the first.[31] In this context, the ability to dispose of resources is an essential element in politics, because it provides the means to bestow, deny, or deprive others of something that they value. Control of military resources, control of the means of production, and control of the fate of personnel and populations provide the means by which something of value can be used in different ways to modify or influence the behaviour of another. Military resources can deprive others of their military power, as well as their means of production or the lives of populations. Military resources can also be used to deny others of something valuable, as in the imposition of an embargo on goods going into a country or restrictions on the travel of its citizens. Control of economic resources can inflict deprivation, for example by denying another energy supplies, but by the same token it can bestow on others an inducement to behave in a certain way, as with an offer to supply natural resources like minerals essential for certain productive processes. In terms of personnel, the taking of hostages gives bargaining power to those who hold them, and the use of a human shield may deprive an opponent of power they would otherwise have. The ability to mobilize mass numbers on the streets is often itself an important instrument of power.

Control of resources should not be understood in a simple physical way, for two reasons. The first is that there are many examples of institutional power, understood as the authority under a set of rules to make a certain type of determination. The police have the power to make an arrest; judges have the power to sentence criminals to prison; adults have the power to marry or enter into contracts; parliaments have the power to pass legislation. Power in this institutional sense derives from occupying a role within a rule-governed institution, with the rules bestowing authority to make a decision or inaugurate an action. Institutional power is typically a precondition for the exercise of the control of military or economic resources. Within an army there have to be well-functioning systems of command otherwise the military resources cannot be deployed effectively and an economic system requires that individuals have the authority to coordinate the actions of others or dispose of resources to achieve their ends. This leads to the second reason why power should not be understood merely as a physical phenomenon. To exercise power in relation to others through military or economic means requires the acceptance of authority under a set of institutional rules or conventions. As Hume correctly pointed out: 'The soldan of EGYPT, or the emperor of ROME, might drive his harmless subjects, like brute beasts, against their sentiments and inclination: But he must, at least, have led his *mamalukes*, or *praetorian bands*, like men, by their opinion.'[32]

Power as a capacity to make a threat does not have to be exercised in order to be effective. It may be sufficient to induce someone to conformity to threaten to inflict harm by producing a setback to their interests by denial or deprivation.[33] This is the power of the strike, the boycott, or the military blockade. Interests can be set back by the exercise of the power of physical compulsion, as illustrated by the case of the frog-march; but the power, as a capacity, resides in the ability credibly to threaten such action. Interests do not actually have to be set back in order for power as threat to be operative. Indeed, because threats can be costly to administer, it is often better for the power-holder not to have to exercise them, even at the cost of losing something of value. Landowners can threaten legal action for trespass, but their interests are best served by people taking the warning and not trespassing in consequence, so saving on legal fees. If this means that some trespass occurs, then this may be the price to be paid. However, threats do not have to be so costly to administer that they cease to be credible. By contrast, power as bestowal does have to be exercised in order to be effective, at least in more than casual interactions. To promise an incentive to someone to behave in a certain way and then not to deliver on the promise is a certain way of making sure that one's exercise of power in the future is reduced. Threats can be held in reserve; promises have to be delivered, unless the person promising can find ways to go on making false promises that are nonetheless believed.

A situation in which there is a balance of power is one in which agents have the ability to offer credible threats or promises on a reciprocal basis. Schelling points out that even in situations of conflict, where parties have the ability to inflict considerable damage on one another, there are joint interests to be advanced, if only the joint interest in avoiding that mutual damage. A successful strike is not one that destroys the company in which the union's members work. A successful defence strategy is not one that leads to intolerable damage to one's own population, even if destruction is imposed on the opponent's population.[34] So it does not follow from each participant having some power to inflict damage upon others that there are no joint gains to be made. Indeed, it is precisely the possibility of avoiding the general damage that gives rise to the bargain. As Glaucon noted, from this perspective, justice emerges in the mutual agreement not to inflict damage upon one another. Each wishes to avoid a setback to interests, because many could create such a setback. However, in order for such bargains to be struck, there has to be the ability to make a credible commitment to cooperative action as an inducement to the other to conform to the terms of the agreement.

Inducements and threats are pervasive and typical modes of power, but they do not exhaust all forms. Another form of power is the power of persuasion, including the persuasion of example. This is the power of the orator, the advocate, and the preacher, or, in the case of the power of example, the saint. It is power by attraction and can be thought of as 'soft power', the ability of one country to influence others not by acting on their interests through threats or promises, but the ability to alter or modify the values by which countries define their interests, so that the one comes to want what another also wants.[35] As with promises and threats, this can be thought of as an asymmetrical form of power, in which one agent comes to acquire the value scheme of another agent. However, it also has a reciprocal form, as when a pattern of cooperation among agents leads them to value the relationship that they have jointly established as an integral part of the identity of each.

Promises and threats are forms of persuasion because they work through deliberation and choice. It thus might seem that we cannot distinguish power as persuasion from power as promises and threats. However, whereas all forms of promises and threats can be regarded as species of persuasion, not all forms of persuasion work through promises or threats. When you are persuaded of the proof of a mathematical theorem or of the appropriateness of the sentiment of a poem, the effect is not worked through inducements or threats, but by the logical and aesthetic merits of the work in question, rather than the accompanying features of the way in which those merits are portrayed. Indeed, Habermas's appeal to the 'force of the better argument' as being the decisive element in political justification has to rely upon a distinction of this kind, linking to the Kantian formulation of public reasoning in terms of 'the argumentative practices of a republic of letters'.[36] On this account, to free politics from threats and inducements, we have to rely solely upon arguments that are persuasive by virtue of their intrinsic merits.

From this point of view, it might seem a mistake to build a theory of justice upon the assumption of a balance of power understood as interdependence in outcomes among participants in a social contract were their threats or promises to be realized. Justification, it might be urged, should depend upon the intrinsic merits of the arguments advanced by each of the parties and not their ability to threaten retaliation in case an acceptable agreement is not forthcoming. Yet, just as Joseph Butler thought that there were arguments of benevolence that we could best appreciate in 'a cool hour' of reflection, so there may be arguments of justice that are best appreciated in circumstances in which a symmetry of power convinces some participants in a social contract that what is in the general interest is also in their separate interests.[37]

How is the condition of equal power related to the requirement of rationality? If each party is rational, and each knows that the other is rational, then no party can expect the other to entertain a concession or restriction that is not mutual. Both power and rationality are needed to make the contract one in which common rules are agreed. Equal power over advantages and disadvantages without the equal rationality to use that equal power will result in one-sided outcomes, for the one who is more rational in the deployment of resources can effect outcomes that the less rational agent cannot. Conversely, if each agent is as rational as the other, then each agent has to find a way of collaborating with others as equals.[38] Joint rationality may thus impose a form of universalizability. A universalizable reason is one such that, if it is a reason for one agent, it is a reason for all (under suitable conditions). Reasons may be distinguished from desires. So, even if agents had a desire for relative advantage, their acknowledgement that they were on common terms with other agents would give them a reason to act that was distinct from that desire. Since it would be a universalizable reason, it would be a reason that all similarly situated agents could share. Acting on universalizable principles would seem to enable players in a prisoner's dilemma to solve the collective action problem by reason alone.

Yet a requirement of generalizability or universalizability is not sufficient of itself to resolve the collective action problem. Indeed, the logic of mutual defection in a prisoner's dilemma rests on understanding that each agent has the same reason to defect. In a one-shot prisoner's dilemma there can be no reason for thinking that if you defect those playing with you will cooperate, since any reasoning that applies to you applies to them with equal force (unless they are somehow placed in a different situation to you, say by not sharing common knowledge about the structure of the game). Thus a maxim to the effect that one can only will what others could also will at the same time would lead to a policy of defection on the part of each agent. To be sure, there is an air of paradox about the thought that a generalizable pattern of reasoning will leave both players worse off than they need to be, because if both could agree to cooperate both would be better off. Yet this says nothing about the value of generalizable reasoning; it merely underscores the vicious situation in which the participants find themselves in the absence of their being able to make an enforceable contract. Generalizability and optimality come apart.

There is a distinction between unconditional and conditional universalizability. Unconditional universalizability is the principle that one should always act on those principles or maxims that could be universally willed. Onora O'Neill has shown that this approach will validly yield practical conclusions of the form that no one should coerce or deceive others.[39] Yet even these principles would be compatible with suboptimal outcomes in respect of collective action problems. Those subject to such dilemmas might well honestly, but regretfully, say to one another that they have no choice but to defect and to recognize that others have no choice but to defect. Indeed, on some occasions such honesty might be the prologue to attempts to change the rules of the game. To move towards an optimal outcome for all requires the logic of conditional cooperation according to which each person agrees to cooperate provided that others will do so. Here another level of universalizability arises, since there would be a contradiction, akin to the contradictions that O'Neill noted in respect of deception and coercion, if agents sought to commit themselves via a maxim of conditional cooperation without acknowledging that they could not do so unless they were prepared to bear the burdens just as they expected others to bear the burdens of such cooperation. From this point of view, the logic of conditional cooperation is a universalizable logic of commitment. The only condition under which one could rationally expect cooperation from others is that one is able to give a firm and credible commitment to cooperation oneself. And this requirement is also tied to the role of equality power in the social contract, as well as the capacity for normative self-direction.

If political associates are in a situation of rough equality of power, at least in the sense that non-compliance by only a few will deprive the members of the association of joint benefits, then the relevant form of reasoning over the rules to be followed by all will be one that addresses itself to the common issues facing the association and pays due attention to the need for the relevant rule-governed practice to be fair between participants. Public reasoning is the process by which associates deliberate upon the solutions to the common problems facing them. The reasoning does not stem from a putative agreement motive in which there is a desire to justify one's conduct to others; rather it stems from the need to legislate a rule to common advantage.

4.4. Practical public reasoning

In characterizing the social contract for democratic justice, we have already characterized a form of democracy. Among the various forms of democratic institutions and the conditions under which democracies exist, we have exploited the variation in form and circumstance to identify those that satisfy the circumstances of justice as widely understood. Such a democracy is egalitarian, participatory, oriented towards the securing of common interests, and rests upon a deliberative account of rationality. A complementary argument shows that the features of political equality, common interests, and fallible, that is to say defeasible, public reasoning constitutes a political system that is justifiable relative to the most feasible and defensible non-democratic form of government.[40] The social contract for democratic justice models the basic logic of political life. Competition and conflict are inevitable given scarce resources. At the same time cooperation in the production of certain public goods is required if competition and conflict are not to create a war of all against all. Ostrom, for example, highlighted the importance of the distinction between the act of appropriating a resource by a member of the community—for example catching fish or abstracting water from a river basin—where there is competition, and the maintenance of the resource system itself—for example stocks of fish or river basin management requiring the engineering of water abstraction—where producers have a common interest in maintaining the integrity and functioning of the system.[41] Participants in a common pool resource regime are in a situation of scarcity not abundance, but they need to cooperate with one another to maintain the stock of resources on which they all depend in being.

The account of rationality developed so far has sought to outline what assumptions we need to make about agents and the knowledge that they possess in order to understand how it is that they could enter into arrangements of conditional cooperation with one another to mutual advantage. In formulating an account of empirical social contracts, we saw that the rationality of such contracts had to be a deliberative rationality rather than the formal rationality of choice rankings. The elements of deliberative rationality included reflective distance, deliberative competence, the ability to understand particular specifications as means towards determined ends, including specifications that are novel, and the ability to give oneself reasons and to recognize the temptations associated with compliance in respect of those reasons. The principal rationale of this account was that individuals facing collective action dilemmas had to be capable of appreciating the situation that they were in and responding to that situation through the construction of innovative sets of rules embodied in social agreements and in committing themselves to the terms of those agreements. Moreover, defeasibility means the need to ensure that crafted rules are appropriate to local conditions and that participation captures dispersed knowledge. To cooperate is to cooperate in a set of practices under specific and definite circumstances.

The collective action problem that is faced by those in the social contract is how to achieve the end of resource conservation in such a way that the legitimate, but competing, claims of each associate are respected. As an issue of practical rationality, this can be seen as a problem of finding agreed minor premisses in a practical syllogism. The remodelling of the situation that deliberative reflection allows requires the selection and specification of means to bring about agreed ends together with the ability to demonstrate meaningful normative self-direction to the point where others have good reasons for finding the commitment credible, all against a background of the reasoning being defeasible. The account of practical public reasoning has to be consistent with these elements.

It may be argued that this focus on the minor premiss of the practical syllogism necessarily leads to an inadequate account of public reasoning. If public reasoning turns on the minor premiss of a practical syllogism, that would seem to rule out the discussion of ends as well as means in political judgement, and it might be urged that there is no reason to constrain public reasoning in this way. Democratic autonomy means that the choices of the collective should reflect the freely chosen ends of political associates, but unless those ends can be debated, then public reasoning is not being given full play. To focus the minor premisses of a practical syllogism unjustifiably limits the scope of public debate. The use of common property resource regimes as a model of justice is similarly restrictive, it might be argued, since the end of collective action, conserving the natural resources for future use, is taken as a given and is, to a large degree, uncontroversial.

However, to suppose that to focus on the minor premiss of a practical syllogism is unnecessarily narrow is to misconstrue the character of public reason. Even in situations in which deep differences in conceptions of the good are at issue, the problem of public reason is, in effect, a problem of determining such minor premisses. To illustrate this point, consider the way in which Rawls construes the problem of public reason. The principle of public reason within liberal constitutionalism is that no 'citizen, or association of citizens, should have the right to use state power to decide constitutional essentials as that person's, or that association's, comprehensive doctrine directs'.[42] In consequence, the considerations justifiably invoked to direct the use of public authority within a liberal constitutional regime should not make essential reference to controversial religious or philosophical ideals and doctrines, but rely instead on an overlapping consensus of reasons. Rawls's model for this account of public reason derives from the historical development of the principle of toleration as a result of the European Reformation.[43] The modern understanding of liberty of conscience grew out of an attempt to escape the wars of religion of the sixteenth and seventeenth centuries, reflection upon which led to a new possibility, namely the peaceful practice of toleration in liberal societies.

The justification of the Rawlsian conception of public reason therefore presumes an agreed public end, namely the maintenance of a reasonably harmonious and peaceful society, and derives an account of the conditions that would need to be satisfied in public discourse in order for this end to be realized. This is to regard the practices of toleration and its form of public reasoning either as a means to social peace or as a more detailed specification of what social peace requires. Either way, the form of argument can be fitted into the model of the practical syllogism. (The minor premiss of a practical syllogism does not have to be about minor matters.) In fact, the Rawlsian prescription of a separation of church and state is only one way of specifying the means to bring about social peace in the face of deep philosophical and religious divisions. An alternative is the pillarization of public power practised in the consociational regime of the Netherlands for much of the twentieth century by which public resources were assigned to separate religious corporate bodies to finance education and public services.[44] More generally, deep ethnic and other divisions can be resolved by such consociational devices, sometimes with the need to ensure that elite bargaining is softened by institutions that foster an interplay between political representatives and civil society.[45]

The approach to public reasoning via the premisses of the practical syllogism in relation to agreed ends also enables us to make sense of the claims that have been advanced under the label 'epistemic democracy'. Epistemic democracy requires that there are procedure-independent standards for better or worse political decisions.[46] In line with this view, Richardson, for example, has written as follows:

> 'Deliberation' is a truer sense, however—that which is needed to make deliberative democracy a view distinct from liberal proceduralism—will count as practical reasoning, reasoning that is oriented to figuring out the truth about what ought to be done. As we might more colloquially say, practical reasoning aims to figure out what really ought to be done.[47]

Put in this form, this seems to many like too strong a requirement on the possibility of normative argument. For example, some hold that imperatives to action can be neither true nor false in themselves, but have to refer to some antecedent desire. Even those who think that reasons for action are statements of fact distinguish between 'truth' with respect to theoretical statements and 'justified, correct or well grounded' with respect to ought statements.[48] In fact, if public reasoning is about filling out the specification of what is involved in broadly accepted public goals, we can provide an analysis both of how its constituents can be understood in a procedure-independent way and how political procedures are required to settle differences of view as to what is normatively required.

Consider the specification of a norm to resolve a coordination problem. A coordination problem has a structure in which all the parties have an agreed end, but they need to agree on their actions in order to realize that end. One obvious example of normative rules in this sense is rules of the road, many of which exist solely to coordinate drivers' expectations about the behaviour of other drivers. One example of such a rule was used in France for much of the twentieth century, namely that all drivers should give priority to vehicles coming from the right, except when the contrary was indicated. For many years this was a very effective rule. It had wide applicability (in towns and in the country, at roundabouts and junctions, and for heavy or for light traffic) and so avoided the need to make numerous specific decisions in particular localities. It was simple to state and simple to follow. It economized on the use of traffic signs and road markings, since it could be applied generally and could be presumed to be common knowledge among motorists. It therefore served a number of public ends very well. It provided the direction to drivers necessary to achieve coordination, and did so in a way that the use of scarce resources was avoided. However, it also had disadvantages. It relied on drivers coming out of minor roads to be suitably cautious when approaching major roads. It was premissed on there not being too great a volume of traffic, particularly on roundabouts, where those already on the roundabout had to give way to those coming on, so making for gridlock. And the assumption of common knowledge was less plausible as the number of foreign motorists on French roads increased.

Practical deliberative rationality directed at this issue would therefore have to encompass both questions of fact and the relative weight to be given to different values. The questions of fact concern such matters as the extent to which it is reasonable to believe that motorists do understand and operate the rule, whether the problems of accidental collisions are limited to certain types of junction (in which case the rule allows for an alternative provided that it is signed), what would be the costs of providing signage, and what projections there were for the increase in the volume of vehicles using the road. However, the deliberation would also have to encompass issues in which the relative weight to be given to certain values was important. How serious are the collisions compared to the amount of money that would need to be spent to make specific provision at each junction for which local direction was required? Since private insurance picks up much of the cost of collisions, is there an argument that there is no reason to take the expense of signage onto the public budget? What responsibilities do public authorities have to compensate for lack of drivers' (including foreign drivers') care and attention, who might otherwise be expected to know and follow the rules of road?

These are, of course, only a small portion of the policy questions that need to be addressed in such a change. The truth in the claim of epistemic democracy is that a conception of public reason that was merely defined in terms of procedures, without attention to the substantive merits of the reasoning that was offered in those procedures, would be misleading. The notions of truth and falsity have to be applied to decision premisses, otherwise the public reasoning of a democracy would not be functioning well. Were the overwhelming majority of those involved in the decision to hold false beliefs about any of the relevant matters of fact relevant to the decision, for example in over-estimating the costs of making the transition, it would not justify the use of those beliefs as reasons for the decision, even if the process by which the decision was made conformed to due process. A parallel argument applies to the relative weighing of values, even if we do not think that values can be ascribed properties of truth and falsehood. An unreasonable weight given to some values over others would not make for a justified decision, even if that relative weighing of the options was widely shared among those making the decision, as might be the case if no weight was given, for example, to the interests of foreign drivers.

Public deliberation, then, has to be a form of *reasoning*. That is to say, public reasoning has to be more than the uttering of sounds or marks on paper or a computer screen. The sounds and marks have to have meaning, they have to be linked in ways that makes their sequences intelligible and it has to be possible to make reliable inferences from the sounds or marks. In short, public reasoning has to conform to minimum standards of meaningfulness, inference, and evidence. Chambers has drawn attention to this aspect of public reason, labelling it the 'Socratic' as distinct from the 'democratic' element in public reasoning.[49] However, although from one point of view we can make a logical separation between the Socratic and the democratic aspects of deliberation, there is a line of argument that suggests that they are still linked in a very specific way.

The epistemic interpretation of democracy requires that the deliberation aim at the truth. Suppose, however, that we do not hold the view that for a proposition to be true it must represent something else, accepting Kant's critique that we cannot have knowledge of the thing in itself. As Hacking points out, this means that to be objectivist, one must find a surrogate for the represented thing that preserves the values of truth and reality without pre-critical naiveté. One solution to this dilemma is to be found in the thought often ascribed to Peirce that there is an objective surrogate for truth to be found in method, so that truth emerges as the consensus of a group of enquirers following a method.[50] It is this idea that Habermas took up, arguing, with Peirce, that the metaphysical (that is, pre-critical) conception of truth is replaced by the consensus of an unlimited 'audience of competent interpreters that extends ideally across social space and time'.[51] If we accept this understanding of what it means for a proposition to be true, then the original claim of epistemic democracy, which relied upon a distinction between truth and procedure, seems to unravel, since truth becomes the consensual upshot of a certain type of procedure. The notion that there are procedure-independent standards for better or worse political decisions is undercut, since those standards are themselves the product of a certain sort of procedure.

Even if we accept this line of argument, it does not follow that the procedures of liberal democracy are the right procedures for securing good decisions. It may even be that we do not have to accept the claim that the notion of truth has to be understood as the consensus of enquirers. Peirce himself appears to have withdrawn from this strong position, arguing that 'Real things, whose characters are entirely independent of our opinions about them... affect our senses according to regular laws, and... we can ascertain by reasoning how things really and truly are'.[52] Yet these more realist thoughts do not preclude our saying that, even if truth is more than the consensus that would be arrived at through a certain method, there are some methods that are more likely to enable us to secure the truth than others. Richard Braithwaite once defended induction as a method of science on the grounds of its effectiveness (inductively established), pointing out that no other method—for example, heavy breathing followed by free association or consulting a savant—achieved equal predictive success.[53] There is a parallel argument to be made in the case of democratic procedures and the rationality of public deliberation. There may be other methods of taking political decisions than ones that satisfy conditions of democratic principles, for example decision by expert committee or the monarch's advisers, but, though it is plausible that such methods are appropriate for certain issues, they are so only in the context of the open public discussion that democratic procedures, properly construed, provide. In particular, where democratic procedures embody accountability, the possibility of public challenge and political representation, there are reasons for thinking that they provide a method for practical public rationality.

Accountability can be captured by the principle that for any decision it should be possible for all political associates with the requisite skill and time to follow the train of reasoning that led to a practical policy conclusion without finding fault in the reasoning. On this test, a valid form of public reasoning is one where anyone can reconstruct the steps of the practical syllogism that led to the decision that was taken. The original process of reasoning may have had its origins in the views of one associate, but it will be publicly rational to the extent that others can follow it. This does not mean that others will agree, since there may be disagreement with the empirical claims contained in the premisses upon which the reasoning is based or with the ways that different values are weighed against one another. However, to be the product of public reasoning, the grounds of a decision should meet minimal standards of logicality: sufficient conditions should not be confused with necessary conditions, so that relevant alternatives are not considered; attributions of causality should avoid *post hoc ergo, propter hoc* reasoning; and sufficient statistics should be given.

The requirement of public challenge is closely associated with the defeasible character of practical reasoning. In the world of common property resource regimes, this is linked to the condition of participation because collective success depends upon associates being able to participate in formulating and modifying the rules to which they are subject. Where information about what works and what does not work is dispersed among a number of different actors, then the logic of defeasible reasoning has special significance, since no single decision maker is in a position to understand the full implications of adopting any particular rule so that their knowledge, being necessarily incomplete, needs supplementing by those who are familiar with the relevant facts and circumstances. This is not just a case of only the wearer of the shoe knowing where it pinches, though that is important. It is also at the core of Mill's argument that no one person could rule a community satisfactorily, since without omniscience, as well as benevolence, no one person can rule anywhere satisfactorily.[54]

Information will also be incomplete when creative decisions are possible, since by definition the technical solution to a problem—the content of the minor premiss of the practical syllogism—will not be known to participants in the regime. Within the theory of non-monotonic logic, this element of defeasibility is related to the so-called 'closed-world' database assumption.[55] If decision makers can assume that they have access to a closed database that contained all relevant information, then their reasoning could proceed on the assumption that the premisses of their decision making would not be overturned. There would be nothing further that could be learnt that would lead to a revision of beliefs and associated actions. However, securing confidence that one has access to a closed-world database is hard in practice, and, although people may act as though their database were closed, they will find that there are circumstances in which it is not. Where innovation is possible, then the closed database assumption cannot hold. By the familiar argument, discovery is not something that can be predicted, since if it were predicted, then it will already have been invented. So, if the creativity to which Arendt and Shackle refer is employed, then defeasibility will have to be a feature of any rule that is adopted rationally and the scope and application of the rule will always be challengeable.

Gutmann and Thompson argue that one of the requirements of deliberative democracy is that the members of an association are disposed to seek fair terms of cooperation with one another, within a framework in which the key principle is reciprocity.[56] One element of reciprocity is the recognition of partial understandings, since by 'their nature, reasonable differences contain partial understandings' of which each 'alone is likely to be mistaken if taken comprehensively, all together are likely to be incoherent if taken completely, but all together are likely to be instructive if taken partially'.[57] One justification for this conception of deliberative reciprocity is to be found both in the epistemic need to identify warranted premisses for practical action and in the principle of fairness as motivating deliberative interventions.

Ideally, within a contract theory public reasoning is framed in such a way that associates can find reasons from within their own point of view for accepting a proposed rule or policy. The reasoning needs to be one with which each associate can identify, at least in the sense of recognizing that although restrictions on individual freedom have to be accepted, they are negotiated in such a way that they are fair. The good of all has to be compatible with the good of each. It is reasoning that each person can accept as an equal. This condition does not require that all be advantaged by a particular decision. There may be circumstances in which some people are asked to bear a heavy burden in the public interest. However, it does require that there be a meaningful sense that whenever any such burdens need to be imposed they are potentially imposed upon any of the associates and not simply on a designated group. In this sense, practical public reasoning is reasoning from a public point of view, taking into account the need to ensure that the interests of each and every person are represented in the process of decision making. In this sense it captures the element of political equality in democracy as well as the element of practical rationality.

CHAPTER 5

The great transformation

5.1. Justice and the great transformation

In developing our account of justice and democracy, we have relied upon the analysis of the social contracts found in small-scale societies that are agricultural in their primary mode of production. Social cooperation in such societies takes place under conditions in which production necessarily involves spillover effects from one producer to another. Given the approximate equality of power of all producers, some form of collective governance is needed to fix agreeable rules of cooperation. Without the restraint implied by these rules, resource depletion would ensue to the disadvantage of all. Although cooperation is possible, limited altruism means that no spontaneous agreement on rules of appropriation will occur, since each agent has interests in resource acquisition that are contrary to those of other agents. Justice has value in situations of moderate scarcity as it would not have in situations of superabundance, where there is no competition for resources, or extreme scarcity, where the competition for resources is as fierce as it can be. Approximate equality of power means that no one group is in a position to secure a privileged position in access to the means of production by comparison with other groups. These conditions together mean that the cautious, jealous virtue of justice is required.

The same societies institutionalize forms of decision making in which those affected by the rules are able to shape the rules and in which interference by external political authorities is relatively low. There is, then, direct participation in the making of collective decisions, thus replicating one of the standard conditions of social contract theory, by which each associate is able to shape the terms of social cooperation. There is also collective control over conditions governing the basic structure of productive activity, which is also an important element of social contract theory. To be sure, some of the common property regimes are attenuated democracies, in which certain members of society, for example wage-labourers, are excluded from the collective decision making. However, given the inevitable shortcomings of functioning polities by reference to democratic values, common property regimes provide us with plausible empirical models of the principle that a community of equals would institutionalize if they had to make a social contract to mutual advantage.

The main principle of economic justice to emerge from the analysis of the social contracts embodied in such regimes is that producers keep the full fruits of their labour when all have equal access to the means of production. This principle can be seen as the agreed bargain among those of equal power concerned to protect their ability to earn a livelihood. It represented a balance between a form of individualism and a form of collectivism. The individualism is that of the Hohfeldian liberties, the exercise of which means that individuals can adversely affect one another through direct spillovers or the cumulative consequences of uncoordinated action. The collectivism is that of the political authority implicit in the need to govern access to resources. Collective control of common property, with equal access assured to each, but also with individual ownership of the fruits of labour, means that free choice was preserved between different forms of economic activity. Each producer is free to decide when marginal effort was equal to marginal returns. Justifiable marginal returns—that is to say marginal returns to which associates have a claim in justice—are those that derive from work effort in a situation in which every agent has a roughly equal chance of securing access to the relevant means of production. Since those means of production are embedded in governance arrangements that resemble those of a procedural democracy, the social contract that underlies the institutions of governance is a democratic social contract.

However, we cannot simply read off a general theory of justice and democracy from the experience of common property resource regimes. No theory is plausible that looks to an alleged simpler form of society in order to provide a practical model to follow for a more complex form. To say of such regimes that they can provide models of democratic justice is not to say that they provide models in the sense of prototypes that need to be imitated. We have to supplement the empirical analysis with a reconstruction of the underlying logic of cooperation, but the examples of such embodied social contracts in such societies provide us with a reference point for our theoretical reasoning. The requirements of collective practical deliberation in managing externalities and securing the gains of social cooperation require an open and defeasible form of reasoning that is central to any meaningful account of democratic deliberation. If the theoretical reconstruction of their logic is correct, they provide us with a model of democratic justice. They also embody, in one specific form, the principles of a property-owning democracy, defined as a political economy in which citizens are put 'in a position to manage their own affairs and to take part in social cooperation on a footing of mutual respect under appropriately equal conditions'.[1] Wade captures their self-governing feature with his designation of some communities as 'village republics'.[2] Yet, how far, and in what ways, can common property regimes be used to inform our reasoning about justice and democracy in larger and economically more complex societies?

The question arises because Hayek famously denied that we can apply principles suitable to small-scale societies to what he termed, taking the notion from Adam Smith, 'great societies'. As part of his more general critique of the idea of social justice, Hayek wrote:

> I believe that 'social justice' will ultimately be recognized as a will-o'-the-wisp which has lured men to abandon many of the values which in the past have inspired the development of civilization—an attempt to satisfy a craving inherited from the traditions of the small group but which is meaningless in the Great Society of free men.[3]

Alongside this distinction between small and great societies, Hayek also makes distinction between government by legislation and government by the rule of law. Government by the rule of law is supposedly characteristic of justice, whereas government by legislation supposedly rests upon false assumptions about the role of knowledge in society. If these twin distinctions—between the traditions of small groups and the great society on the one hand and between government by the rule of law and government by legislation on the other—can be made good, there are strict limits on the extent to which we can infer anything general from the example of small-scale common property resource regimes.

This brings us to the second reason why we cannot simply read off from the examples of the common pool resource regimes a full theory of democratic justice. So far, democratic institutions have been presupposed in the theory of the social contract. The governance structures of common pool resource regimes are taken as models of what is involved in a democratic social contract. Participation in rule-formation and rule-modification, equality of standing among participants, and agreements the commitment to which can be monitored illustrate what is involved in democratic governance. However, we cannot simply transpose these elements onto governance structures in large societies. In common property resource regimes participation in the making of rules is essential. In great societies mass participation in the making and modifying of legislation is impossible. So a social contract theory of governance in great societies cannot presuppose that full participation is essential to justifiable public reasoning. A central element in the political authority of common property regimes cannot be replicated in great societies. Theoretically what is needed, instead, is an analysis that shows how the political functions performed in common pool resources can be instituted in great societies.

It may be urged in this context that there is no difference between an empirical and a hypothetical theory of the social contract. Whether placed behind a veil of ignorance or located in bargaining situations of equality, modern social contract theory sees individuals as potential partners in a social contract determining the political constitution by which they shall live. Such a construction assumes that all relevant individuals can speak to one another. If such a theory is acceptable in its hypothetical versions, why should it also not be acceptable in its empirical versions? However, there is one important difference. In hypothetical contracting theory, the contracting parties are suppose to apply the principles upon which they can agree to the evaluation of alternative social arrangements in the light of their understanding of the laws and conditions governing social organization. The theory assumes that the contracting parties have access to all the social scientific understanding that there is. However, such an understanding of social and economic organization is not present in the minds of the contracting parties; being purely hypothetical, they strictly speaking have no minds. Rather, it is the theorist constructing the hypothetical contract who supplies the understanding of social and economic organization. By contrast, in the empirical version of the social contract, the theorist has to rely upon an understanding of the principles of organization that can be inductively derived from a range of cases, illustrated in Ostrom's conditions for regime success. Consequently, one can have no assurance that the same principles will carry over to different types of society that involve a larger political scale or corporate forms of economic organization. Of course, theorists of the empirical approach might feel that this puts them in a better position than purely hypothetical theorists, who may have little by way of empirical verification of the assumptions that they make about social organization. But it may preclude the principles identified in small-scale societies in any way carrying over to large-scale societies.

Hayek's insistence that we need to attend to the difference in the principles of organization between large-scale and small-scale societies thus raises important issues of method and substance. Fully to understand these, we need to consider the grounds and logic of Hayek's own argument.

5.2. Hayek on justice and democracy

In Hayek's contrast between the traditions of a small group and the idea of a great society, there is supposed to lay a basic distinction of kind. To apply the principles from one order to those of another is to commit a fundamental category mistake. The distinction between small groups and great societies forecloses on the possibility of using principles derived from the one type of case to apply to the another. Hayek presents his thesis as a strong one. In the words of the title of the second volume of *Law, Legislation and Liberty*, we are confronted with *The Mirage of Social Justice*. On this view, *any* attempt to construct an account of social justice that applied to large-scale societies would be an attempt to perform the impossible. More importantly, it would also threaten the maintenance of freedom that the principles of constitutional and limited government uphold. Hayek's thesis about social justice is thus bound up with his thesis that a free society is one characterized not by democratic legislation but by individual freedom secured through the guarantee of the rule of law.[4] From this point of view, the idea of modelling democratic justice in terms of small-scale common pool resource regimes looks a mistake, not only because it transposes the circumstances of small societies onto great ones, but also because it incorporates an assumption that democratic legislation can provide a basis for justice. The substantive challenges to the principles of democratic legislation and to the idea of social justice complement the methodological scepticism about using small-scale societies to inform our judgements about large-scale ones.

To understand Hayek's scepticism about social justice and democracy, it is necessary to understand one of the principal distinctions to be found in his theory, namely that between a social order that is the product of design and a social order that is the product of evolution.[5] For Hayek, societies cannot be designed, because no one person is in a position to command the knowledge that would be required for organizing the world according to a plan. Instead, we should see societies as having evolved their customs and norms in a spontaneous way. Such customs and norms are the product of the myriad of interactions between parties who contract with one another for mutual benefit. Thus his preferred view is:

> [T]hat the orderliness of society which greatly increased the effectiveness of individual action was not due solely to institutions and practices which had been invented or designed for that purpose, but was largely due to a process first described as 'growth' and later as 'evolution', a process in which practices which had first been adopted for other reasons, or even purely accidentally, were preserved because they enabled the group in which they had arisen to prevail over others.[6]

Social institutions are thus, in the words of Adam Ferguson quoted by Hayek, 'the result of human action but not of human design'.[7]

Corresponding to this contrast between two ways of thinking about social order, there is a distinction for Hayek between the justice characteristic of a free society on the one hand and the idea of social justice on the other. The idea of social justice presupposes a claim to a synoptic understanding of society, a claim not required for justice in a free society. In a free society, government takes place by the rule of law. The requirements of justice comprise rules applicable to individuals in respect of their conduct towards one another. By contrast, the synoptic claims of social justice are an attempt to impose a single vision of a good society upon the complexity of actual societies. In a free society there are no social purposes; the function of political rule is the promotion of the general good, which consists in the facilitation of individual purposes. The synoptic delusion is to suppose that a flourishing society can be anything other than a free society, in which government is limited in what it can do and in which the plurality of different substantive purposes can be pursued.[8] Since in the great society information is dispersed, no one is in a position to determine the outcome of economic processes. It follows that, if a principle of social justice requires the outcome of the myriad of transactions to conform to a single pattern, theorists of social justice are asking the impossible. Given this intellectual background, it is easy to see why Hayek would be sceptical of any principle that appeared to impose a common set of principles upon the organization of society as a whole, rather than general rules that were common to the individuals within a society. For Hayek, pursuit of the mirage of social justice is precisely such an attempt.

Taken literally, such a view undermines any place for deliberated legislation in the making of public policy. Government would take a judicialized form rather than that of a parliament or popular assembly in which public purposes were discussed and negotiated. Hayek quotes Duncan Forbes to the effect that Ferguson, together with other luminaries of the Scottish Enlightenment, dispensed with the 'Legislator myth', according to which states were founded by conscious acts of legislation.[9] In short, Hayek thinks that the evolutionary development of society precludes the success of any form of conscious and deliberated legislation.

Section 2.2 argued that such a view would make effective government subject to various disadvantages, of which the inability to anticipate problems and deal in advance with their consequences was one principal instance. For example, it would preclude legislating for pollution control by setting standards that all manufacturers should meet instead of requiring each agent suffering pollution to sue for damages each and every time it occurred. Moreover, precluding the possibility of agreement on public purposes denies not only the myth of the legislative origins of states, accurate for many states, but also allows no place for legislation on matters to do with the basic structure of a society, where the basic structure includes any institutional arrangement that plays a fundamental role in determining the patterns of social and economic life for citizens. Whilst it may be implausible to suppose that anything but a handful of polities is the product of conscious construction by legislators, it is equally implausible to suppose that deliberated legislation has played no part in creating institutions that constitute crucial and determining elements in the basic structure of society. To take just one example, consider the debates surrounding the introduction of limited liability in Gladstone's Companies Act of 1844. The example is significant, because the principle of limited liability is the basis for the modern corporation and its ability to enter into extensive contractual relationships. As Atiyah notes, because the partisans of the different sides recognized the significance and scale of the issues involved, there was considerable debate around this change in the law, even though many of the subsequently identified pertinent issues were not fully discussed.[10] Both those in favour of limited liability and those opposed advanced arguments about the consequences of such legislation, not least its implications for freedom of contract and the risks that individuals would incur as a result of limited liability. The debate may have been of a low level and the legislation now appear to have an air of inevitability, as Atiyah himself believed, but that the legislative change would have significant consequences affecting the basic structure of economic relations was not in dispute. One need not be subject to the synoptic delusion to think that it is possible to have some reasonable estimate of what the range of consequences in general will be of planned public action, at least in the medium term.

In fact, when looked at carefully, Hayek's actual position on social justice does not take so uncompromising a form as to preclude its application completely to important social institutions. For example, he accepts that Rawls's theory of social justice is compatible with his own views, on the grounds that Rawlsian principles apply to the basic structure of society and not to individual transactions within it.[11] Just as strikingly, in *The Constitution of Liberty* Hayek not only assigns a substantial role to national institutions to assure income support in old age, unemployment or sickness, he takes it as 'an obvious corollary' of the state's role that it is right to compel individuals to insure or otherwise provide against the common hazards of life because 'by neglecting to make such provision, they would become a charge to the public'.[12] To be sure, Hayek does not literally say in this passage that there would be an injustice to those who do provide for themselves if those who do not become a charge on them. So his position could be justified purely on grounds of prudence in public expenditure. However, his argument is certainly consistent with the claim there is an injustice if those who could have provided for themselves, but did not, became a charge on who had provided for themselves, and it is the task of the state to prevent such injustices. Finally, in a passage that uses a veil of ignorance argument, Hayek suggests that where people are in competition for scarce resources, they can find it advantageous, particularly where they are ignorant about future outcomes, to submit to lotteries or queues as a way of allocating resources.[13]

How, then, does Hayek think that social justice is a mirage? The answer is that he is relying upon a sharp distinction between rules governing the basic order of a society and rules for allocating resources within a society. For Hayek, it is futile to think that anyone will ever be in a position to secure rewards to individuals that correspond precisely to those individuals' needs or deserts. Any arrangement that sought to ensure such a correspondence would have to put a great deal of discretionary power into the hands of public officials, and this would be incompatible with government acting in accordance with the principle of the rule of law, in which general rules are applied to all individuals. Moreover, since no one is responsible for determining the rewards that people secure, it makes no sense to say that there is an injustice in the distribution of rewards. Any distribution is the product of human action but not of human design. Hence, we should not assume that it is right, even if it were feasible, for the structure of rewards to be tailored so as to conform to a specific set of distributive principles.

It is possible to accept much of Hayek's line of analysis and still hold that common property resource regimes provide a model of social justice. In fact, Hayek himself, perhaps rather inconsistently, appeals to the experience of agricultural and other small-scale societies when discussing the place that desert considerations might have in our thinking:

> The contention that all differences in earnings must be justified by some corresponding difference in deserts is one which would certainly not have been thought to be obvious in a community of farmers or merchants or artisans, that is, in a society in which success or failure were clearly seen to depend only in part on skill and industry, and in part on pure accident which might hit anyone—although even in such societies individuals were known to complain to God or fortune about the injustice of their fate.[14]

As this quotation shows, the distinction that is really doing the work in Hayek's account of social justice is not that between application of the principles of justice to society and acceptance that any outcome is just, but that between the detailed adjustments of rewards to the particular circumstances of individuals and the general conditions under which individuals secure a return on their efforts.

A similar distinction informs Hayek's analysis of political constitutions. Hayek holds that the idea of legislation was originally associated with the idea of the separation of powers.[15] Legislation, properly so called, is concerned with the formation of general rules applicable to all individuals across an indefinite range of circumstances. By contrast, legislation, as it has come to be understood in the context of parliamentary sovereignty, is the direction of conduct by instruction. He marks this distinction with the terms *nomos*, denoting rules taking a general form, and *thesis*, denoting rules that provide instructions to particular individuals. Whereas one has to obey a law in the former (*nomos*) sense, that is to say constrain one's conduct in relation to the rules the law contains, one has to carry out an instruction in the *thesis* sense. Rules understood as general laws state the conditions to which all are subject; legislation understood as rules is to be carried out through executive action.

This general distinction underlies Hayek's account of the distortions of the political order that accompany the search for social justice. Properly understood democracy is the principle 'that coercion should be allowed only for the purpose of ensuring obedience to rules of just conduct approved by most, or at least by a majority' and such democracy is seen as 'the essential condition for the absence of arbitrary power and therefore of freedom'.[16] However, as it is practiced, democracy, according to Hayek, has come to mean a system in which elected assemblies with unlimited powers become the 'playball of group interests'.[17] As a result, instead of political representatives thinking of themselves as legislating in a general way, they come to see themselves as responding to the particular demands of special interests, making laws in the sense of *thesis* rather than in the sense of *nomos*. Given this diagnosis, it is hardly surprising that Hayek recommends the construction of a constitution in which the legislature is insulated from the demands of popular sentiment by being elected at a relatively mature age (45 to 60), for long periods (15 years is suggested), but its members are ineligible for re-election and instead allowed to retire at public expense to such positions as lay magistrates.[18]

Despite Hayek's ostensible attack on social justice and parliamentary democracy, there is one element in his thought that the proponent of democratic justice can support. Justice should not be thought of as an assignment of economic claims to individuals by a central authority or social planner. Instead, justice must grow out of the relations of individuals and groups—although the democratic contractarian insists those groups must have access to the means of production and political authority on equal terms. The democratic contractarian also shares with Hayek the view that there is no reason to suppose that a central plan could provide a final and uncontentious ordering of social and economic arrangements. Hayek's insight that we cannot move straightforwardly from the principles that govern small-scale societies to the principles that should govern great societies is an important one. It suggests that, not only do we need to reformulate our account of economic justice, but we also need to consider the features of social organization that arise in the move from small-scale to large-scale societies. To borrow Karl Polanyi's phrase, we need to understand 'the great transformation' from agricultural to industrial and post-industrial societies and the normative significance of the transition.[19] In particular, we need to understand the transformation of the three central institutions that make up the basic structure of society: the political system; the economic system; and the household.

5.3. The political transformation

The most significant political effect of the great society is upon its scale of organization. The common property resource regimes studied by Ostrom were based in communities with a maximum size of around 15,000 people. A community of this size would barely constitute a small town in great societies. Indeed, such communities are small even by the standards of the classical city-state on which so much participatory democratic theorizing has been built. At the time of Pericles in the fifth century BCE, Athens had an adult male population of about 60,000. A hundred years later, at the time of Demosthenes, this had dropped to 30,000, because the requirements for citizenship had been tightened.[20] Thus the largest of the common pool resource regimes that Ostrom examined was half the size of the Athenian adult male population under relatively restricted circumstances. Modern states are significantly larger, and are on a scale that until the nineteenth century would have been seen to be incompatible with democracy.

Modern states are now the principal form of political organization in the world, covering virtually the entire land surface of the earth. However, as Birch has pointed out, this development is relatively recent. Some two hundred years ago, there were fewer than 20 such entities, the rest being divided between empires, city-states, and principalities, as well as the homes of tribal communities without formal boundaries.[21] The birthplace of the modern state is Europe, the history of which gave the state its characteristic form from *c.*1450 CE onwards.[22] States arose as a result of political consolidation and the centralization of authority by monarchs gaining military ascendancy over nobles and magnates incorporating formerly politically independent states into common systems of political authority.[23] They involved the development of a professional class of state bureaucrats and military forces under the monarch, who was able to use increased power to extract revenues from the governed territories. Outside Europe, state-formation comes about as a result of imperial colonization, creating a central authority that is then bestowed on indigenous groups or descendants of colonizers when empires fade or are overturned.

The scale and pace of these developments varied within Europe, but the long-term consequence of this centralization of authority is that each state develops its own system of uniform law to replace the varied patchwork of local and clerical law that had been a feature of the medieval period. Moreover, and also by contrast with the medieval period, political authority becomes detached from the person of the monarch. Medieval monarchs were expected 'to live off their own', with there being no clear separation between the personal finances of the royal household and the public finances associated with the running of the state. In England, parliaments were called irregularly when the monarch required extraordinary revenue, but the monies passed through an administrative office that worked to the personal direction of the king. In France, Philip IV, the richest king in Europe, maintained at his own expense the diplomatic missions from the rest of Europe.[24] In the modern state, public administration loses this personal element. Public finance becomes the full-time responsibility of parliaments. Law ceases to be the prerogative of the monarch. With the decline of the dynastic principle and the rise of democracy, political authority is desacralized, and public authority becomes the property of the nation. Democratic authority is seen to occupy the role of the sovereign.

How should that democratic authority be conceived? As Hart once argued, there is a logical incoherence in supposing the people can stand in a relation of sovereignty to itself in the same way as a people formerly did in relation to the person of the monarch.[25] Within a monarchy, monarch and people can be thought of as separate persons. But if popular opinion is the origin of law in a democracy, it makes no sense to say that a people is obeying itself in obeying the law. We can only speak of a set of rules and conventions that define the rights and powers by which law is made. Strictly speaking, in place of a relation between the person of the sovereign and the people as subject, we should think of the modern democratic as resting on that body of rules and conventions together with the associated habit of citizens in stable conditions to recognize the authority of laws made in accordance with the constitutionally defined process.

The rise of the principle of the modern democratic state is associated with the ideology of nationalism, understood as the doctrine that each nation is entitled to its own state and each state should be made up of one nation.[26] However, because the historic centralization of political authority took place through territorial consolidation, modern states typically contain groups who differ in respect of their cultural identification, language, or religion. The legacy of territorial consolidation also creates a source of conflict between centre and periphery, as territorial units that were previously autonomous vie with the instruments and interests of the central state, perhaps overlain by a more general tension between town and country.

The great economy (section 5.3) creates a division of economic classes, between landowners and others and between owners of capital and workers. Each of these distinct and separate economic and social groups may share some interests in common with other groups and some interests that are distinct and opposed to those of other social groups. Interacting with the territorial and cultural differences in complex ways, these differences form the basis for political organization and mobilization. For example, religion may reinforce the cleavages arising from distinctions of economic class, as was true in nineteenth and early twentieth century Ireland, or it may counter-act them, as it has done in Germany. Agricultural interests, particularly landholders, may see themselves as politically aligned with the interests of industrial capital, as has been true in Latin America, or farmers may join forces with workers, as was true in Sweden in the 1930s. Religious differences may produce a pillarization in cases where adherents of different faiths are territorially intermingled, as in the Netherlands. Differences of language may push towards bilingualism as in Canada or territorial concentration as in Belgium, Switzerland, and Spain.

Ideologies may be defined, following Freeden, as 'systems of political thinking, loose or rigid, deliberate or unintended, through which individuals and groups construct an understanding of the political world they... inhabit, and then act on that understanding'.[27] As Freeden explains, such ideologies are fused from various conceptual elements in ways that decontest those elements to provide a pattern of understanding. The ideologies of modern politics (liberalism, socialism, nationalism, social Catholicism, conservatism) can be thought of as the means by which different and competing social groups both construct and articulate their interests and identities in ways that frame detailed political arguments and policy proposals. The vehicles for such articulation are political parties together with associated pressure groups and social movements. Political democracies, therefore, contain not only a pluralism of interests but also a pluralism of political doctrines that are irreconcilable with one another. However, by contrast with religious and metaphysical doctrines, proponents of competing ideologies typically enter into coalition with one another, either through their respective political parties in government or less formally in the positions that they take in public discussions about policy proposals, so that political competition for public office joins forces that would otherwise be distinct.

The principal instrument for securing public office is through elections. Political parties compete for a share of the popular vote for representation in the legislature. A subset of parties, in some systems usually only one, then form the government that is dependent upon the legislature for its tenure in office. Its policy-making capacity is shaped by the political institutions through which it has to work. Political institutions provide the forum and the channel for those advocating different policy positions both within and around government. Institutions matter. They act as channels through which decision making, power, and influence occur. As David Truman put it in relation to the institutions of the USA, 'The formal institutions of government in the United States do not prescribe all the meandering of the stream of politics. They do mark some of its limits, however, and designate certain points through which it must flow whatever uncharted courses it may follow between these limits.'[28] Comparative work in political science has developed various typologies of political institutions depending upon their forms of decision making. However, for normative political theory, a particularly useful typology can be derived from the work of, respectively, Lijphart and Powell.[29]

Using these approaches, representative democracies can be classified by reference to two principal criteria. The first is the design of the electoral system and in particular on the extent to which it is constructed on the basis either of proportional representation on the one hand or of a winner-takes-all plurality rule on the other. The second criterion of classification is the extent to which the executive dominates the legislature, in such a way that the government can usually be assured that it can pass its programme into law, or by contrast is counterbalanced by a strong parliament in which extensive negotiation has to take place among leading legislative actors. If we cross-classify countries by these two criteria, we can assign countries to one of two dominant classes. Those countries that use the simple plurality rule for elections with strong executives typically include the Westminster democracies like Australia, the UK, and New Zealand (before 1996). Those countries that use proportional electoral systems and that encourage the sharing of power in the legislative chamber include the continental European democracies, such as Austria, Belgium, Denmark, the Netherlands, Norway, Sweden, and Switzerland.[30] Those countries that are 'off-diagonal', like Canada and Finland, have a placement that can be understood in terms of their distinctive institutional characteristics. Simple plurality/strong executive systems may be called 'Westminster systems' and systems using proportional representation and the sharing of power between executive and legislature may be called 'representational democracies'.[31]

Within the categories there can be considerable variation. For example, proportional representation systems vary in the extent to which they produce a direct correspondence between votes and seats, depending on such variables as the size of the threshold required for parties to enter parliament, the average size of the electoral district, and the exact formula for translating votes into seats.[32] Nonetheless, even allowing for this variation, the classification of representative democracies into two broad classes depending upon their electoral systems and the degree of executive dominance does pick out an important distinction for a wide range of purposes, and is particularly helpful in the context of normative evaluation.

There is, however, one major qualification, which concerns how one classifies systems that combine a plurality electoral system with strong constraints upon the executive, of which the USA is the most obvious example. The issue is theoretically important and there are good normative reasons for taking the USA as forming the paradigm of a distinctive group, namely that of liberal constitutionalist regime. The distinctive feature of such regimes is the institutionalization of strong counter-majoritarian devices, most notably in the case of the USA a strong second chamber in the Senate, Presidential veto power, a Supreme Court capable of declaring unconstitutional legislation that has duly passed through all its legislative stages, and a Federal Reserve given the responsibility for running monetary policy. As Anthony King has most recently shown, these strong counter-majoritarian devices have been intellectually justified by a distinctive tradition of American political thought.[33] That tradition has received strong support from Rawlsian social contract theory (see section 6.5). So it is helpful to treat liberal constitutionalism as a distinctive set of practices in its own right. Certainly, there is no empirical reason why we should not, and some good empirical reasons why we should.

5.4. The great economy

The social and economic features that made common property resource regimes models for democratic social contracts involved a direct relationship between production and consumption so that the value of labour is clear to participants. Such regimes also involve broad access to the means of production, including access to resources managed in common, no extensive division of labour, relatively flat hierarchies in the organization of production, and the centrality of households to the means of production. All these elements are transformed in the transition to the great society.

A great society has moved from agricultural production to commodity and service production. Historically, for those societies that have made the transition, there will have been at some point a sufficiently large agricultural surplus to allow for the capital investment in new forms of production or access to foreign capital. As the proportion of the population engaged in subsistence agriculture drops, processes of corporately organized production and market exchange become more important to total social product. As a result, income derived from market transactions comes to predominate over the returns from direct production of the means of livelihood. Moreover, this change has in turn implications for the centrality of the household as a unit of production, consumption, and risk-sharing.

It is its enhanced scale, stemming from the modern rise of population, that marks out the great society.[34] Enhanced size permits the extensive division of labour, which in the analysis of Adam Smith is the origin of the wealth of nations. There is a dispute among economists as to the exact ways in which the division of labour brings about greater productivity, as well as about the relative merits of the various forms in which it can be organized, and it should certainly not be assumed that only the capitalist firm is capable of realizing the gains in productivity.[35] Nevertheless, the division of labour allows the assignment of producers to the tasks for which they are best suited and enables the more effective utilization of equipment.

This was at the core of Smith's own analysis, in which he contrasted the output of one worker undertaking all the operations of pin-making alone with the output of a team of workers among whom the tasks are divided up. Also, to the extent to which greater productivity enables an enterprise to build up buffer stocks and hedge against fluctuations in the market, the division of labour will facilitate greater economic efficiency.[36]

As a result, productive techniques come to depend upon specialization and the division of labour that such specialization presupposes. Economies that rely upon a division of highly specialist labour require individuals to occupy highly skilled niches. Alongside financial and physical capital, therefore, great societies have members who have high levels of human capital in general, and specialist skills in particular. As Arrow puts it, with the division of labour '[f]undamentally similar people become different to complement one another'.[37] Adam Smith himself already recognized this phenomenon with his observation that there was less between the street porter and the philosopher than the latter liked to think.[38] As great societies increase their productivity, so the division of skills becomes greater. Sources of wealth and productivity are to be found in the interactions of large groups of people, such that the factors of production only achieve their value in a particular social context. Another way of putting the same point is that the human capital created through the division of labour often takes the form of asset-specific human capital, that is to say, sets of skills the value of which reside in their use in specific forms of production.[39] Professional graphic designers or surgeons presuppose an economy that already has a high degree of specialist labour.

Thus, by contrast with common property resource regimes, no one individual, or even reasonably large set of individuals has the power to make a decisive impact upon overall social production. In common property regimes, the maintenance of productive resources through land, water, or stock conservation was central to their functioning, and such conservation was sensitive to the behaviour of individuals. A misuse of water or a failure to terrace one's land properly could have severe adverse effects on many others within the community. Within a great society, comparable power is hard to find. To be sure, there can be workers in strategic sectors of the economy who can be disruptive. At times in the modern world the list has included doctors, airline pilots, utility workers, and transport workers, and the extent to which particular groups can be effective will depend not only on their position in the economy but also on the laws that allow combinations to form. However, within a large economy there is in principle the capacity for those who rely upon such groups to make alternative arrangements for supply of goods and services, thus diminishing or entirely negating their power. Moreover, if power is wielded with the short-term effect of raising income returns above the level that the economy at large can sustain through effective demand, one long-term effect is the decline in economic importance of that sector, particularly where there can be an import of goods from alternative suppliers—a phenomenon that many industrial groups in developed economies have experienced.

Alongside the division of labour a great society substitutes market relations for the relations of barter, haggling, patronage, and familial cooperation found in small-scale societies. In smaller-scale societies there are possibilities of mutual gains from trade, but the relevant terms of trade often have to be negotiated individual bargain by individual bargain, as individuals seek to shift as much of the cooperative surplus to themselves as possible. In a great society, with many buyers and many sellers in competition with one another, the price mechanism can substitute for direct haggling or negotiation and participants become price-takers reasoning in a parametric way when confronted with alternatives. The consequence is that the output of production appears in the form of a vast set of commodities to be traded. The conditions of production are correspondingly those of markets in which producers compete with one another on the basis of the returns that they anticipate receiving. The value of any one individual's productive output becomes the sum of the valuations that those willing to purchase his or her labour will put on that output.

Although great societies are often characterized as market economies, the term is misleading. A great society is a system of hierarchies as well as of markets, since it is in firms that most production takes place. As Coase explained, within the firm market transactions are eliminated and instead of a complicated arrangement of market exchange the coordination of activity is achieved through management.[40] Similarly, Wiles noted that 'every enterprise is a small command economy' comprising 'any group of people among whom methods of command or administration are used, and who are not expected to respond in the short term to market stimuli'.[41] It follows that an important emerging form of power is organizational power, that is to say that power that comes with holding a position in a corporate hierarchy. The returns that a firm makes are returns to it regarded as a team and it is not easy to assign some fraction of the return to particular individuals. Nor should it be assumed that what is assigned in practice is equal to marginal product. Marshall characterized the income of the firm in this sense as 'composite quasi-rent', which would be divisible among the different persons in the business 'by bargaining, supplemented by custom and by notions of fairness'.[42] However, within such an organization, those who are in control in the firm have discretionary power, arising from the specialist possession of information as well as authority over resources that fall to their discretionary spending. Where there is a separation of ownership and control, as there typically is with highly developed firms, then those who control the organization are able to determine the flow of a significant proportion of the returns that they manage. This has implications for their ability to engage in rent-seeking behaviour not only from other workers in the firm but also from its formal owners, the shareholders.

If ownership is separated from organizational control in the great society, it is also separated from labour. In common pool resource regimes there is direct access to productive resources so that households have the means needed for production. The economy of a great society provides no such general access to the physical means of production, whether natural or manufactured. Sometimes the origin of industrial society is traced back to the expropriation of common land from agricultural workers, taking place at different times and places. In England it dates back to the sixteenth century and when it is said to have constituted 'a revolution of the rich against the poor'.[43] More recent scholarship suggests that the role of enclosures is exaggerated in this picture. Laslett notes, for example, that both 'before and after enclosure, some peasants did well', securing better crops and more land to till.[44] Yet, however the historical transformation came about, a significant feature of the great society is that workers lack both ownership and control of the means of production in which they are employed. Firms are typically owned by a different set of actors from those who work in them. There are, of course, good reasons why workers, who have their human capital tied up in a particular sector of the economy, would wish to diversify their savings into other sectors of the economy to spread the risks of economic failure. However, this pattern is also conjoined with a form of contracting by which capital in general hires labour rather than labour hiring capital. Quite why the relationship should take this form is a matter of discussion among economists. Whatever the explanation, it has significance for our understanding of the normative properties of the great society.

The combination of markets and hierarchy that is characteristic of production in the great society brings with it one further feature, namely the importance of the network of relations in which producers are related to one another. The relevant distinction in this regard is between the internal and external elements of the productive process. The distinction is Marshall's, who contrasted the *internal* economies of economic organization that firms have to make for themselves with 'those *external* economies which result from the general progress of the industrial environment'. In explaining this distinction he cites as examples of external economies the 'value which a site derives from the growth of a rich and active population close to it, or from the opening up of railways and other good means of communication with existing markets'.[45] Marshall also noted how 'barren heath land may suddenly acquire a high value from the growth of an industrial population near it'.[46] If one form of productive activity can be related in a network to other forms of productive activity, then there can be an enhancement of output over and above what each could achieve singly. Prior to industrialization, there was production for markets with clothiers giving spinning work to agricultural households in a form of proto-industrialization.[47] Yet distances could be such that household members would be underemployed because there was no industry to hand.[48] In the language of Marshall, productive resources languished for want of external economies.

The place of such externalities in generating the economic surplus of a great society is both large in practice and has normative significance. In one of those seemingly offhand, but insightful, remarks at which he is so expert, Arrow writes that 'in some deep sense there are increasing returns to scale' in a large economy, so that there 'are significant gains to social interaction above and beyond what individuals and subgroups can achieve on their own'.[49] Increasing returns to scale exist when the marginal costs of production remain below the average costs of production, so that it is profitable to expand output. Such situations arise from networked interactions in which the existence of the network means that costs such as the costs of distribution and collection are low or close to zero. Thus, once an extensive computer network has been created, the costs of electronic publishing are low and many items can be added to published stock. In great societies, it is possible to identify a number of positive external effects that arise from linking producers together, particularly through means of transport, communication, and the spatial concentration of production. What this suggests is that the total product of a society is attributable not simply to the productive effect and skill of its members, but also to the way in which those members are linked to one another in mutually beneficial relations.

5.5. The household transformation

In analyzing common property resource regimes as models of a social contract, mention was made more than once of the centrality of the household in the productive activities of society. The reason is that participants in such societies are subject to constraints arising from the mode of agricultural production. As Peter Wiles noted, in societies with agricultural forms of production farmers typically 'live above the shop' and family members are involved in processes of production. The phenomenon arises because the internal distances of production are all important—it is generally crucial to be near the place of harvesting—and this fact alone in turn limits the potential for economies of scale.[50] Planting, cultivating, harvesting, child-rearing, nursing, food preparation, daily care, and maintenance are part of one and the same process of production and reproduction. Although the means of production do not determine the mode of production—since property rights can vary among agricultural communities of otherwise similar types—they place constraints on what forms of life can be sustained in such communities. Where the conditions that Wiles specifies apply, the household organization of labour is thus a functional social necessity in the sense that, given a certain mode of production, it will typically be more advantageous to organize social life around the household as the unit of production than in some other way.

This fact is important not only in itself, but also for the empirical method within social contract theory. With the empirical method we use particular types of society to model the social contract. When we use common property resource regimes as examples of societies in which the circumstances of justice obtain, we are focusing upon the balance of power that they exemplify. Within the household, by contrast, we expect there to be an imbalance of power, where relations inside the household are gendered. So the question arises as to how far such societies can be treated as models of justice. The particular issue in the case of common property resource regimes echoes the general doubts that have been advanced about the gender bias of social contract arguments. In *The Sexual Contract* Carole Pateman suggested that the original story of the social contract should be understood as a social-sexual pact, in which the story of the sexual contract had been suppressed.[51] As a result, social contract theory is not an account of social and political freedom but instead disguises patterns of domination within the household. From this point of view, social contract theory constitutes an ideology in one of the classical senses of that term, namely a system of thought that through its representation of social life systematically distorts the understanding of that social life. The emancipatory ambitions of social contract theory being undermined by the tacit assumptions it contains about families, gender roles, and, more generally, the place of women in society.

Pateman's interpretation of the social contract as a 'fraternal pact' is primarily directed at those historical versions of the theory that ascribed the origins of society to a social contract. According to Pateman, such accounts of the origins of society and government contain tacit assumptions about differences in bodily strength, the interdependence of mother and child and the conditions under which access to political power is granted. The seemingly free association that is supposed to be a feature of the contract is underpinned by structural inequality.[52] Moreover, according to Pateman, the problems run deeper still. Acknowledging that among contract theorists Hobbes avoids the conventional assumptions of his day about gendered roles, Pateman insists that this does not rescue contract theory. For, if the fundamental assumption of contract theory is that human relations in general can be understood in contractual terms, this will obscure the significant fact that interdependence and vulnerability in household relations limit the extent to which those relations can be freely contractual. Commitments are not only occasioned by contractual relationships; some forms of commitment precede and need to inform contractual relationships.

In modern social contract theory, the importance of tacit assumptions about relations within the household is exemplified in Rawls's treatment of the family in *A Theory of Justice*. There, Rawls regarded the monogamous family as part of the basic structure of society, which is itself the object of justice.[53] However, in order to deal with the problem of intergenerational justice, he conceived the parties to the contract 'as representing a continuing line of claims. For example, one might assume that they are heads of families and therefore have a desire to further the well-being of at least their more immediate descendants.'[54] In effect, Rawls made one part of the basic structure not the object of the theory of justice but part of its construction, potentially confirming a public/private dichotomy that precludes the theory of justice being used to evaluate the distribution of power within the family.[55] In *A Theory of Justice*, as Okin and others have pointed out, the effect was to preclude the analysis of domestic relations as beyond the principles of justice—including such matters as the household division of labour, fair opportunities, and the distribution of burdens and benefits.[56]

Rawls's reply to this criticism was to distinguish sharply between the principles that applied to the internal relations of the family and the principles that were to govern the basis structure of society. The latter guarantee the basic rights and liberties together with fair opportunities to all its members, and family forms that prevent those conditions being met are unjust.[57] However, seeing the family and the household as a unit of production as in the common property resource regimes underlines the extent to which there is no simple distinction to be made between the internal life of the family on the one hand and the wider social structure on the other. As a unit of production, the family or the household is part of the basic structure of social organization.

At a more general level, a proponent of social contract theory might seek to defend the approach by admitting that a number of particular (though important) theorists have made tacit assumptions about gender roles within the family, but deny that this is a problem for social contract theory as a normative enterprise. There is a distinction to be made between the logic and force of the theory on the one hand and any particular instantiations of that theory on the other. Thus Mills distinguishes between the descriptive contracts of non-ideal states and the normative use of the idea of a contract to identify what is demanded of agents as moral persons.[58] From this perspective, the idea of a social contract can be used to criticize regimes of domination. However, even if such a line of defence works for particular historical versions of social contract theory, it is more difficult to apply to an empirical method that takes common property resource regimes to model a social contract, since those contracts would seem to presuppose just the structure of dominating human relationships that Pateman identified in classical contract theory. If social contract theory is advanced as an emancipatory theory, then it would seem that the centrality of household, rather than the individual, as the unit of production undermines that ambition.

However, rather than assume this problem away, democratic contractarianism can be interpreted in such a way as both to support and to qualify the feminist critique of the family in social contract theory. It supports it because historically speaking a social contract between households on equal terms is compatible with highly unequal relations within the household. However, as agricultural societies develop to become 'great societies', in which there are substantial economies of scale and extensive division of labour, patterns in the family and household organization of work change. The original functional requirement for household production in an agricultural economy drop away. In the empirical contract, we can observe the unit of production ceasing to be the household as a matter of functional necessity and enabling an individualization in patterns of relationships. To see this, consider the organization of the household as work unit prior to the great society.

In pre-industrial societies the distinction between family and household is difficult to draw, because those living together in the same dwelling would include not only husband, wife, and children, but also servants, apprentices, and employees who slept and ate together.[59] Agricultural production at subsistence, near subsistence, or within only limited markets keeps individuals in such 'family' units, but the same was true for enterprises, like bakeries, in cities in pre-industrial societies. Moreover, these units were strongly gendered in their mode of operation. Laslett characterizes the typical household work unit as follows:

> The man at the head of the group, the entrepreneur, the employer, or the manager, was then known as the master or head of the family. He was father to some of its members and in place of father to the rest. There was no sharp distinction between his domestic and his economic functions. His wife was both his partner and his subordinate, a partner because she ran the family, took charge of the food and managed the women-servants, a subordinate because she was woman and wife, mother and in place of mother to the rest.[60]

There is a serious historical discussion as to how accurate such generalizations are when applied to the pre-industrial world. Laslett himself notes that one fifth of households in England between the sixteenth and the nineteenth centuries were headed by women, and money in the household was often pooled and managed by the wife.[61] Moreover, widows would often carry on the trades of their dead husbands.[62] Laslett also cites an eighteenth century observer noting that in long winter evenings, the husband cobbles shoes, mends clothes, and looks after the children while the wife spins.[63] Clearly we should be careful about the generalizations that we make about the division of labour and authority in the pre-industrial world. But, even allowing for the qualification and counter-examples, the great transformation has, in general, shifted the locus of production from the household, with its gendered structure of roles, to formal organizations, firms or teams of workers in the market place. In doing this it treats labour as something to be supplied by individuals rather than households.

In pre-industrial societies, the role of the family in social care, in particular the care of the sick and the elderly, is also complex. Sometimes there were high rates of geographical mobility in the later middle ages as well as explicit contracts between parents and children by which parents promise to bring up the children in return for the children looking after them when they are old, the latter at least suggesting an individualist moral outlook.[64] Laslett also underlines the extent to which we should not assume that in the pre-industrial age that the family was the primary unit of social care. For example, he cites the example of the outbreak of plague in 1604 in Salisbury when 411 out of some 2,000 households had to be supported by the civic authorities.[65] So, even in the seventeenth century, the security of the individual could not be assured by the household and the same was true in cases of crop failure. However, and allowing for these exceptions, the household remains the location of social care, with large parts of responsibility falling upon wives and daughters. In the great society, by contrast, although much care is still undertaken by women in the household, there is also much care provided through formal organizations like hospitals and nursing homes or agencies. There will be emotional ties that bind family members together in care relationships, but care can also be embodied in wider sets of transactions.

The family is the primary unit of reproduction. Laslett suggested that a good 70 per cent of all English pre-industrial households contained children. He pointed out that in a pre-industrial community children were everywhere, and were expected to take part in agricultural or other forms of production when of a suitable age.[66] Long periods of suckling meant that the number of children a household contained would not be large, but by the same token implied limitations on the freedom with which mothers could take up different occupations. In the great society, the family retains its role as the primary unit for social reproduction, even though relatively high rates of divorce and remarriage mean that the legal parents of children are less frequently the biological parents. Changes in numbers of births, suckling, and child-rearing theoretically mean that women can be freer than they were in pre-industrial communities of those responsibilities, but in practice the tasks of social reproduction remain structured by gender differences.

An important aspect of social reproduction in the great society is that formal school education has become more significant as the human capital needed for the economy has risen to a higher standard. A high level of human capital means an extended period of education. Some productive work can be combined with high level education, but there is a limit to the extent to which this is so. Hence, whilst a high level of human capital enables individuals to have a wider range of occupational choice, so making those individuals more free, it also makes them more dependent during the course of education because a high level of attainment demands exclusive attention. That being so, individuals are economically dependent upon others during the course of their education.

The transformations wrought by the development of the great society have lifted pressures that bound members of a household together within a functioning productive unit. However, responsibilities of care and child-rearing still involve interdependency in complex patterns of family and household responsibility. Indeed, because family responsibilities can only ever be partially incurred voluntarily (adults marry one another, but children and in-laws come as part of the package), there is necessarily only a limited sense in which individualism is possible. The extent to which interdependence can be freely chosen is limited. It may even be the case that in a society in which it is generally assumed that individuals are free to move house or job, the obligations of caring with little choice are more burdensome than they would be in a society where occupational roles are more fixed. The implication for the theory of justice, as we shall see (section 7.4–7.5), is that the continuing imbalances of power such dependency creates needs to be relieved by effective means of social savings.

5.6. The contractarian agenda

The great transformation is sometimes characterized in terms of the distinction between two types of society, those exhibiting strong social solidarity and those exhibiting the logic of contractual relations among otherwise free individuals. These transitions are of course those that Maine sought to capture in his claim that societies had moved from status to contract and Tönnies sought to describe in the contrast between *Gemeinschaft* and *Gesellschaft*.[67] After the great transformation, individuals may work away from home, wage labour and money relations become more important and different members of the same household can be engaged in different parts of the wider economy. There is thus potentially greater individual freedom from the bonds of the family unit of production and the communities in which those families were embedded.[68]

However, even if the growth of individualism is taken as a broadly accurate characterization, there are respects in which we should not see the great transformation at the linear progression of freedom.

As we have seen, continuing responsibilities for care create their own forms of dependency within the household. Increasing length of life and high levels of production create different forms of dependency affecting members of society at large. Sometimes the dependency arises through secular effects on whole societies, of which the fluctuations in the business cycle is the most conspicuous in great societies. Such fluctuations mean that potentially even highly skilled people are vulnerable to having their interests set back as a consequence of the spillover effects of the behaviour of others, since they cannot guarantee that the sector of the economy in which they work will survive. Thus it is not surprising that the 'individualism' of the modern era is itself complex, with various forms of class and occupational solidarity being created in mutual insurance organizations, trades unions, and welfare clubs of various sorts, as ways of dealing with the risks of economic organization.

These various forms of dependency exhibit the logic of externalities, if we use that term to mean the extent to which the well-being of one group of people depends, either for good or for ill, upon the well-being of another group of people. The existence of externalities makes it impossible for people to avoid damage to their interests by decentralized interaction and piecemeal adjustment. There is a need of a regime of public choice if the requisite coordination and adjustment is to be achieved. Alongside these functions of coordination and adjustment, the political institutions of the great society also need to ensure the protection of natural resources not least because the scale of potential damage to natural resources is high given modern methods of production. In addition, great societies need police and military security, good transport infrastructure, high general levels of literacy and numeracy, scientific research, and good public services if the network effects of externalities are to play their part in raising prosperity. The economic differentiation of the economy of the great society increases the need for political institutions to secure public goods.

In common property resource regimes, participants were seen as having two types of interests. The first was in the need to secure access to natural resources for their own use, an interest where participants were in competition with one another. The second was in the maintenance of the stock of common property to which each had access, where the interests were shared among the participants. The same logic applies in the great society. A great society needs to be able to supply the public goods upon which any economy depends and it needs to regulate the access and use of resources to competing claims. How common, yet differentiated and potentially competitive, interests are to be served in a representative political democracy is the first question for contractarian institutional design.

CHAPTER 6

Political democracy in the great society

6.1. Participation, deliberation, and representation

Common property resource regimes are village republics. They embody, if only imperfectly, the features that make a system of collective decision making democratic in a procedural sense. The rules they make determine the conditions under which productive activity is undertaken. Those affected by the rules are able to participate in their making. In such a regime, participants have two interests. The first is in their own capacity for resource extraction, where all are in competition with all. The second is in the conservation of common natural resource, where there is a joint interest in cooperation. Democratic decision making is best understood in terms of the stake that political equals have in securing their common interests under conditions of fallibility, whilst at the same time protecting their separate interests. The requirements of practical rationality mean that joint legislation should have the warrant of deliberation as well as respecting the equal standing of each member of the community.

The village republics are participatory democracies. Participation is important because compliance with agreed rules, a necessary condition of common resource management, is enhanced if those subject to the rules are able to modify them. It is also necessary to enable communal decision making to draw upon the practical experience of members of the community in the design of rules that are appropriate to the circumstances in which those rules have to be applied. Netting, for example, refers to vigorous debates in the village meetings of Törbel.[1] The underlying logic of this requirement can be related to the defeasible character of practical reasoning.

Defeasible practical reasoning has a bias towards specificity, in the sense that one is likely to reason more accurately knowing the details of a case rather than simply following general prescriptions. In managing natural resources, a prescription may be valid in the general case but fail to apply in particular circumstances. For example, rules for harvesting or abstraction may be valid in most circumstances but fail in application when the stocks from which harvests are being taken are either abnormally high or low. The ability to modify the collective agreement through experience is therefore important to the applicability of the rule. Since no one can expect compliance with rules that are inapplicable to the situation in which they are supposed to be operative, participation in rule-modification is a rational requirement of agreement on a social contract.

In an almost canonical definition of deliberative democracy, Dryzek claimed a deliberative democratic theory holds 'that outcomes are legitimate to the extent to which they receive assent through participation by all those subject to the decision in question'.[2] In the limit this would imply that no public decision was legitimate unless it rested on a full consensus within a society. In a similar vein, Richardson links the idea of government through public discussion to the liberal demand that persons be treated as autonomous. For Richardson, this gives rise to three requirements on political processes: they should publicly address each citizen as someone capable of joining in the discussion; they should solicit the participation of each citizen as a potential agent of political decision; and they should treat each person as a self-originating agent of claims.[3] Cohen too suggests that political outcomes are legitimate, if they could be regarded as the object of free and reasoned agreement among equals.[4] Leading theorists of deliberative democracy thus link the notion of political deliberation with a requirement of participation in politics. Considerations of consent, autonomy, or equality suggest that political participation in deliberated public decisions is a condition for the legitimacy of a political system. This link between deliberation and participation is not a gratuitous one, but is grounded in a view about the requirements for political legitimacy.

Yet in great societies this condition of participation cannot be met for obvious and familiar reasons: there is no physical space large enough for all to meet; discussion would take too much time; and the costs of participation are too high for each individual given the low probability of making any difference. As a result, a large portion of political decision making in great societies has to be undertaken by political representatives. To be sure, this claim about the impossibility of participation in great societies has been contested. Ian Budge has argued that modern information technology could dramatically extend the number of issues over which there was mass participation compared to what is normal in representative democracies, including those representative democracies, like Switzerland or some states of the USA, in which the use of referendums to make public policy is common.[5] Budge envisages information and communications technology enabling mass participation in online voting, as well as the transmission of information about policy issues and the evidence and reasoning associated with the alternatives that are up for policy decision. However, if this proposal were implemented, even under ideal circumstances, it would only solve the problem of participation, not the problem of deliberation. To enable all to vote on public policy measures up for decision does not show that the participation has arisen as a result of deliberated consideration. Nor does it address the issue of unanimous consent that is implicit in strong theories of deliberative democracy, since mass political participation of the sort that Budge envisages presupposes the mechanism of voting to resolve cases where there is continuing disagreement about the best policy to follow.

Because there are clear practical difficulties with securing mass participation in politics, the claim that the assent of all is necessary for political legitimacy cannot be plausibly maintained. Consequently, the claims to deliberative legitimacy are sometimes couched in terms of potential or hypothetical agreement. On this revised account, we do not have to suppose actual participation. We merely have to suppose that deliberated decisions could be the object of reasoned agreement, even if they are not in fact so. We might imagine that were, contrary to fact, everyone able to participate in a social conversation, then they would agree. However, such an interpretation of the claim recapitulates for deliberative democracy the principal problem of hypothetical social contract theory. It is one thing to find that people unanimously agree under some circumstances; it is another to suppose that they would agree without our having some independent evidence about what the terms of that agreement would be. If this is true for hypothetical contract theory, it is equally true of deliberative democratic theory. To the extent to which the test of deliberative legitimacy is a purely hypothetical test, it is compatible with an indeterminately large range of outcomes.[6]

Concerns about the ascription of assent to mass populations in the absence of direct participation can be assuaged provided that one has confidence in the system of political representation. If political representatives faithfully represent the views of their constituents, then ascribing hypothetical consent becomes more plausible. Representatives say and do what those citizens who support them would say and do, were they to have participated directly. If representatives stand for important and distinct currents of political opinion in a society, and they present and argue for the views of their constituents in ways that those constituents regularly endorse, then a political decision that is agreed by those representatives can be said to be one that has received the equivalent of assent by all those subject to the decision in question.

It is plausible to hold that public decisions will be better if the general body of citizens takes an intelligent interest in public affairs, has a high level of familiarity with the relevant issues and considerations and takes the trouble to engage in discussion and interchange with their representatives. Discussion of political issues among friends and acquaintances and in social networks is therefore likely to raise the quality of political decision making through a variety of means. Habermas has argued that extensive political deliberation in civil society strengthens the democratic legitimacy of a political system, suggesting that there is a dual system of public discussion. The domain of civil society links with and influences the formal domain of political representation, thus strengthening the legitimacy of representation.[7] Political discussion among friends and acquaintances may be taken as part of a broader 'deliberative system' within which political decision-making processes take place.[8] Moreover, a noteworthy feature of the movement for deliberative democracy is that its advocates include not only political theorists but also policy analysts and even practising politicians, with attempts by policy makers to improve democratic performance through innovations in decision making. For example, at the practical level many experiments in different countries have taken place, with such innovations as citizen juries, deliberative polling, and other forms of public consultation under the influence of deliberative democratic theory.[9] Such innovations can be seen as both reflecting and stimulating political deliberation in civil society. General public discussion and consultation can play an important part in the policy-making process.

To note these points, however, is to note that deliberative participation is an important and valuable supplement to political representation, not a substitute for it. Deliberative participation through consultation presupposes that there is a differentiated and representative system of decision making to which public discussion is related. It is not to imagine that mass public participation can replace the role of representation within a political system. Moreover, widespread and well conducted political discussion is unlikely to lead to unanimity on a decision. Social, economic, and cultural differentiation in great societies means that there is no consensus on many practical matters of public policy, even when participants in the policy-making process approach it conscientiously and with good faith attempts to resolve differences. Thus the requirement for such a high degree of reasoned consensus among citizens implied by some accounts of deliberative democracy is incompatible with both the scale and the differentiation of political democracies in great societies. Scale precludes universal participation in public discussion, at least if that public discussion is understood as a contribution to the final decision process rather than political discussion among friends and acquaintances. Functional differentiation means that the degree of agreement found in small-scale communities cannot be replicated at a larger scale. We cannot simply transpose the principles of village republics to great societies.

If we cannot simply read off from common property resource regimes a political design for representative democracies, the alternative is to take the values exemplified in those regimes and ask how best they could be satisfied within a representative system. The task then is to identify the type of institutional and political conditions that would allow the embodying of public reasoning oriented towards issues of common interest in ways that respected the requirement of political equality. Can we find a set of political arrangements in representative democracies that embody these values?

The Lijphart-Powell typology discussed in section 5.3 identified the key elements of those institutional alternatives found in representative democracies. Westminster systems are distinguished from representational systems by reference to both the electoral formula and the relationship between legislature and executive. In Westminster systems, the first-past-the-post formula combined with single-member districts encourages one party government. The party forming the government controls the legislature through its parliamentary majority in a situation in which legislative committees are relatively weak. In representational systems, by contrast, the electoral formula rarely delivers one party with an overall majority in the legislature, so that the formation of government depends upon coalition bargaining. Legislative oversight of government policy is complemented by relatively strong committees. To this twofold classification must be added the institutional arrangements of liberal constitutionalism, in which a high degree of legislative coordination is needed between different branches of government. The same legislative powers are found in separate institutions.

In practice, few countries exhibit in pure form the features of any one of the types. However, close approximations to Westminster systems include Australia, the UK, and New Zealand (before 1996). Close approximations to representational democracies include Austria, Belgium, Denmark, the Netherlands, Norway, Sweden, and Switzerland. The USA provides the clearest example of a liberal constitutionalist regime. The allocation of countries to the different categories is interesting both in its own right and in relation to social contract theory. Barry suggested that the representational democracies of Western Europe, particularly those of the Netherlands and Scandinavia, exhibited politics conducted in circumstances of impartiality, with each section of the population being able to articulate its interests, open methods of communication, and a political culture of solidarity and problem solving.[10] By contrast, Rawls argued that in a liberal constitutionalist regime with the separation of powers, the US Supreme Court could be seen as an exemplar of public reason but in a form that respected the 'political ideal of a people to govern itself in a certain way'.[11] For Rawls, the Court is the body responsible for that aspect of public reasoning issuing from the constituent power of the body of citizens within a democracy, so that its decision making could stand as a model of deliberative democracy.

These contrasting evaluations prompt the question as to whether some types of representative democracy are more in accord with the principles of a democratic social contract than others. Of course, there is no need to suppose that we are confronted with the necessity of an either/or choice in response to this question. There may be more than one way of institutionalizing the values of political equality and deliberation oriented towards the common interest. The equivalent of a uniqueness theorem is not required. It is not necessary to show that there is one and only one type of institutional democratic arrangement that would meet the relevant conditions. Moreover, although institutional design is important, it may only be one part of what is needed to ensure political deliberation oriented in an egalitarian way to the public interest. Political culture, attitudes among political elites, and historical contingency may play a vital role in determining the effective function of the political system according to the norms of democratic justice. Yet, even with these caveats, there are still grounds for asking whether there are reasons for favouring one type of institutional design over another. Before looking at these arguments in detail, however, it will be useful to consider the concept and functions of political representation as a preliminary.

6.2. The functions of political representation

The general concept of representation is given by the notion of one thing standing for another. Contour lines represent hills on a map, and a flag can stand for a country.[12] However, associated with this concept there are a number of distinct conceptions, each of which highlights the different ways in which one thing or person can stand for another. Adapting Pitkin we can say that the 'standing for' in political representation potentially has six different senses: authorization; accountability; descriptive similarity; symbolic representation; substantive interest representation; and responsiveness.[13] Each of these senses is logically distinct from the others. A person or body representative in one sense need not be representative in another sense. For example, an authorized representative may not have a duty of accountability to constituents, a possibility exemplified in Hobbes's theory of political obligation, where the sovereign acts for subjects but is not accountable to those subjects.[14] Similarly, a representative body may be accountable to an electorate, but not be descriptively representative of the electorate in statistical terms—indeed, none are. It is not even essential that a body or agent be democratic to be a representative.[15] In international relations, non-democratic representation is common and rests upon a convention in terms of which diplomatic representatives can speak and act on behalf of the countries that they represent. Similarly, we cannot assimilate a substantive notion of representation, in which someone acts in the interests of another, either to authorization or to accountability, since one may act for someone's interests without being either authorized by or accountable to that person.

However, to say that there are different conceptions of representation is not to deny that those different conceptions can be linked with one another, as Pitkin herself pointed out.[16] Indeed, different theories of representation are formed from the different conceptions compounded in particular ways. Heads of states or elected representatives may be treated as authorized agents for certain purposes, yet they are only democratically representative when they account for their actions to citizens. Some heads of state, such as the French president, have a role both in terms of authorization as when they sign international treaties and symbolically as standing for the nation on ceremonial occasions. And there is an obvious sense in which political representatives in a democracy are supposed to act in the substantive interests of their constituents but also to demonstrate this by being responsive or at least accountable. On the different conceptions of representation can be built different theories of how it is that political representatives should behave in order to represent. Pitkin's own definition of democratic representation comprised a mixture of authorization, accountability, and substantive representation.[17] Whatever the merits of her specific account, her general analysis that any conception of representation is compounded of different element seems correct.[18]

An important aspect of representation, mentioned by Pitkin almost in passing, is that political representation may be best achieved not through the detailed specification of the role of any one person or agent in a political system, but through the way the system operates as a whole.[19] This distinction between the properties exhibited at the level of individual or roles and the properties exhibited at the level of the system is an important one. At the level of individuals we can ask whether the substantive representation of interests is best secured by individual representatives being delegates, held strictly to account by their constituents, or by their being independent capable of freedom of action, say, negotiating with other representatives about packages of proposals to be legislated on. At the system level, we can ask whether substantive representation is better secured through institutions in which decision making is concentrated in an executive that is relatively free of parliamentary control during its period of office or a set of institutions in which power is divided. The character of the decision-making process is a property of the system as a whole, not of the performance of the individuals within the system. To the extent to which system-level properties constrain and shape the behaviour of individuals and groups within the system, specification at the level of the system will have implications for the behaviour of those individuals and groups.

The institutions of democratic government are supposed to serve the interests of the governed. Democratic contractarianism conceives these interests as falling into two categories: the separate interests of associates in the good of themselves and their kith and kin, and the collective interests that all associates have in the public goods of a society. Given these twin interests, what functions does a system of political representation need to serve?

The interest in collective goods entails an interest in the deliberative capacity of the political system, in particular in its capacity to formulate and evaluate putative solutions to collective problems. A political system that serves the interests of the governed must be able to identify the alternative ways in which public goods can be provided. Even when public goods are quintessentially within the province of government, the identification and evaluation of alternative policies to supply them are not straightforward and will require policy deliberation to assess arguments and evidence. Consider, for example, problems of coastal flooding and erosion, protection against which is an obvious form of public good. Within the policy communities related to coastal protection, there are technical debates, for example, about the comparative merits of hard barriers versus managed retreat allowing tidal action to create its own barriers from coastal material. Moreover, resolving these disputes can involve further technical knowledge of currents, coastal geography, and the economic value of enterprises liable to damage. So, even with something as self-evidently useful as protection against flooding, the form that the public good should take is something that requires policy deliberation, often of a complex kind.

Technical discussions of policy design shade into discussions about the social values that are involved. Issues of coastal protection again provide a good example. Whatever the effectiveness of any proposed flood defence scheme, there will be questions about its untoward side-effects, including possible physical and economic damage to communities affected by the form of coastal defence adopted or damage to wildlife species that are important in the culture of the community. Political deliberation is therefore needed as to establish how to balance any technical merits that particular schemes might have against wider questions about how to evaluate their broader effects. Thus, in terms of its deliberative function, a representative system needs the capacity to institutionalize the problem-solving capacity that is required to deal with such issues.

A meaningful representative system not only needs to provide the deliberative forums within which the merits of alternative policy solutions can be addressed, but also to do so in a way that enables the practical problem to be addressed. In addition to deliberation there is practical action, with a choice having being made between the alternatives. Normally, to be effective, policies have to avoid frequent changes with their needing time to take effect. So not only must a choice be made, it should also be immune to frequent revision. In some cases, this condition is met by the nature of the solution that is adopted. Where public policy involves high levels of capital investment, then immunity to change is literally built into the system, the example of flood protection providing a good example. However, time-inconsistency is possible with a wide range of important policies, and a good representative system will avoid such outcomes, not least by ensuring that all relevant objections have been articulated and responded to in the formulation of the policy.

Every political choice needs to be made in the presence of persistent and continuing disagreements about the merits of the choice. Given such disagreements, a representative system needs to be able to aggregate different views providing a way of coming to a collective decision in the face of continuing disagreement. One reason that this is important is that the technical issues of policy choice shade into political questions about the balance of interests that need to be struck where there is competition. Consequently, a representative system will also need to be able to institutionalize negotiation and bargaining about the allocation of costs and benefits that any provision of public goods entails in such a way that the legitimate interests of all affected parties are respected. For example, those liable to pay the costs of provision will need assurance that those costs are reasonable given the benefits that are being supplied. This assurance is only possible in a representative system in which representatives can secure the confidence of their constituents. If political representation is to be effective in such situations, then representatives need to be able to enter into commitments on behalf of their constituents, and those with whom they are negotiating will need assurance that these commitments can be honoured. This in turn will require representatives to be sufficiently responsive and accountable to their constituents that it is reasonable to believe that collective commitments entered into can be met.

A good representative system will be one that combines these functions to a high degree and to do this means that it meet both deliberative and aggregative requirements. The Lijphart-Powell typology largely makes the classification of systems turn upon the way in which differences of view and opinion are aggregated to form a public policy. However, if we place these aggregative features in the context of a broader theory of representation, then we can see that there is also a need to make sure that our theory of aggregation coheres with our theory of deliberation.

If we accept the persistence of political and policy disagreement, then we need to be concerned with the way in which those differences are reconciled in practical decision making, and this means finding an account of political institutions that brings together principles for the evaluation of aggregation as well as deliberation. The need for a reconciliation of the theory of deliberation with the theory of aggregation was recognized by deliberative democratic theorists some time ago.[20] One basis upon which the theoretical reconciliation may be made is to distinguish between, on the one hand, the fit between some measure of collective preferences and what is decided for public policy and, on the other hand, the way in which those preferences are formed. Within the deliberative theory of democracy, this distinction has been recognized. As Joshua Cohen has written, 'the deliberative conception [of democracy] emphasizes that collective choices should be *made in a deliberative way*, and not only that those choices should have a desirable fit with the preferences of citizens'.[21] In this context, the task is to show that there is a conception of democracy in which processes of aggregation and processes of deliberation can be regarded as elements in a broader conception that stresses both the centrality of political equality and the importance of institutionalizing credible processes of public reasoning.

6.3. Aggregation and deliberative rationality

Since the concept of political equality is central to any conception of democracy, it makes sense to begin with the implications of that value in the institutional evaluation. In an important argument, Anthony McGann has proposed that forms of representational democracy, as instanced in some European countries, embody to a significant degree the democratic values of political equality.[22] Central to his argument is a distinction between a seat share allocation rule and a social decision rule. A social decision rule is applicable to the problem of how to determine a single best or rank-ordered list of public policies. Such a rule does this by imposing restrictions on the function that maps a statement of individual preferences into a social choice. A seat share allocation rule, by contrast, is a way of determining a set of agents, from a pool of eligible candidates, to represent citizens in parliament. One way in which we might think about this distinction is to note that whereas the function of a social decision is typically to indicate which is the 'best' policy (as a function of the preferences of individual citizens), the function of a seat share rule is to identify a set of representatives without indicating any rank-order of preference among them.

McGann shows that seat share rules based upon the principle of proportional representation satisfy formal requirements that can be interpreted as stipulations deriving from the principle of political equality.[23] The rule should be anonymous, in the sense that it should not be biased in favour of the votes of some voters rather than others, and it should be neutral, in the sense that it should not favour preferences for any particular type of alternative over any other alternative. The rule should also be positively responsive, meaning that if voter preferences shift in a particular direction, then the pattern of seat share allocation should reflect that shift in the same direction. Given these conditions, a seat share allocation rule will have the property that it will increase the proportionate seat share of candidates in line with the proportion of votes received. If vote shares are equal, then an anonymous and neutral seat share rule must give an equal number of seats to each party and if the share rule is positively responsive it will increase the share of the party that has gained votes. By an extension of the argument, the same is true of coalitions of parties in a parliament.[24] In short, a concern with equality in the political representation of citizens will imply that proportional representation systems of voting should be used. The fair treatment of individual voters requires proportional representation. Under proportional representation, each voter is given the same chance of increasing the representation of those opinions in the parliament with which he or she agrees. This is a weaker condition than that of the ability to block or spoil outcomes, which was the operational meaning of equality of power in common property resource regimes, but it is a strong condition within the context of rules of preference aggregation.

If we could stop at this point of the argument, we could move directly to the conclusion that political equality favours the representational alternatives of the Lijphart-Powell typology and so conclude with Brian Barry that these systems embody the circumstances of justice (which Barry would of course have understood in terms of impartiality). Of course, we should have to admit that there was some distance between a theoretical ideal of proportional representation and the way in which it was implemented in practice, simply because for practical reasons it is impossible to make seat share systems fully proportional in character. However, exactly the same can be said of any real world institutions compared to its theoretical ideal-type. Allowing for this factor, do we not have a complete argument for favouring representational designs for democracy?

The answer is negative, because, in addition to showing that a representative parliament elected by proportional representation would satisfy conditions of political equality, we also have to consider the rule by which parties in parliament vote. Let us suppose that issues are determined by majority rule in a parliament. In a well-known result, it can be shown that, if preferences are single-peaked, with the preferences of those voting declining monotonically from an ideal-point, then the preferences of the median voter will be a Condorcet winner, meaning that it is an alternative that will beat any other alternative under a majority vote when placed in direct competition with that alternative.[25] This too is a rule of equality; since majority decision is anonymous between voters and positively responsive to their changes in preference, both properties that can be associated with equality.[26] Hence, if we think that proportional representation preserves political equality for electors choosing parties and a rule of majority voting in parliament preserves political equality among the parties selected by those voters, we can say that a parliament elected by proportional representation and using the majority principle is the only system that will preserve political equality at both levels of decision making.

However, there is a long-standing argument that multi-party parliaments produce instability, with competing coalitions successively seeking to form governments that replace previous occupants to the detriment of viable decision making. The National Assembly in the French Fourth Republic is a well studied and much commented upon example. Moreover, the concern with stability intersects with a concern about deliberative rationality. One element of deliberative rationality is accountability. A requirement of accountability means that it ought to be possible for anyone to retrace the chain of reasoning within a practical syllogism as to why a government has adopted the policy it has. Yet unstable parliamentary coalitions may undermine the conditions for accountability. Legislative decisions would fail to exhibit the rationality that was required for the accountability. The implication would be that, resting on only a plurality of the vote, Westminster systems may not make decisions that reflect the preference of the majority of the electorate, but their policy making might at least exhibit the coherence necessary for political accountability.

To understand this line of argument, we need to consider the phenomenon of majority rule cycling. Between two alternatives, the majority principle will always produce a clear decision. However, with three alternatives it is prone to cycling, in the sense that alternative x may be preferred to alternative y, alternative y preferred to alternative z, but alternative z preferred to alternative x. When this happens, it seems impossible to determine which alternative should be chosen. The circumstances under which this can happen are many, but the general logic is easy to illustrate with a simple example. Imagine a parliament in which there are three political parties of roughly equal size, A, B, and C. A and B may form a majority preferring x to y. A and C may form a majority preferring y to z. But B and C form a majority preferring z to x. If x, y, and z are all on the agenda of decision making, then an underlying pattern of cyclical preferences means that potentially any alternative could be chosen. If we think about a sequence of decisions over time, then the observed outcome of such a cycle would be a lack of stability in choice as the composition of majority coalitions changed. Empirically, if cycling is important in parliamentary politics, its effects will show in the instability of governing coalitions as different combinations of parties seek to realise their most preferred alternative by joining with others in a succession of agreements. The governmental instability of the Fourth French Republic would be one such instance and short-lived governments in post-war Italy another. There is in-built conflict between giving equal power to different parliamentary groups, making the collective choice responsive to their preferences, and securing the coherence of those collective choices over time.

Do we have to worry about the cycling of majority rule if we adopt a deliberative account of rationality? To say that intransitivity of choice is irrational might be thought to rest upon a definition of rationality solely in terms of consistency conditions on choices. If so, it might not seem that cycling was a problem in a framework of deliberative rationality. Yet it is. If majority preference gives us a reason to prefer x to y and it also gives us reason to prefer y to z, then it should give us *even more* reason to prefer x to z. If a parliament has reason to prioritize the hospital building programme over road improvements, and reason to prioritize road improvements over new warships, then it would seem to have more reason to prioritize the hospital building programme over the new warships that it does to prioritize road building over the warships. Coherence in public reasoning seems threatened if we cannot make inferences of this sort. If coherence is threatened, then so is credibility, in the sense that we cannot provide an intellectually satisfactory account of public choices. The requirements of political accountability cannot be met. If majority rule cycling is important in multi-party parliaments, we need to think about its implications for the requirements of deliberative rationality.

The cycling of political choice is usually a product of there being more than one dimension of contention in political decisions. Within great societies, there are potentially many bases of difference and contest. For example, alongside economic differences in a society, there may be cultural differences, for example of religion, or ethnic differences. The distinct interests associated with underlying social cleavages can be thought of in dimensional terms. Each social cleavage (economic, linguistic, religious, territorial, and so on) can be thought of as a potential dimension of conflict. Moreover, those who are agreed in one dimension may disagree on other dimensions. For example, in many democracies, those who are economically liberal favouring a low tax economy are divided between those who are socially conservative, favouring traditional morality, and those who are social liberal, favouring gay rights, abortion, and liberal laws on recreational drug use.

The dimensionality of political conflict is not something that is solely determined by social cleavages outside the political system, but can be affected by strategic action within the political process. Seeing a latent dimension of conflict, politicians can have an incentive to turn it into a salient issue of political competition.[27] Where the members of an electorate are divided on more than one set of issues, groups will arise that express those others sources of controversy and discontent and the principle of political equality suggests that those who share an interest should be able to form an association that can be effective in advancing that interest. Hence, in any great society we should expect political controversy to exist along more than one dimension. Citizens and their political representatives, who would naturally form a coalition of interests with others on one issue, may find themselves diametrically opposed on other issues. As different issues come up for decision, so we would expect different majorities to form. The logic of equal representation implies a multi-party legislature in which winning coalitions are shifting, but is this compatible with the coherence that accountable practical public reasoning might seem to require? If public policy is made by shifting coalitions, in what sense can we say that it is deliberatively rational?

To consider the question, let us consider a pure case of proportional representation, where political agendas include more than one dimension of issues. Suppose a parliament operating with the rule that the median party in parliament on any one issue dimension is decisive, although the same party may not be decisive on other issues. For example, a party may be the pivotal party in respect of finance and taxation but not in respect of environmental regulation. Such a situation existed in Denmark in the 1980s, when a conservative government secured a majority of economic and financial policies, but had to concede policy on environmental matters to an alternative 'green majority' made up of governing and non-governing parties.[28] Indeed, the practice of Nordic minority governments in general illustrates a similar phenomenon, since the willingness of parties outside of the governing coalition to support the government programme depends upon a willingness of the government not to bring forward measures that the smaller parties would veto.[29] The principle here is that support for a government does not have to be support for the whole combination of policies that it advances but can vary depending upon particular policies. Formally, in our hypothesized case, the decision rule that authorizes public policy is the product of the issue-by-issue median.[30] This is the rule that makes public policy the result of a majority choice in parliament on each issue taken one by one. There is no constraint that a governing coalition of parties has to sign up to an agreed programme of policies across different issues that they all have to support. It can be shown formally that the rule of issue-by-issue median voting is the only rule that is anonymous, responsive, and strategy-proof, so exhibiting a form of political equality.[31]

Taking this as our reference point, in what sense is there a lack of political accountability in such a system? It is certainly true that there is no one point of view from which it is possible to lay out a chain of reasoning that provides a coherent set of reasons for favouring the policy bundle that emerges from a sequence of votes decided by the majority principle. If one thought of oneself as a social planner, for example, there would be no single rank-order that one could construct to represent what the parliament was doing. The upshot of the voting process would lack global transitivity as the dimensions were amalgamated. However, this would only be an objection to the practice if it were plausible to assume that anyone could take up the position of such a social planner. However, by familiar arguments from bounded rationality such a point of view is impossible. Arrow's theorem shows that there is an inherent tension between rational coherence and responsiveness to the preferences of those who are voting.[32] This is nothing especially to do with majority rule; there is *no* social choice function satisfying the Arrowian conditions. The global intransivity that results from using the issue-by-issue median is a consequence of the pluralism that exists in society that is then faithfully represented in the parliament.

There is no one chain of reasoning, starting from agreed premisses, that rationalizes the results of the issue-by-issue median. The rule is non-monotonic. Adding a new dimension of issues leads us to revise what is globally rational. Nonetheless, there is a simple justification that can be offered for the bundle of policies that result from the issue-by-issue median, namely that it is the aggregate of each party sincerely voting according to its views on the issue in front of it at the time. The majority of representatives found the arguments favoured one policy position in one dimension, and a different majority found argument persuasive to favour a particular policy position on another dimension, thereby modifying the implication of the first agreement as a result. When you put the results together, the bundle defined by the issue-by-issue median is just the result that you get.

The approach to public decision making using the issue-by-issue median relies on being able to separate the issues (say, conservative on finance, green on defence and environment) and it may be argued that there are limits to such unbundling. Across a range of issues, globally preferred alternatives must be found. McGann suggests that this restriction applies most notably in the area of budgetary decisions.[33] Where a global budget has to be agreed, the division of items in that budget means that each item has effects upon the others. Decisions about spending on health cannot be detached from decision about spending on defence, education, or other items. No doubt it is right to say that global budgeting does impose these interdependencies. However, the extent to which a political system should operate a global budgeting approach in its public expenditure is itself a matter of institutional choice and design. For example, in social insurance systems of health care, decisions on financing and expenditure are made by decision processes outside of those of the government budget, so that a decision to reimburse a particular set of medical interventions does not of itself have implications for public spending. Indeed, the autonomy of financing agents in social insurance systems appears to be one of their operating features that participants value highly.[34] Even where government makes the budgetary decisions, rather than separate social agencies, it is possible to argue for more extensive use of hypothecated taxation, by which the finance raised is ear-marked for particular items of expenditure, so that decisions on such matters can be detached from global budgetary decisions. None of this is to say that disaggregating budgetary decisions provides an easy solution to the problem of coherence in public reasoning, but equally one should not underestimate the extent to which some institutional practices reduce the problem.

Moreover, as McGann himself has argued, following Nicholas Miller, although cycling, and so global intransitivity, may exist, its scope is limited under plausible conditions. This line of argument relies upon the concept of the 'uncovered set'.[35] An alternative *x* is uncovered if there is no *y* that beats *x* and all the alternatives that *x* itself beats. The uncovered set is the collection of alternatives that satisfy this condition. Cycling can occur within the uncovered set, but the set of points that are covered will by definition be beaten by some points in the uncovered set. The implication for political competition is that a party seeking office is unlikely to occupy a position that would lead it to adopt an alternative in the covered set, since it would know it could be beaten by parties that adopted alternatives in the uncovered set. Party competition will therefore take place within the uncovered set and this set will be quite small and central to the dimensions of competition. If cycling takes place in a small space that is centrally located, it may be hard to observe and small in scope. Over successive years governing coalitions may prioritize hospital spending over road, roads over defence, and then defence over hospital spending. This would lead to oscillations in capital budgets and fluctuations in staff numbers in each line of activity, but if the margins were small enough they would not be noticed within the general fluctuations of the economy.

Of course, 'small' and 'centrally located' in graph-theoretical terms does not imply insignificant in political terms. If parties are distinct in ideological or programmatic terms, the area of their competition will be bounded by the uncovered set that is formed by the intersection of points that are feasibly in competition with one another. However, this is still compatible with large fluctuations in terms of political ideology. In post-1945 democracies, far right parties and extreme libertarian parties have adopted positions well outside the uncovered set, but that does not mean that the fluctuations between neo-liberal and social democratic parties within the uncovered set were not large in practical terms. One implication is that cycling within the uncovered set is less likely to be practically problematic if it demarcates enough of the overlapping consensus that forms the political culture of accommodative problem solving. Although the rules are important, so are the preferences that parties bring to the forum of voting.

Majority rule cycling is not nearly the bugbear that it is sometimes made out to be. It is compatible with a form of non-monotonic rationality that recognizes pluralism as inherent in any complex great society. Moreover, the fact that different majorities can form on different issues precludes there being the likelihood of a permanent majority that can tyrannize over a permanent minority.[36] Cross-cutting cleavages sustain pluralism in a way that a solid indivisible majority does not. The tyranny of majority rule is not a feature of representational democracies. Does this give sufficient protection for minority rights, however? The condition of equal power in the common property resource regimes effectively gave each participant the opportunity to spoil the bargain if it was not sufficiently advantageous. In representational parliamentary democracies, with fluctuating coalitions, that notion of power has been replaced with one in which equal power means having the same opportunity as others to join a majority coalition on a subset of issues. It may be that protection of civil and political rights is in the uncovered set of preferred political positions, but that makes rights potentially subject to the calculus of political advantage. The liberal constitutionalist argues that such rights should have stronger constitutional protection than the way they figure in the preference orderings of political actors. Is that a plausible position?

6.4. The liberal constitutionalist alternative

Suppose we hold that the only way in which the civil and political rights of citizens can be protected is by making them a component of a constitution that is itself hard, if not impossible, to change. The implication of this position is that the scope of government should be explicitly limited and nothing government is allowed to do should exceed those limits. The purpose of providing for constitutional protection in this way is to prevent individuals being subject to the tyranny of majority rule. Without such constitutional protection, it is argued, majorities can pass legislation to the detriment of minorities. There might be various ways of fettering majority supported governments, for example by strong concurrent majority requirements in the passing of legislation between different legislative houses, as well as a strong doctrine of the right of constituent units within a political system to nullify decisions that are taken at a higher level. However, one obvious means of fettering is to have a bill of rights, protected by a constitutional court, to which minorities can appeal. Political equality, it is argued, requires counter-majoritarian institutions.

One problem in general with fettering government with the aim of protecting minority rights is that it assumes that tyranny comes only from decisions that a majority might make, and not from a failure to make a decision. Suppose, for example, that a minority has its rights threatened by a government failure to secure certain goods on its behalf. Perhaps, for example, it lacks the flood protection that it needs, and so faces a threat to its right to property through natural hazard. Suppose also that the best way of dealing with this problem would be government-provided flood protection. It will be much harder for the legislature to vote the funds for such a measure if a super-majority is required than if it is not, since super-majority requirements always favour the status quo. However, it may be argued that this is to look at the matter in too aggregative a way. Institutions with considerable veto powers will constrain government decision making to the status quo, but the same may not be true when seen from a deliberative perspective, if we interpret the jurisprudence of constitutional courts in such a way that it is consistent with the democratic will and not contrary to it. The most sophisticated version of this argument was offered by John Rawls in his defence of the claim that the US Supreme Court could be an instrument of deliberative democracy.

Rawls argued that the US Supreme Court could be seen as an exemplar of public reason but in a form that respected the 'political ideal of a people to govern itself in a certain way'.[37] For Rawls, the Court is the body responsible for that aspect of public reasoning issuing from the constituent power of the body of citizens within a democracy. Relying upon Locke's distinction between the constituent power of a body of citizens to establish a new regime and the ordinary powers of citizens and officers of government, Rawls identifies a difference between 'higher' and 'ordinary' law, with higher law stemming from the people's constituent power and ordinary law stemming from the powers given under that higher law. A democratic constitution is the expression in higher law of the ideal of popular self-government and the 'aim of public reason is to articulate this ideal'. Within this account, the constitutional basics are the outcome of particular constitutional moments in the development of democracy, in which the citizen body by a democratically ratified constitution 'fixes once and for all certain constitutional essentials', especially equal civil and political rights and the rule of law.[38] The task of the Supreme Court is to apply and extend the relevant constitutional principles to matters of public policy and concern. The jurisprudence of the Supreme Court is monotonic: new issues may add to that jurisprudence but they cannot modify it.

On this account constitutional democracy is dualist. There is a distinction to be made between a political power that flows from a people, which forms a higher law, and the form of political power that is exercised as ordinary law in everyday legislation. Acting as the interpreter of the higher law, the Supreme Court reinforces and upholds the authority of the people. Faithfulness to the constitution, as mandated periodically by the people, is what gives the Supreme Court the claim to be a servant of democracy. In carrying out this mandate, the Supreme Court is an institutional exemplar of public reason as well as the guardian of civil and political rights (although Rawls notes that it is not the only exemplar). Its exemplary status is revealed in three features. First, the only basis upon which justices in the Supreme Court are allowed to reason is that of public reasoning; they cannot invoke their particular comprehensive views as citizens as political representatives may do in ordinary law-making. Secondly, the reasoned opinions of the justices have to reflect the best interpretation of the constitution that they can offer. Thirdly, by its judgements on fundamental constitutional questions, the Court gives 'public reason vividness and vitality in the public forum' when it interprets the constitution in a reasonable way.[39]

One essential implication of the Rawlsian argument is that changes in the constitution have to be construed as bringing out public values that were implicit in the founding constitutional moment, so that valid constitutional amendments bring 'the Constitution more in line with its original promise'.[40] Rawls saw the founding moment of the US constitution in contractual terms and it provided an analogue to the idea of the original position. Thus, in the development of his idea of a four-stage sequence of contractualist reasoning in *A Theory of Justice*, Rawls imagines the parties to a social contract moving to a constitutional convention where 'they are to decide upon the justice of political forms and choose a constitution', explicitly noting that it was the history of the US constitution which inspired the idea.[41] However, it follows from this construction that the idea of an original constitution has to be made compatible with the evolution of a democratic political culture.

To secure this compatibility, Rawls relied upon Ackerman's interpretation of the history of the US constitution.[42] Ackerman argued that there have been certain moments of constitutional politics in the US in which existing political principles were redefined, to be applied and acted on over subsequent decades. In particular, in his version of events, the three crucial turning points were the Federalist founding regime, the Republican reconstruction regime and the Democrat New Deal regime. All three of these changes should be seen as collective popular transformations in which majorities are mobilized. Thus, on this account, when the Supreme Court appears to be making law without legislative sanction, as it did in *Brown v. Board of Education* in 1954, it is not asserting its own authority, but rather interpreting and applying the authority of the people stemming from the Roosevelt New Deal regime change. The judges do not usurp the authority of the people but preserve the achievements of popular sovereignty. From this point of view, though being unaccountable to the electorate, the Court is an instrument of public reason in a democratic society. It is acting to uphold the authority of the people, where that authority is understood in terms of the higher constitutive authority of the people.

However, if this theory is to be made to work, it has to be consistent with the historical record. Consider the claim that the various constitutional moments of US political developments should be seen as expression of collective transformations in which popular majorities are mobilized. On this account, Reconstruction and the New Deal, and the constitutional changes that accompanied them, were events that took place at the level of the people. For this to be true would imply that certain elections are 'critical elections' marking turning points in popular opinion and political coalitions. Although the theory of critical elections has been a widespread view in US electoral studies, it has been seriously challenged by David Mayhew.[43] On Mayhew's account 1932 certainly stands out in terms of the major policy initiatives associated with the New Deal, although civil rights do not feature until 1948, which on no one's account is a critical election. But, when judged by turn-out, which is an obvious measure of popular mobilization, 1932 is a disappointing election as evidence of a fundamental transformation of popular sentiment, since it exhibited a comparatively low figure even for the twentieth century. For the constitutional turning-point of the Civil War and Reconstruction, it is difficult to find strong evidence for 1860 as a critical election, and, more worryingly for the higher law thesis, there is something of a case for the elections of 1874 (mid-term), 1876, and 1880 as marking the end of Reconstruction and ushering in what Mayhew calls the 'consociational republic' of North and South, which might equally be called the era of peaceful co-existence between North and South based on malign neglect by the federal government.

There may of course be other evidence of constitutional moments in US politics, but to interpret the jurisprudence of the Supreme Court as an expression of democratic public reason would require that evidence to be distinct from, though related to, changes in public opinion and political orientation of a fundamental kind. Otherwise, the most natural way to understand the Supreme Court is as a non-majoritarian institution the authority of which is to be found in its own tradition of reasoning, of which one version is Dworkin's 'chain novel' metaphor.[44] That is consistent with making the Court a deliberative institution, but not a deliberative democratic institution. The Supreme Court's well-known pro-business decisions, as in *Lochner*, between the end of the Civil War and the

New Deal seem to be unassociated with popular political feeling, except negatively. In this context, Richard Bellamy has persuasively argued that, insofar as constitutional courts seek to remove issues of political rights from the realm of democratic discussion and debate, they deny an essential feature of such rights, namely that when they come into conflict a reasonable pluralism can make different judgements as to how the balance is to be struck, and the best way of representing this reasonable pluralism is through the parliamentary process.[45] If the case for liberal constitutionalism is going to be advanced, it has to be on grounds other than that it is the outcome of a democratic contract.

6.5. The public reasoning of representatives

Representative democracies involve a mixture of conflict and cooperation. Given the functional differentiation of a great society, conflict arises from the differences of interests thereby generated. However, even with entrenched differences of interest, great societies still have to solve problems to do with the supply of public goods, in particular a functioning system of law and regulation, protection of natural resources and the environment, and protection from external threats. They also need to ensure that they can facilitate the achievement by individuals and groups of interests that they have in common, as well as provide procedures that broker a fair compromise where interests cannot be harmonized. I have argued that, from an aggregative point of view, political equality requires that public policy be made in accordance with a rule of median correspondence. However, this claim needs to be reconciled with the deliberative argument that correspondence is not enough and that what is needed is that the preferences be formed in a deliberative way. What sort of deliberative formation of preferences is compatible with the recognition of the two interests of associates in a social contract, namely the separate interests that are potentially in competition and the common interests that require cooperation?

Within representative democracies, the determination of policy is a competitive process. Parties compete with one another for seats in the legislature, and then transact with one another for a share of government power. There is also a competition among interest groups and social movements over the definition of the public agenda, and the priority to be accorded to different policies. In discursive terms it is useful to think of public policy formation as a competition among different advocacy coalitions, who may be defined as groups of actors united in sharing policy positions that they explain and justify by reference to core beliefs.[46] The actors joined in a policy coalition can be very diverse, including firms, policy think-tanks and research units, social movements, pressure groups, charities and other non-governmental organizations, sections of the media, members of the legislature, and others. They are linked not by their institutional or material interest in the policy process but by their sharing certain patterns of reasoning, core beliefs as to values, and an understanding of how the world works, together with a willingness to endorse a particular range of policy solutions. They are opposed by opposing advocacy coalitions similarly joined in their pattern of beliefs, but holding contrary policy positions. Other important actors in policy will be neutral, attending to the arguments of the competing advocacy coalitions, but not fully convinced by either side.

In this context, the common interest that all political associates share, whatever their own position in relation to any particular advocacy coalition, is creating the conditions under which this discursive competition identifies the conditions under which public goods can be established and sustained. In turn this requires the system of political deliberation to have the capacity to formulate and evaluate putative solutions to collective action problems in a reliable way. Since the rationality of practical reasoning is defeasible, the debate among competing advocacy coalitions will work well when it identifies faulty decision premisses, shortcomings in the evidence about the effects of different measures and the circumstances under which otherwise generally valid prescriptions will fail in their purpose.

One reason why the system of policy advocacy might fail is that partisans talk past one another. This theory was advanced within the theory of advocacy coalitions by Sabatier, who thought this was a feature of policy systems that he had observed. The notion that political deliberation consists in partisans talking past one another is also implicit in the work of the Comparative Manifestos Project, the basic assumption of which is that in campaigning, political parties treat all issues as valence, rather than positional, matters and stress those issues on which they think they have the competitive advantage.[47] In a similar vein, on the basis of his study of the ratification debates for the US Constitutions, Riker formulated the dominance and dispersion principle to characterize the phenomenon: when one side has the advantage on an issue, the other side will vacate the space of debate; when neither side has the advantage, both will vacate the space.[48]

These claims are all empirical, and they do not address the responsibilities that members of advocacy coalitions might have to play in stringently testing the decision premisses and chains of reasoning that are advanced by their opponents, as well as their obligation to put their own case openly and with attention to its shortcomings. For example, Gutmann and Thompson have proposed a principle of deliberative reciprocity by which, if advocates try to find reasons that are as widely acceptable as possible, they will advance the principles of publicity and accountability.[49] If acted on, the principle of reciprocity would encourage the mutual engagement in debate among advocacy coalitions that would foster the testing of decision premisses. In fact, there may not be quite so sharp a contrast between the processes of policy debate as empirically observed and the normative requirements on advocacy coalitions implied by the principle of reciprocity. The thesis that partisans talk past one another is hard to test. However, it is possible to show that in debates on abortion policy, in the UK House of Commons, opponents do seek to engage with the arguments of the opposition, without abandoning any of the subsets of issues that the policy raises to their opponents.[50] In this sense there is an attempt at deliberative reciprocity in the advocacy of competing positions. Outside legislatures, the presence of neutral apolitical forums, of the type that some charitable foundations provide, can also offset the tendency for proponents of competing policies to talk past one another.[51]

A further way of enhancing the quality of deliberation is to ensure that there are publicly available sets of factual and trend data that can be accepted as common points of reference by those who disagree on policy. Such data includes the obvious economic indicators, but it should also include data on resource use, spatial distribution, patterns of family formation and dissolution, details of educational attainments, health status and other indicators of social welfare. Maintaining the integrity and scope of these data sets is important in creating the conditions under which policy debate can enhance its deliberative rationality. Although it is often said that public reasoning requires an orientation towards public goals, this may not be an important condition, since one of the things on which advocacy coalitions typically disagree is how the public good is to be defined. In this context, investment in the sources of evidence, rather than an orientation towards the goals of evidence, is likely to be more important.

The incompleteness of deliberative rationality, by contrast with the completeness of rationality as utility, has important democratic implications. It is this line of thought that lay at the core of Mill's argument that no one person, unless *per impossibile* possessed of omniscience, could rule a community satisfactorily.[52] Similarly, it is this reasoning that justifies Barry's insistence on the importance of policy making being transparent and open, with measures consulted upon openly and with a chance that the consultation will make a difference. By the same line of argument, openness and transparency are enhanced if citizens are well informed and educated, and where there is no monopoly of the means of communication, and policy makers respect expert opinion. In the legislature, political representatives need to be able to follow the logic of the arguments advanced rather than the requirements purely of party discipline.

Maintaining the deliberative quality of representational democracies is still compatible with decision making by majority voting, as a way of reconciling disagreements about how separate and competing interests are to be balanced. Indeed, the argument from political equality for such systems was that they provided a means for realizing the preferences of the median party in a broadly representative parliament. However, it might be argued that in matters of policies regarding the basis structure of society, a more demanding condition than correspondence with median preferences was required. Arguing rather than bargaining, it may be urged, presupposes that unanimity is the implicit decision rule for basic constitutional matters, and that, in the words of Habermas, majority rule 'only represents a caesura in an ongoing discussion; the decision records so to speak, the interim result of a discursive opinion-forming process'.[53] The principle of unanimity implicit in this claim would have to be taken as a regulative ideal rather than a practical rule of choice. Applied in real world societies, the principle of unanimity and super-majoritarian rules that tend to unanimity have the effect of privileging the interests of those with a large stake in the status quo.[54] The requirement of general agreement in order to secure legitimacy has as its base the idea that unless a proposal can secure general agreement it will not be just because the majority will be able to dominate the minority. The twin requirements of equal power and deliberative rationality appear to favour a criterion of unanimity in legislation, even if only as a regulative ideal.

However, whilst the requirement of unanimity expresses an aspiration towards inclusive legitimacy on grounds of political equality, as a practical rule of policy making it is inconsistent with the functional differentiation of a great society, in which there are ineradicable differences of view and interest. As a result, bargaining and negotiation are irreducible elements of the constitution of political democracy, since they enable those parties that can agree with one another to converge on policy solutions without being required to share all their decision premisses. In political bargaining, parties to a negotiation recognize that they have a different point of view, usually based on competing interests and evaluations, and they are searching for a course of action that makes them both better off in terms of whatever values and interests they have. If they could get their own way, each would; but recognizing the need to deal with the other, they are looking for mutually agreeable solutions. A successful bargain can be thought of as the identification of a minor premiss in a practical syllogism that combined with different major premisses of two different parties leads them to act in an agreed way.

In this context, one fallacy, to which Richard Bellamy has drawn attention, is to assume that bargaining is purely about interests.[55] Sometimes bargaining is simply about interests, and devices like splitting the difference in wage-negotiations or house sales illustrate the principle very well. On the other hand, bargaining may arise where there are values that people care about, but are in a situation where others can block the realization of those values unless there is some agreement. Secularists may not like the state funding of church schools, but if they have to agree to the policy in order to improve funding for state schools, then they may be prepared to accept that solution as the outcome of a bargained compromise. Indeed, bargaining may be said to carry its own intrinsic value in the sense that it does not require one party to seek to change the mind of the other, but search for some point that is acceptable to the other. In political cultures in which maintaining consensus across different social groups is important and in which there is a political culture of compromise, there may be strong incentives leading to constitutional designs in which the majority principle is delayed in its use or modified in its application to ensure that enough has been done to explore the possibility of agreement beyond a winning political majority.

In this respect, representational democracies form a varied class, with some being unicameral and others bicameral with a number of legislative veto points built into their operation. In this respect representational democracies span a range of systems that balance the need for deliberated agreement and equality of aggregation in different ways. On the basis of a comparative study of four legislatures (Switzerland, Germany, the UK, and the US Congress), Jürg Steiner and his colleagues suggest that the favourable institutional antecedents of deliberative quality are present in the representational democracies of Switzerland and Germany in a way in which they are not in the Westminster system of the UK or the liberal constitutionalist regime of the USA.[56] The conditions include consensus institutions, the presence of veto players, debate in second chambers, and debate in non-public arenas.[57] It would be interesting to know if the Nordic systems exhibited an equal degree of deliberative quality, since their less institutionally constrained decision making may be associated with their more universalistic welfare states by comparison with the more status-differentiated Bismarckian regimes of Germany and Switzerland.[58] What the exact contours of the trade-off are, if there are any, is something still open for examination. The result is suggestive; it would be interesting to know whether the deliberative quality of some representational democracies could be linked to the institutions of the sort we are about to consider.

6.6. The constitution of political equality

Requiring that governance for public goods meets conditions of deliberation and balanced representation is a way of applying the logic of democratic contractarianism. That logic sees the social contract for the provision of public goods as involving conditions of practical rationality and equality of power. Decisions that are practically rational are sensitive to the truth or falsity of their decision premisses. Since human agents are only boundedly rational, their practical rationality is defeasible and their judgements are always open to revision in the light of new information. Justly constrained contractarian logic also respects the equality of power condition. Insofar as collective deliberation takes place under the circumstances of justice, the most important of which is the equality of power condition, its upshot will constitute policies respecting the principles of justice. The twin conditions of collective and defeasible practical reasoning under conditions of the equality of power gives us a distinctive conception of public reasoning. Reasoning is public when it meets conditions of practical rationality and takes place under conditions in which the premisses and principles of public decisions can be challenged by associates who stand in a relation of equality with respect to one another.

If the argument of this chapter is correct, then one set of political institutions that incorporate these values are parliamentary democracies whose rules of aggregation are based upon proportional representation and whose political culture is oriented towards collective problem solving in the common interest. It is beyond the scope of a normative theory to say that these are the only institutions to provide a justifiable embodiment of these values. For one thing, such a view would be contrary to the defeasible character of practical rationality as that might be applied to constitutional design. We simply do not know what innovations in the design of political institutions are awaiting discovery (although we do know that such institutional design changes are rare compared to, say, industrial design). However, in as much as we are considering what might be the features of a property-owning democracy, we can say that flourishing parliamentary systems exhibit an important variant of the possibilities.

CHAPTER 7

Just returns in the great society

7.1. Full fruits transformed

The contractarian logic of association in common property resource regimes means that producers who had common, but rule-governed, access to the means of production are entitled to the full fruits of their labour. Each productive unit is assured of access to the means of production on terms that are equal to anyone else who is a participant in the regime, but there are only few circumstances in which harvested product is required to be shared with others as a condition of participation. Natural resources were managed under collective control using schemes of rotation of access to even out fluctuations of luck or fortune in the productivity of a resource. As a matter of empirical conjecture, such a set of arrangements leads to only a relatively narrow span of economic differences among participants given the similarity of skills and abilities operating within the mode of production. There is no rule of distribution formulated in accordance with a social plan that determines an overall allocation or shares of benefit and no collective choice of a profile of returns, as would be required if skills and abilities were regarded as a common asset. Implicitly, the principle of economic justice is: equal access to the means of production and free inequality in the fruits of labour within the limits of overall resource protection.

In systems of agricultural production, the principle that producers are entitled to the fruits of their labour has a literal interpretation. The fish they net, the rice they grow, the animals they rear, the wood they harvest belong to those who have laboured for a return. If there were a system of collective accounting in the economy, which added up the amount of fish, rice, cattle, and felled wood, then each productive unit would be making its contribution to the total of the community. Each producer's total would then be their marginal contribution to that total, that is to say the amount that they add given the activities of everyone else. Their willingness to produce the amount they do is a consequence of the amount and value of the productive activity that they undertake. They produce up to the point at which their marginal product is just equal to the amount of effort and activity that they are prepared to expend.

Within a great society the principle that producers should be able to garner the fruits of their labour can no longer be given the literal meaning it had in the common property resource regimes. Because monetary transactions have replaced the harvesting of produce, the full fruits of labour can no longer be represented by physical goods. Instead it refers to the marginal contribution that individuals make to the overall social product defined as the sum of consumers' willingness to pay for the goods and services they produce. Standard elementary economic theory is that producers receive in their earnings the marginal value of what they produce. What people add to the economy is the sum of what others are willing to pay for what they produce in goods or services. Thus the correct measure of marginal product is the earnings that individuals receive. In a fully competitive economy, with no economies of scale, externalities, or asymmetries of information, one's market wage will equal one's marginal product. The sum of other people's willingness to pay for the goods or services that you produce will equal the value of the goods and services that you produce.

To see why this is so, consider a simple example, adapted from Robert Frank.[1] Suppose that clay to make brick is in plentiful supply and free of charge, and a firm employs brick-makers to mould the clay into bricks. Suppose each moulded brick sells for £1. Some workers will make 10 bricks in a day, some 20, and others 30. Each brick-maker's marginal product is equal to the number of bricks made and expressed in cash terms is equal to the number of bricks made multiplied by the value of each brick. (For the purposes of this example, the fixed costs of entering production that the firm has to recover for itself are assumed away.) If the firm paid the worker who makes 20 bricks in a day the same as the worker who only made 10 bricks—say £15 each—then the more productive worker would simply gravitate to another firm that paid a daily rate closer to that person's marginal product. This would result in less income for the firm and so the income of the less productive workers would have to drop, for labour costs could no longer be covered by income. After a while, depending on how long the sorting of pay and productivity took, we should expect each worker to be receiving the value of the their marginal product. Had they been fishers in a common property resource regime, they would have kept or sold the fish they caught and that would have been their marginal product. For fish substitute the value of the bricks.

If the principle of common property resource regimes was that producers keep the fruits of their labour as the upshot of a democratic contract, it would seem that the principle of just returns in the great society is that workers are entitled to the value of their marginal product in the market. Of course, such an inference presupposes that earnings in a market economy are equivalent to the marginal value of what each worker produces. Ricardian socialists like Thomas Hodgskin questioned the inference, noting that part of the return of the product went not to those who produced it but to those who own the means of production. However, let us for the present suspend discussion on this point, and focus on the issues of principle prompted by the claim that just returns equal marginal product. There are at least two cases to consider: redistribution from the more productive to the less productive and redistribution from those who work, no matter what their relative productivity, to those in need because they are not able to work.

If we make the assumption that people are only entitled in justice (charity or voluntary giving is another matter) to the full fruits of their own labour, it follows that any forcible redistribution of income from those who are more productive and so have earned more to those who are less productive is contrary to the requirements of justice. Opposed to this claim is the view that if the more productive through market bargaining are insisting on higher returns in exchange for the exercise of their skills, then they are behaving unjustly because they could be exercising those skills for the common good at the same rate of earnings as any other worker. Thus G.A. Cohen wrote that in 'a culture of justice shaped by the difference principle, talented people would not expect (what they usually have to power to obtain) the high salaries whose level reflects high demand for their talent (as opposed to the special needs or special burdens of their jobs)'.[2] On this view, the relevant principle of justice is not one of returns according to marginal productivity but one of averaging of returns across all workers in society. So this first objection to the justice of the marginal productivity principle is that justice is being ignored if the more productive extract the full fruits of their labour, when they could exercise their skills and talents for the same reward as everyone else.

The second case involves the redistribution of the fruits of labour from those who work to produce those fruits, to those who are not able to work. Among the latter groups will be those who are in need because they are not able to work through illness, disability, immaturity, or old age. Those who fall into these groups will form a high proportion of those in absolute poverty, which may be defined as the level at which the basic needs of a decent human life is impossible. If justice means that those who work are entitled to the full fruits of their labour and it also means meeting needs—an important principle in many modern theories of social justice—then there appears to be a contradiction at the centre of the theory of democratic justice. As we saw in section 3.7, Cohen worried that the needs and non-exploitation principles came apart, a concern that is logically distinct from the concern with differential incentives.[3] A structurally similar conflict is evident in the contrast between the principle of justice as requiting desert, where desert is understood in terms of work effort, and the principle of justice as meeting needs. Miller has identified this tension in contemporary public opinion and it would seem to be a natural consequence of taking both the returns to work principle and the needs principle seriously.[4] The social and economic differentiation that accompanies the division of labour in the great society creates a situation in which the claims to the fruits of one's own labour and the claims of need come apart, creating distinct and conflicting principles of justice to which appeal can be made in a great society.

These two cases present potentially troubling examples to any theory of justice that allows workers to retain the value of their marginal product. Each suggests that their may be considerations of economic justice that would disallow any principle that permitted workers to keep the fruits of their labour. This is both a substantive and a methodological challenge. The substantive issues are whether there are alternative principles—whether of equality or the obligation to meet need—that should trump the principle of marginal productivity. The methodological challenge is at least as serious. If retaining the full fruits of one's labour is implied by the logic of contractarian association, but some other principles trump the full fruits principle, it would follow that there is something amiss with the contractarian approach. After all, the full fruits principle follows from the logic of mutual advantage; if mutual advantage leads to injustice, then this casts a shadow on any theory in which mutual advantage is central. So it is important to consider whether concerns about equality or need can displace the *prima facie* rationale for the full fruits principle.

Properly to confront those questions, we need to consider the prior question of how far we can assume that wages in a market economy do provide a measure of workers' marginal product. This is important because intuitions about the justification of the full fruits principle are likely to be strongly influenced by perceptions about the very wide inequality of incomes that great societies typically produce. In the common pool resource regimes, we conjectured that inequalities of return could not be that great because the mode of production did not allow for anything other than relatively similar differences in skills and talent to determine returns. The same is clearly not true of the market economies of great societies. We can only transpose the contractarian logic of association to mutual benefit from societies in which the fruits of labour have a literal embodiment to a society in which monetary returns are earned through complex contractual relations, if we believe that those complex contractual relationships preserve a close relationship between marginal produce and earnings. For one alternative to rejecting the full fruits principle is to reject the claim that a great society does reward workers according to their marginal product. Market returns do not equal full marginal product if we allow some of the output of productive economic activity is not captured by market transactions.

7.2. Marginal productivity in the market?

In Chapter 5 we followed Coase noting that, within the firm, market transactions are eliminated. In place of an extended series of bilateral contracts, the coordination of activity within the firm is achieved through hierarchy and command.[5] Wiles underlines this aspect of economic organization, noting that 'every enterprise is a small command economy' comprising 'any group of people among whom methods of command or administration are used, and who are not expected to respond in the short term to market stimuli'.[6] The effect of these internal organizational features of the firm is that the income of enterprises should be regarded as what Marshall termed 'composite quasi-rent'. Composite quasi-rent is defined by Marshall as the income a firm derives from its wares in the market, 'but with little reference to the cost of preparing for their work the various things and persons engaged in it'. In other words, there is no true accounting of the costs of employing each element in the factor of production as distinct from simply treating the work team as a whole and for whom the income is divided among its different persons 'by bargaining, supplemented by custom and by notions of fairness'.[7]

In this situation we should not necessarily assume that what individuals receive is equal to their marginal product. Marshall's own example is a good one. He writes that the head clerk of a firm may have a knowledge of its personnel and affairs that could be sold to a rival firm at a high price. However, if the information is of no value to anyone but the firm itself, then the head clerk's departure would injure the firm by a value larger than the clerk's salary whilst the clerk himself might not be able to secure half the original salary elsewhere. The logic here is that the maximum salary that anyone can command is one that will be just sufficient to induce them to move their employment from one line of activity to another. However, if skills are particularly related to one firm but not to others, the firm for whom those skills are not of special value will not need to pay as much by way of market reward as they would if the skills more generally useful. Williamson, who cites this example, gives it as an instance of the centrality of asset-specificity in economic organization.[8] Asset-specificity means that skills suitable for one line of economic activity may be suitable for few others. Its effect is to make the return from alternative sources of employment a poor estimate of the value that an employee brings to the firm. These restrictions arising from features of human capital may be reinforced by institutional arrangements, for example restrictive covenants on the use of information gained in one firm for employment in another, that also reduce the potential market returns of some classes of worker.

Robert Frank offers a contrasting set of cases in which there is a departure from the principle of marginal returns, but in which some workers are paid more than their marginal product. Within many organizations, wage scales may be compressed so that those with comparatively high rates of productivity are not paid in proportion to their value to the firm. In many jobs, for example, there are salary scales that depend upon seniority within the organization, so that older workers are paid much more than younger workers, even though their productivity may not warrant such differences. (Those in academic departments may recognize something of this phenomenon.) Wages to commercial airline pilots show a strong gradient associated with length of service, although it seems implausible to suppose that the returns to their flying planes differs by virtue of seniority, not least because commercial pilots usually have many years of flying experience before they start to work for their airline. Finally, at the opposite end of the spectrum to Marshall's example of the clerk, Frank cites evidence of the compression of differentials among car salespeople, even though the skills of selling are likely to be pretty transferable across different businesses and so there is no restriction arising from asset-specificity. (Probably all of us know people who could sell booze to teetotallers and chocolate to those slimming.)[9]

Alfred Marshall suggested that organization can sometimes be viewed as the fourth factor of production, alongside land, labour, and capital.[10] It is also possible to hold with Michels that 'who says organization, says oligarchy'.[11] Organization allows for the detachment of personal effort from a share of organizational returns. Opportunistic behaviour in a context of asymmetric information means that some individuals will derive more benefit than their marginal contribution and others less.[12] The returns that a firm makes are returns to it as a team and it is not easy to assign some fraction of the return to particular individuals, nor should it be assumed that what is assigned in practice is equal to marginal product. Moreover, those who are in control in the firm have discretionary power, arising from the specialist possession of information as well as authority over resources that fall to their discretionary spending. When there is a separation of ownership and control, as typically there is with highly developed firms, then those who control the organization are able to exercise discretionary power over a significant proportion of the returns that they manage. This has implications for their ability to engage in rent-seeking behaviour not only from other workers in the firm but also from its formal owners.

This line of argument offers a modern version of the argument advanced by Thomas Hodgskin within the framework of Ricardian socialism. Hodgskin recognised the justice in the economic return of the exercise of skills of management. Organizing workers into productive teams is the exercise of a skill from which one is properly entitled to a return. What he denied was that there should be any return to ownership as such. Mere ownership of the means of production by virtue of artificial legal title involves no exercise of effort, and so in justice is not owed any economic return. Hodgskin's was a world in which ownership and control of the enterprise were largely joined together. The updating of his claim would augment his worries about the return to mere ownership with a concern about a return premissed not on contribution to the product of an enterprise but merely on occupancy of position within the organizational hierarchy of an enterprise, so that managers had the opportunity to divert a disproportionate share of the product to their own returns.

Sometimes the divergence between marginal product and organizationally determined wage-returns can be ascribed to an implicit contract between subordinate workers and those occupying higher positions on the rungs of management. Consider for example the implicit inter-generational contract between junior employees and older partners of professional firms. Young lawyers, for example, will work long and hard on tedious work that still brings in high economic returns, much of which go to the partners who may do little of the actual work. The implicit contract in these arrangements may be reconstructed as one in which the young are prepared to take less than the value of their marginal product on the understanding that in time they will be promoted and be able in turn to enjoy more pleasurable work—for example lunching potential clients in so-called marketing exercises—in return for their ability to extract the surplus from those who will be younger than they are.

It may be very difficult to disentangle that portion of returns that is an effect of increasing marginal product and that portion that derives from exploiting the power of hierarchical position within an organization. Consider the case of very high returns to chief executives and members of the senior management team within many large organizations, returns that have grown relatively in value over a number of recent decades. One explanation links this growth to the expansion of markets through better communications and the increase in the cost of capital, meaning that new forms of debt, for example buy-outs dependent on loans, force the performance of managers into securing high returns. In this environment, it might be true that employing person A as chief executive rather than person B could be worth a great deal of money to the firm.[13] An alternative explanation points to the discretionary power that comes with position within an organizational hierarchy and the system of closed and inter-locking remuneration committees that have not internalized the interests of shareholders and other workers in the firm. On this latter explanation, highly paid chief executives are in the opposite position to Marshall's clerk: they are taking a sizeable proportion of the firm's composite quasi-rent as private income and when the firm fails they are insulated against the effects. With luck they privatize the gains and socialize the losses. Knowing when high returns do or do not correspond to marginal productivity may be very difficult.

Suppose, however, that we can identify cases in which there is a divergence between market returns and marginal product: what does this imply for the marginal productivity principle as a principle of justice? Rather than undermine that principle, it seems to reinforce its legitimacy. To say that market returns do not correspond to marginal product means that, insofar as we can discern an injustice, it is that market returns do not reward the value of the work that each producer contributes. Instead, there is an appropriation from those producing at a certain value to those not producing at the value at which they are paid. Those knowledgeable about the details of business would have higher incomes if there were fewer restrictive covenants on their being able to use the information that they have acquired, whereas chief executives and senior management teams would earn lower incomes if they were rewarded according to the genuine marginal increment they brought to the firm or organization. Those who are sceptical about the justice of market returns may be sceptical because they do not think the principle of marginal productivity sufficiently accounts for our considered judgements about economic justice. On the other hand, however, they might be sceptical because they do not think that markets, as constituted through the hierarchies that make up its firms, adequately reward the full range of productive outputs that individuals actually deliver. If we adopt the latter view, then we are endorsing the relevance of the full fruits principle, but denying that it is realised under certain institutional conditions.

Once we have freed ourselves from the mistaken thought that actually existing market societies incorporate the principle of marginal productivity, we are in a better position to examine the merits and the shortcomings of that principle itself. Why should we assume that in a great society workers are entitled to the fruits of the labour, even if we could modify the operation of the market to bring such a result about? In other words, are there other ways of thinking about the justice of production and distribution that would be sufficient to overturn the marginal productivity principle even if it could be reliably embodied in institutional arrangements?

7.3. Marginal productivity and economies of scale

An important source of value stems from what Marshall termed 'external' economies by contrast with the 'internal' economies of the firm's organization.[14] External economies result from falls in costs that are a consequence of where firms are located or the networks in which they are embedded. As argued in Chapter 5, one of the distinguishing features of a great society is that there are increasing returns to scale, brought about largely as a consequence of Marshall's external economies. According to Arrow, increasing returns to scale provide some justification for redistribution. He writes as follows:

> There are significant gains to social interaction above and beyond what individuals and sub-groups can achieve on their own. The owners of scarce personal assets do not have the substantial private use of these assets; it is only their value in a large system which makes

> these assets valuable. Hence, there is a surplus created by the existence of society as such which is available for redistribution.[15]

On this view, since my marginal product is only a part, and perhaps only a minor part, of the value of my own personal efforts and to a large degree is a consequence of the large economy in which my actions take place, I have no entitlement to the full value of my marginal product. Our brick-makers may differ in their productivity, but the productivity of all would be much lower if there were no furnaces in which to heat the clay, no banks to lend the firm capital, fewer houses to build, no architects to design large buildings, no transport to take the bricks to market, no system of accounting, and so on.

The phenomenon is a general one. Scarce personal talents can only realize their full economic value in a large society. One reason is that a large society both depends upon and fosters an extensive division of labour. This extensive division of labour enables the cultivation of the talents of individuals, because it frees most individuals from the obligation to provide for their own subsistence and basic needs. Computer programmers, opera singers, specialist surgeons, and skilled engineers cannot exist where there is no division of labour that enables these occupations to occupy a niche in a larger economy. That larger economy will also supply the scale of returns that will encourage individuals to undertake the training necessary to achieve the requisite standard to perform in these roles. In the absence of the larger market, the returns to specialization are simply not great enough to induce individuals into any particular line of work for which the rewards are contingent upon extensive training. As Thomas Gray noted, in his *Elegy Written in a Country Churchyard*, it was in a 'neglected spot' that 'some mute inglorious Milton' was laid to rest.

The principles of economic justice for large societies cannot be read directly off the circumstances of common pool resource regimes, because the economies in which those regimes are located are small-scale and do not allow for much division of labour. However, the underlying principles of such regimes show the way in which the securing by individuals of the fruits of their own labour is dependent upon forms of social cooperation that maintain the sources of production in being. The relevant contribution may involve keeping to the agreed rules of use and refraining from interfering with others' appropriation. It may also require participants to undertake various forms of labour, for example maintaining communal terracing or ditching, that contribute towards the common stock of resources. However, none of this implies that there is an obligation for individuals to share the fruits of their own labour with anyone else, as distinct from making their contribution to productive infrastructure. In other words, individuals may benefit from the social cooperation of others without being obliged to share the fruits of their labour with others. The cooperation that sustains the communal means of production is a reciprocal cooperation, not a one-way transfer of resources from the more productive to the less productive.

If we transpose this logic to the great society, one in which Arrow's complementarities of skills and talents is developed, then a corresponding obligation upon participants would be an obligation to contribute towards and maintain the social and economic public goods that allow for the division of labour. But what would this mean in terms of principles of redistribution? Would it, for example, justify the redistribution of income among those who earn that income on grounds that, because there were scale economies, the more productive should pool their incomes with the less productive? If the logic is one of network benefits, then it is hard to see how such redistribution is justified by reference to such an argument.

Networks typically create a situation in which there are significant returns to scale and in which marginal cost is below average cost over a large part of the cost curve. In such a situation, we might suppose that the natural set of principles to apply would be those akin to the two-part tariff, as Coase explained with an analogous problem in connection with the marginal cost controversy.[16] In the case of goods, like bridges or telephone networks, the marginal cost of use is below the average cost of use. As a result, some argued that the proper basis of charging for access to the network was that consumers should only be charged the marginal cost of their use of the network. However, where marginal cost remains below average cost, a decision to charge only the marginal cost would not generate sufficient review to pay for the network. The implication, as Coase explained, is not that the difference between the sum of marginal payments and the cost of supply should be covered by an external source like government, but rather that consumers pay a two-part tariff, the first part involving a 'connection charge' that links them to the network and the second part covering the marginal costs that their specific use, for example their telephone call, imposes on the network.

By a parallel line of reasoning, the logic of the economy of scale argument in the case of returns to labour is that it would be just to require contributions to the common provision from that portion of a person's productive output that is attributable to the network effects of living in a sufficiently large society, but not from that proportion of a person's productive output that is attributable to that person's own efforts. In short, marginal product should be identified as *net* of the contribution that is necessary to keep the social infrastructure in good order. There is no assumption that the net marginal product created by individuals is something that is available for redistribution to others. All our brick-makers may have an obligation to contribute to social infrastructure, but none is under an obligation to transfer part of the value of their product to others.

Consider the respective marginal products of two workers, A and B, and let us suppose that A's marginal product is the larger of the two. Let us also suppose that their marginal products arise in a large economy, and both would be less productive in a smaller economy. Can we say that the fact that the marginal product is higher in the large economy than it would have been in the smaller economy means that there is a case for transferring resources between A and B, in either direction? Both have benefittd from the larger economy in the sense that their product is higher in that economy than it would have been in a smaller economy. However, to suppose that a unilateral transfer is called for is to suppose that the logic that generates a joint obligation to contribute to public goods, from which both benefit, will also provide a justification for a transfer of resources from which only one person will benefit. This is to transmute the obligation that each has to contribute to the public good into a unilateral obligation on the part of one of them to benefit the other. If the foundation of justice is a principle of mutual advantage, in which political associates have reciprocal obligations to one another, then it would be unjust to abrogate the joint responsibility to which each ought to be committed.

It is possible that both have some sort of obligation of redistribution arising from the process of economic development. Economic development involves the bringing together of markets that were previously separate. One of the effects of this change is to make certain lines of economic activity obsolete, so creating economic disadvantage for those trapped in occupations that are on the wrong side of economic history, the fate of the handloom weavers in the early part of the nineteenth century in England, and the fate of many other occupations subsequently. In this case, a general growth of economic activity goes along with a decline in economic opportunity for some portion of the population. A large economy in this regard reduces incomes of some rather than increases them. One might argue, in these circumstances, that some compensation should be paid by the beneficiaries to the unwilling victims. Such cases of transitional justice are serious, and there may well be a case under a general insurance principle of redistribution (see next section) for making some compensating adjustment to income financed from a levy on the beneficiaries of the growth. However, it is not clear that there is a general principle to this effect. Whether or not compensation should be paid might well be made to depend upon the specifics of the case rather than a general principle about the circumstances in which large economies give rise to economic returns available for redistribution.

The benefits flowing from the existence of a large economy are less troublesome to the principle of marginal productivity than one might think. If there is an obligation to contribute to the overhead costs of sustaining a large economy, akin to the first part of the two-part network tariff, there is no obligation to pool one's net returns with others, any more than there would be to pick up someone else's bill for their use of metered water, electricity, or telephone use. The case for redistribution, strictly so called, cannot rest on the existence of economies of scale.

7.4. The claims of need

The objection to the principle of marginal productivity that seems most pressing is that deriving from the claims of need. This was the concern expressed by G.A. Cohen. It is possible to construct coherent theories of justice on grounds of need, and there are good reasons for thinking that responsiveness to need is part of a widespread public understanding of what justice requires.[17] Moreover, one reason often advanced against a contractarian theory of justice as mutual advantage is that it would make the weak dependent upon the strong in ways that would leave them vulnerable to exploitation. How significant a line of argument are the claims of need against economic justice defined as the return to marginal productivity?

The principal institutions for addressing claims of need in representative democracies are those of the welfare state.[18] Welfare states take many forms and their modes of organization are correspondingly complex. However, abstracting inductively from the details of well-developed welfare states, it is possible to identify certain general principles of operation that they share. They raise income from those in paid employment and redistribute that income in cash to certain categories of beneficiary, most importantly the elderly, those suffering periods of interruption of unemployment through ill health or accidents at work, those who are disabled, and those with responsibility for caring for children, either as single or as joint parents. With its revenues, the welfare state also finances a range of services, most notably education and health care, those services being provided with the intention of removing financial barriers to access. In the case of health care, for example, the provision may not be free at point of use, since items like pharmaceutical prescriptions are often charged for in many welfare states, but the idea is that such charges, though they may raise revenue and have a deterrent effect on frivolous use, do not prevent those who need the medicines from obtaining them. Similarly, with education, parents may be responsible for paying for transport, school uniforms, and some learning materials, but such payments are intended to be incidental to the financing of the service, not one of its central features.

In developed welfare states, the distribution of cash benefits and services in kind is universal. That is to say, the cash and services are given to those in need—as indicated by age, state of health, or inability to find paid employment—without regard to income or wealth. The benefits are regarded as a right of citizenship rather than as provision merely for the poor or destitute who cannot otherwise provide for themselves. To be sure, in a number of highly developed welfare states the principle of universal allocation is modified by excluding the very wealthy from access to benefits. For example, in Germany and the Netherlands those on very high incomes are excluded from access to the social insurance scheme for health. However, these are modifications to the general principle—and relatively minor ones—rather than a breach of the principle. They do not apply in the case of education.

It follows from these features that the welfare state does not aim at a general redistribution of income across the population at large in conformity to an agreed principle formulated by a benevolent social planner. Indeed, its raising of revenue and then recycling of benefits to those who could afford to cover their own periods of need is sometimes regarded as wasteful. For example, it is sometimes said that it is unnecessary to pay family allowances or child benefit to high-earning parents who can cover the extra cost of their children themselves. However, the basic principle of the welfare state is best understood as a form of income smoothing across the life-cycle rather than an attempt to redistribute income between different social classes. This is what makes intelligible its distinctive policy instrument, namely social insurance. Many welfare state programmes are funded through social insurance, by which compulsory payments are raised from those in paid work and their employers to fund benefits when needed. Social insurance can be thought of as a special case of a more general idea, which White calls shared savings.[19] Whether funded by social insurance or general taxation, the institutions of the welfare state can be thought of as savings shared among the members of society by which the financial risks associated with periods of need at particular points in the life-cycle are pooled among them.

Regarding the welfare as a form of shared savings has implications for the political theory of need, and in particular for the claim that there is an injustice if workers are allowed to keep the full fruits of their labour. Consider, in this context, how needs arise. People are born, and immediately and for many years subsequently are utterly dependent upon others for their sustenance, education, and prospects. At various points in their lives they work and are productive. They share their product among families, households, and friends. They have children, depleting their family or household earnings power. They fall ill, have periods of involuntary unemployment, or suffer disability as a result of injury or accident. They grow old becoming increasingly frail. Only if they are lucky do they avoid a second childhood in old age. They die with the residue of their affairs to be attended to. Need is the name we give to the vulnerable periods. The social contract embodied in the welfare state represents a prudent commitment of each to share the risks of vulnerability with others. The recycling of income through the institutions of the welfare state is not a form of redistribution from the relatively rich to the relatively poor, but a set of devices by which associates enter into a mutual commitment to pool financial risks.

Meeting needs in this sense is also a way of addressing the concerns of Sen, who points to the importance of supplementing a focus on resources in the theory of justice with a focus on capabilities.[20] As Sen correctly points out, the type of life that we can lead is only partially correlated with our control over material resources. Features of our situation, for example difference in the physical or the social environment, or personal characteristics such as disabilities, affect the value of those resources to us. So we should be concerned with capabilities. However, only a subset of those differences that affect capabilities are related to considerations of justice. It cannot be a reason for those living by the Mediterranean to have fewer resources than those living in the chillier climes of northern Europe that it is easier to flourish when the climate is hospitable than when it is grey, although for many people this is clearly true. By contrast, it is a reason to be concerned about capabilities when a reduction in capabilities comes about as a consequence of the needs that are an inevitable feature of the life-course.

Some argue that we do not require a social contract to deal with occasions of need. Periods of vulnerability can be managed through private contractual arrangements. Rational people will foresee the periods of need to which they are going to be subject and will insure themselves against loss of income and financial risk. A great society makes possible such insurance, since risk can be spread among very large numbers. Private insurance is itself a form of social protection through private contract and by itself is sufficient to deal with the problem of need. If we believe that in some sense the full fruits of what people earn belong to them, then there is no place for compulsory redistribution on grounds of need alone. If people have not taken out insurance to cover their needs, then they have simply chosen to spread the costs and benefits of their life-course in a particular way, and it would be wrong to expect others, who have to make provision for their own needs, to pay for the needs of others when those others could have paid for themselves.

In a world of agents with perfect foresight in which the probability of all future events were predictable, this line of argument would carry weight. However, this is not the world of bounded rationality and defeasible practical reasoning. One can only insure against predictable events the incidence of which are unknown. One cannot insure against the intrinsically unpredictable. It follows from this that one cannot insure against the sort of risks that are associated with technical and economic innovation, for example the risks of finding oneself in the middle of life having invested in skills for which there is now no market. Since technical innovation is intrinsically unpredictable—by the familiar argument that if it were predictable it would in effect already have been invented—there is no insurance market protecting individuals from the effects of technological redundancy. By the same token, relevant forms of insurance will not have been invented for unexpected threats to health and well-being, for example the emergence of AIDS or the growth in those suffering dementia.

Moreover, the benefits of large numbers cannot be gained if too many people under-insure themselves, because the number of people among whom the risks can be spread will be too small. If individuals have a systematic bias to the near, so that they discount the future, and suffer from optimism bias, so that they discount the probability that the unfortunate will happen, then they will under-insure.[21] A social contract for collective insurance can be understood as a way of counteracting the deficiencies of individual rationality in this regard. So, although the benefits provided by the welfare state are not public goods in the standard sense (they are rival and exclusive in consumption), the institutions of social saving resemble public goods in that, in providing for common needs without creating financial barriers to access, some way has to be found of protecting their financial integrity, and compulsory contributions are a required way of doing this.

In the face of these barriers to the establishment of successful private insurance markets in respect of the risks associated with the life-course, much of what might otherwise be thought of as vertical redistribution from the better off to the worse off is more aptly regarded as the protection available to each within a social contract. As Barr has crisply put it, 'even if the entire population were middle class, there would still be a need for institutions for people to insure themselves and redistribute income over the life cycle'.[22] In practice, a large part of redistribution that takes place in the welfare state takes this form. The analysis is hard to do, but Falkingham and Hills have shown that, for the UK welfare state in the mid-1980s (and this is not a particularly highly developed welfare state), 'between two-thirds and three-quarters of gross lifetime benefits are effectively self-financed'.[23] Redistribution should not be regarded as a device by which income is transferred from the more productive to the less productive, but as a device by which income is spread over the life-cycle. In this way we can reconcile a commitment to the principle that people are entitled to the full fruits of their labour and the widespread moral intuition that there is a social responsibility to meet human need. Redistribution in the welfare state is a social device for spreading the product of labour over the course of one's life in a way that is both individually prudent and dependent upon a social contract that mandates cooperation.

It may be argued that, even if this analysis is broadly correct, it pays insufficient attention to the claims of need. If two-thirds to three-quarters of redistribution in the welfare state is self-financed, that still leaves one-third to one-quarter that is not. For someone who thinks that justice requires more redistribution in the welfare state than currently obtains, our theory, which seems to imply that there should be about one quarter to one third less, may seem inadequate.[24] It is not implausible to suppose that were spending on welfare state benefits to be cut, the burden of those cuts would fall on the most vulnerable. If this is an implication of contractarian theory, then it would be out of line with many peoples' considered judgements about redistribution. However, this would be to confuse the construction of a theory designed under the assumption of circumstances of justice obtaining with our intuitive judgement about the world as it is. There is no reason to assume that the world as it is is just. Some of what we observe currently in the form of redistribution is occasioned by existing forms of injustice, not least the social deprivation that fails to provide the education and training that would equip individuals to make as much of a productive contribution as they are in principle able to do. To apply intuitions derived from this context to the quite separate case where there is an association between marginal product and effort would be a mistake.

7.5. The socialization of family responsibilities

The social contracts exhibited in common property resource regimes are in conditions in which the functional social necessity of the mode of production requires a household organization of labour. In this form of organization, the economic responsibility for the care of dependants—whether children, the elderly, or the disabled—typically falls upon the family unit. The tightly knit bonds of the family and household unit and the limited alternative economic opportunities mean that alternative ways of organizing labour are limited or non-existent. Outside of a household there is no economic opportunity short of emigration. We can say in this sort of society that the full fruits principle holds literally, but it holds for households rather than for individuals. Another way of putting the same point is that the extent to which individuals can claim a share of produced product outside of the household is limited.

The household was one of the basic institutions of society that underwent change as a result of the great transformation. In the world before the great transformation, the household, often with its extended members around the core of a family, was a crucial unit of production. It was also the primary unit for risk-sharing in childhood, illness, unemployment, and old age. As we saw in section 5.5, it was not always able to perform that function. Laslett's example of the outbreak of plague in 1604 in Salisbury when 411 out of some 2000 households had to be supported by the civic authorities, illustrates that institutions wider than the household would sometimes be needed if risks were to be managed.[25] Nonetheless, in general, before the great transformation, the risks of the life-cycle were primarily borne in the family before their financial aspects were transferred to mutual self-help organizations among workers in the nineteenth century and then the welfare state in the twentieth.

With the development of a 'great society' and its extensive division of labour, this constraint no longer holds. The social necessity of household production ceases to apply and individuals can lay claim to a share of the social product through their individual efforts and the availability of market opportunities. However, although constraints on the social organization of production have been lifted, there remain constraints on the social organization of reproduction. Children need to be cared for when they are young, and therefore some of the labour power that would otherwise have been available for productive labour is absorbed in reproductive labour. Moreover, the services of reproductive labour are not ones that are marketable in any straightforward way. Even if, *per impossibile*, we leave aside the natural affection that parents have for their children, the transactions-cost minimizing solution to the problem of how to allocate the burdens of reproduction and child care is one in which parents generally, and leaving aside circumstances like working at a distance and sending remittances home, look after their own children.

Social insurance and other forms of shared savings in the welfare state have traditionally relied upon a model of the family in which the male breadwinner supplies the contribution, with other family members being covered as a result. The effect of this assumption is to give a privileged place to those forms of risk that can be covered by financial contributions from paid work. It is to privilege production over reproduction. Children need to be cared for when young, and therefore some of the labour power that would otherwise have been available for productive labour is absorbed in reproductive labour, predominantly by women. Yet much of the work of women of reproduction is unpaid. If two mothers bring up their own children, their activity does not enter into the national income accounts; if they each pay the other to bring up their children, then that will be entered into the accounts; yet the same level of economic activity has taken place in both situations.[26]

Because reproductive and care responsibilities are not generally marketable, there develops a gender difference in access to wages and income. To the extent to which the family unit functions well, this should not matter. The fruits of marketable labour are shared within the household, just as the benefits of reproductive labour are shared. However, where the family unit does not function well, there opens up a gap between the share of labour that is contributed to its productive and reproductive activities and division of the shares to the return to labour. The problem is augmented by the fact that to the extent to which in a market economy workers are rewarded according to their marginal product, no account is taken of differences in the number of dependants that they might have. If wages are so low as to require the mother to work without being able to pay for adequate replacement child care, then the socially valuable activity of raising children is not receiving the amount of work that it requires. Under these conditions, heads of households could not adequately represent the members of the household in a social contract.

These arguments might be used to assert that some of the costs of reproduction should be socialized such that they are shared by a wider group in the community than the parents of the children. The core of the argument is that, when one moves from an agricultural mode of production to a more extended mode of production, those who work are not being secured the full fruits of their labour to the extent to which their reproductive work is unremunerated in markets. These are among the arguments that were used in the twentieth century to support the introduction of family allowances. Thus Eleanor Rathbone argued that whereas the introduction of social insurance in the UK had made provision for the unemployed and the sick, no provision was made for the widowed mother bringing up children, who ought to be regarded as earning money by undertaking services as valuable to the community as those provided by paid labour. She then generalized this to the argument that the well-being of children and the economic status of motherhood required support in an economy in which the stream of purchasing power is distributed on the basis of personal service.[27] They were not, of course, the only arguments. In some societies like France in the inter-war period, the case turned on the need to repopulate the country after the war and to deal with threats to military security. However, though historically relevant, this is not an argument available in contractarian theory, whereas an appeal to the importance of the full fruits principle is compatible with the approach.

Yet noting the possible imbalances in the return to labour would not by itself imply that the socialization of some of the economic responsibility for child care was justified. After all, it could be argued that the only arrangement consistent with the full fruits principle was that individuals should save before they formed families, so that the costs associated with child care were absorbed across their lifetime earnings, and more generally that wage earners should only have families that their incomes allowed them adequately to support unaided. Under this arrangement, so it might be argued, each person keeps the full fruits of his or her labour and is not required to share some of that fruit with others for the purpose of raising the children of others. Of course, this would not address the problem of the badly functioning family in which the wage earner was not fairly sharing income with other members of the family, but it might be urged in this case that such neglect was a matter for individual social work, not a justification for designing institutions that socialized child care costs. On the core argument that wage earners should only have those children that they could support unaided, Mary Stocks once commented that this was a recipe for 'a regime of sterility for the poor compensated by polygamy for the rich'.[28] Yet, insofar as a social contract theory is committed to the full fruits principle, is it not also committed to the non-socialization of the costs of child care, whatever intuitively unattractive consequences that principle might seem to have?

One reply to this question is to note that the full fruits principle does not absolve anyone from paying a fair share towards the costs of providing collective goods from which the members of one's society benefit. Having a well-educated replacement generation coming into the workforce is to the general advantage, even to those who themselves do not have children. Since individuals are unlikely to abide by Malthusian constraints, there can be no assurance that a generation is well looked after in economic terms unless there are means for supplementing the incomes of those families and supplying educational and social services beyond what those families could afford themselves.

Secondly, the full fruits principle is not the only principle to emerge from the common pool resource regime contract. In addition, there is the equal opportunity principle exemplified in the practices of securing rotating or random access to natural resources. Issues of child support prompt similar concerns. If the opportunity to raise children is dependent solely upon one's own resources, then for those with low incomes, that opportunity will have to be deferred—and biology being what it is, that means for some denied. Theoretically, this problem could be avoided if parents could draw down against their future incomes after the raising of their children. However, it is difficult to imagine how a suitable draw down institution could be devised. It would require assurance that the draw down would be repaid, and this in turn would require some credible commitment to repay. The most credible commitment to repay is a scheme of compulsory taxation, but this is in effect a form of socialization.

One argument that has historically played a prominent role in justifying the case for the socializing of child care costs is that financial support in particular plays an important role in maintaining the status of women who disproportionately take responsibility for such care. Insofar as the care prevents women earning in the labour market, their economic position is weakened compared to their husbands or partners, who have access to the advantages that a market income brings. If male members of the family fail to share their income fairly with their female partners, then socializing some of the financial costs of child care can provide a basis upon which the bargaining position of women in the household is maintained. When the man drinks away his wages, then at least the mother has the means to buy the children's shoes.

It might be urged that this was again a second-best argument. To be sure where individuals fail in their obligations of justice, then public policy may need to find remedies for those who are liable to those injustices. Where a man fails to provide adequate support within the means of his income for his children and the mother of his children, then he has wronged his family members. He has also failed in his obligation to society at large, since those who are not members of his family have a right that he behave in a responsible way. However, these considerations do not provide theoretical reasons for socializing child care costs in general where more general conditions of justice are maintained. At best, they would be arguments in rectificatory justice for ensuring that those who failed in their obligations were obliged to make some form of restitution. They would not provide arguments for designing policies and institutions such that those responsibilities were shared come what may.

Looking at the issue of redistribution in this way helps us resolve what would otherwise be an embarrassment for the general approach taken in our theory. Although we have modified the rationality assumption and placed contracting parties in an empirical equivalent of the circumstances of justice strengthened by Mill's equality of power condition, we have followed Gauthier, who in turn saw himself as following Rawls—as well ultimately as Hobbes and Glaucon—in characterizing justice as a form of cooperation among equals to mutual advantage, with the consequence that it becomes hard in terms of contractarian reasoning to deal with the congenitally disabled.[29] It was this implication of the mutual advantage approach that Brian Barry drew attention to as being an obvious deficiency, since it left the weakest members of society with no claims of justice against the stronger.[30] Barry allows that an argument might be created by which it is the families of the congenitally disabled who have a claim of justice, but thinks this is insufficient since it makes such individuals only the derivative beneficiaries of those claims. However, the embarrassment is not as great as Barry's line of argument supposes. Those who are congenitally disabled are not a separate class of beings from others. They come into the world through natural biological processes and stand in familial relationships with parents, siblings, and other relatives. The disadvantages suffered by the congenitally disabled are therefore shared by their relations. We can construe the injustice here not as one done directly to the disabled—for unless the disability were deliberately or negligently induced it is a misfortune, not an injustice—but as one to the disabled as part of the network within which they stand. If there is a failure of justice on this analysis, it is a failure that attaches to a failure of associates to share the risks associated with reproduction with others. A system of care for the congenitally disabled would take the form of sharing the burdens that any such disability brings about (which is not to say that disability only brings about burdens).

This is still a mutual advantage conception of justice. A mutual advantage conception does not say that justice involves being treated by the principles that the more powerful can impose upon the less powerful. It is the requirement that the more powerful behave to the less powerful as though they were equally powerful. The mutual advantage that is gained by individuals through redistribution is protection against risks that occur in the life-course given the fact of family interdependence. If adequate protection is not provided, it is not simply that the heads of households can complain of an injustice because the burdens of care have unduly fallen upon them, it is also true that those who need the care can complain that they are being excluded from the advantages that would accompany a redistributive scheme.

7.6. Ownership, capital, and the property-owning democracy?

Common property resource regimes are in large measure one-class societies. Their members have access to the natural resources that are a crucial element of the means of production on roughly equal terms. The trees to be felled in the forests, the grazing to be had on the mountains, or access to the seas to fish are available to all members of the community as part of the social contract on similar terms. In being managed as a collective resource for the good of all, access to the means of production is open to each. This does not prevent there being private property in the means of production and some of that private productive property being unequally distributed. Some associates may have more livestock or better forms of equipment than others. However, these variations in control of the means of production are contained within a more general structure of collective management of the natural resources essential to the productive activities of each individual. In some common property resource regimes, most notably Wade's village republics, there is a separate class of owners contrasted and in opposition to a class of workers.[31] Even so, the general principle of common property resource regimes is that the equality of political power among participants is complemented by a rough equality in the ownership of the means of production alongside common management of the shared natural resource. Insofar as this is true, the regimes can be said to embody in one form the principles of a property-owning democracy, in which according to Rawls's definition citizens are put 'in a position to manage their own affairs and to take part in social cooperation on a footing of mutual respect under appropriately equal conditions'.[32]

In their historical development, great societies have not been one-class societies. Although there is some disagreement among historians of the great transformation about the scale and effects of the agricultural enclosures that concentrated land ownership and control in a separate class of landowners, the growth of great societies has involved the creation of class-divided societies. Where private ownership has predominated, this has meant control by a small number of 'great families' or corporations in which legal control is vested. Where economic development was state-led, it has meant a division between state bureaucracies on the one hand and workers on the other. The growth of these divisions reflects the differential ability of individuals and groups to take advantage of the economic opportunities that arose under the pressure of modernization.

In this context, to carry the argument forward, it is tempting to quote John Stuart Mill:

> The opinion expressed in a former part of this treatise respecting small landed properties and peasant proprietors, may have made the reader anticipate that a wide diffusion of property in land is the resource on which I rely for exempting at least the agricultural labourers from exclusive dependence on labour for hire.[33]

But, after noting that small-scale proprietorship is too much decried, Mill goes on to write that 'a people who have once adopted the large system of production, either in manufactures or in agriculture, are not likely to recede from it.... Labour is unquestionably more productive on the system of large enterprises.'[34] In short, the benefits of a great society are such that it would not make sense for the mass of the population to return to the conditions of the one-class societies in which common property resource regimes are found. As with the discussion of political democracy, the use of common pool regimes as empirical models of justifiable social contracts does not imply that those models are to be treated in a prescriptive way, providing a blueprint for the organizational form that a just society would take. Rather they are to be taken as a model embodying the logic of contractual association and principles that need to be adapted to the circumstances of particular social and historical conditions. The normative task is to identify the functional equivalents of those conditions in the one-class common property resource regimes that make them candidates for models of democratic justice. Another way of posing the same question is to ask what it would mean for a great society to become a property-owning democracy.

In this context, it might be argued that a natural counterpart in the great society to communal control in common pool resource regimes is workers' control of their own productive enterprises. Just as in common property resource regimes producers own their own capital equipment, so it might be argued that workers should own the capital of the enterprise in which they work. Such arguments might be supplemented by considerations of deliberative democracy, in which the principal argument would be that the habits of self-government learned in a worker-managed firm have important spillover benefits for the broader functioning of democracy. This is an argument going back at least as far as Mill's own interest in worker-owned and managed firms as providing a form of association 'on terms of equality, collectively owning the capital with which they carry on their operations'.[35] In modern times, the democratic argument for worker-owned and managed firms was revived by Carole Pateman, on the grounds that they allowed for participation within which self-development could take place and more recently Waheed Hussain has urged that the principles of a property-owning democracy would be advanced by a form of democratic corporatism in which workers at least played a co-determining role in the management of the enterprise.[36]

The arguments in favour of increasing worker management and ownership from considerations of democratic self-development are considerable, and yet there are considerable disadvantages if worker ownership is made a condition of social justice. The chief disadvantage is that such a policy requires workers to combine their livelihoods and their saving in the same enterprise and so subject to the same economic risks. A worker-owned firm will often call upon a large proportion of the savings of its members. If that firm experiences problems, then the savings of its members are at risk alongside their occupations. If workers are able to spread the risk of their savings in the form of shares of other enterprises, then economic security is enhanced, since failure in one sector of the economy will not be deepened by the loss of productive resources involved, but will instead be spread around a relatively large number of people, each of whom will lose relatively little rather than a small number of people, each of whom will lose a lot. If ownership of capital is to remain in private hands, then it needs to be widely spread if economic security is to be assured. Here, the appropriate policies involve ensuring widespread access to the means of production through the dispersal of property widely in society. In particular, wealth taxes should aim at the dispersal of concentrated wealth through such devices as consumption taxes, taxes on the imputed income from residential property, inheritance taxes, limits on bequests, and accessions taxes. The effect of such measures is to distribute ownership of productive resources widely among the population. Such measures have been urged within the tradition of thinking that forms the political economy of the property-owning democracy, most notably James Meade.[37]

The widespread ownership of capital available for use in productive enterprise has one further benefit. Much modern capital investment involves the need for large investments that may only pay for themselves over a long period of time, as with railways, roads, or public buildings. If the investment is generated within productive enterprises, the implication is that these need to be large, with all the attendant dangers of monopoly. Conversely, full communal ownership and control would mean that the financing of such projects would have to come out of public expenditure, the availability of which might not coincide with the requirements for investment so that a strain was put on other forms of public expenditure. If private capital sources are able to meet those needs, then these problems are avoided and the returns on the investment accrue to individuals or households in ways that strengthen their economic security. So long as large-scale investments are regulated so as to serve a common interest, their exact method of finance can vary.

We saw that the Ricardian socialist objection to a return to ownership was that ownership was a construction of the law that did not adequately reflect the creation of value by labour. However, at best, this is an objection to inherited wealth and ownership, not an objection to ownership as such, particularly if that ownership is widespread. Where ownership derives from savings, accumulated as deferred consumption during the course of a working life, there is no objection to a return on property as such. The return is simply a way of matching a present need for capital with a present need for holding assets against future contingencies.

Rawls's view was that the principles of the property-owning democracy were to be seen as an alternative to, and superior to, those of the welfare state. James Meade, from whom Rawls took the notion of the property-owning democracy, was an early critic of social insurance, one typical policy instrument of the welfare state.[38] However, widespread ownership of capital can be seen as a complement to the redistribution of income across the life-cycle accomplished by the welfare state rather than a point of opposition. The domain of welfare state policies is distinct from the domain of public policies concerning the distribution of wealth and capital. Widespread capital ownership itself cannot substitute for the economic security of the welfare state. Even substantial capital endowments need to be complemented with welfare state programmes.[39]

In this context, probably the most important element in the widespread ownership of productive resources is the equalization of human capital, so far as this is possible, through high-quality education available to all in accordance with a strong principle of equality of opportunity. In a modern economy human capital constitutes the single most important productive resource that the majority of individuals can control. Equality of educational opportunity, including the opportunity to retrain as economic development alters the occupational structure, therefore becomes a way of equalizing control of productive resources. Moreover, human capital has the characteristic that once it is acquired it cannot be alienated (though of course it may atrophy with lack of use). There are strong limitations on the extent to which ownership of wealth and finance can be widely spread, without substantial controls on disposal, since unless individuals are very prudent with the use of their resource, they will have an incentive to realize the income that is inherent in wealth by selling their share and so creating the conditions under which wealth can be concentrated. By contrast, investment in human capital leaves individuals with an enhancement of their ability to increase their incomes in the future. It also provides them with the skills to participate in the development of a democratic political culture that is associated with the sense of democratic justice.

CHAPTER 8

The sense of democratic justice

8.1. Justice circumstantial and stable

A functioning social contract will promote the common interests of political associates. In advancing the human good, even modest improvements over an anarchic status quo are advantageous, particularly when individuals and households gain the security of knowing that their productive efforts will not be vulnerable to theft and pillage. In societies that are deeply divided by culture or ethnic group, or with social classes locked in intense competition with one another for scarce resources, agents will generally find it to their advantage to establish peaceful ways of resolving their disputes and clarifying the boundaries of their respective rights and obligations. Even in societies that do not have to wrestle with problems of deep ethnic, cultural, or class division, there will be significant gains to the well-being of its members if they can deal adequately with problems of resource depletion, environmental risk, or the positional competition that leads people to wish to avoid paying their taxes or free ride upon the work of others. Where a society devises effective and efficient institutions of social savings, its members are not only relieved of the burdens of economic and social insecurity, they also avoid the waste of resources associated with individual provision at levels that are too low to take advantage of economies of scale. Where public officials are uncorrupt, political competition civilized, even if intense, and the legal system functions so as to resolve disputes effectively, the social and political conditions exist for individuals to deal with one another in a regime of social justice.

Nothing in this description says that there will be political consensus. The balance to be struck between public and private expenditure will be a source of difference, as will the priority to be given, when dealing with questions of savings or resource depletion, to the needs of the future versus the needs of the present. What will seem to one person an extravagance in public provision for dealing with environmental risks will seem to another a prudent precaution. Outside these controversies over public goods, there will be many other divisive political issues, including the place of religion in public life and the authority that a church's doctrines should carry in political deliberation in general and the content of the school curriculum in particular, the moral limits of the criminal law in such matters as sexuality and drug use, as well as matters of defence and foreign policy. There is no reason to suppose that active political deliberation will induce consensus; indeed, it may enhance political disagreement.

In this context, well functioning institutions of public deliberation before the making of political choices become an important public good. On any question of public policy, there will be conflicting evidence and assumptions. The lessons of experience will be differently read, and the possibilities for the future differently evaluated. It is in the collective interest that such differences are resolved in a way that allows all to understand the basis upon which a public decision has been made and what would count as success or failure as a result of adopting one policy rather than another. There need to be ways of generating a consensus on the identification of feasible alternatives, even when there is disagreement about which of those alternatives is desirable, just as there need to be ways of establishing as reliably as possible what the effects of different policies are going to be for different groups.

To perform these functions effectively requires political institutions in which a broad range of opinions and interests find political representation. Chapter 6 argued that multi-party parliaments elected by proportional representation embody the principle of political equality. There are advantages in governments reaching out to form as wide an agreement as possible in passing legislation, but the majority principle, by which the vote of the median party in parliament is decisive, is justifiable as a way of making democratic choices. Although choices across a sequence of decisions may lead to cyclical inconsistency in the making of public policy, there are good reasons for thinking that any such inconsistency will be contained within a set of alternatives that represent the weight of opinion in society as to what feasible alternative policies are desirable. Public policies may be made by different and shifting coalitions, but such a process is an implication of taking political equality seriously in a society where there is a plurality of interests and opinions.

The value of political equality that underlies the democratic contractarian design of political institutions also has implications for the principles of economic justice, as was argued in Chapter 7. Just economic institutions will respect the right of producers to the full fruits of their labour, consistent with those producers supporting the social overhead costs of supplying the network benefits that enhance their productivity. A just society will support redistribution, but such redistribution will be based upon the principle that social saving is necessary to protect against the economic risks associated with fluctuations in the life-cycle. The importance given to these life-cycle effects will be manifested in the economic recognition of the social value of reproduction as well as production. The fairness of rewarding productive activity is buttressed by strong policies to institute and maintain widespread access to capital resources and policies based on equality of social and economic opportunity. In all of these areas of policy there will be disagreements as to priority, urgency, and the best mode of implementation. The achievement of economic justice is, therefore, closely tied to ensuring that political representation is broad and public decisions are taken that embody the principle of political equality.

A contractarian theory of democratic justice is built upon a procedural model of collective decision making. A well functioning democracy institutionalizes practical public deliberation in a situation in which the representatives of social groups negotiate over issues of public policy under conditions of political equality in pursuit of common interests. As a result, there is both bargaining to mutual advantage for separate interests, and political procedures to test and refine what is in the common interest. What makes the upshot of the negotiation just is the equality of power among participants. In having to negotiate with others on equal terms, each has to concede to the claims that are made and none can rely upon using the instruments of political authority to impose a one-sided solution.

Taken as an empirical hypothesis, democratic contractarianism can be interpreted as a theory about how the sense of justice arises. It supposes that a sense of justice emerges in conditions in which political actors in competition with each other have sufficient power to block an agreement that their opponents might otherwise wish to impose, unless it marks a sufficient advance over the status quo, particularly in a situation in which the status quo is highly undesirable for all. Where all must hang together or all hang separately, justice can be the bond that unites. Equality of power among social groups is rare in political societies, however. The empirical method exploits the fact of variation in social organization to identify those societies in which collective negotiation over the production of public goods takes place and in which the negotiating parties have approximately equal power, understood as the capacity to bestow, deny, or deprive advantages to others in relation to their interests. Mill conjectured that the ancient republics were the first political communities in which this condition of equal power was met, so that the social contracts upon which they were built placed human relations under the dominion of a law other than force.[1] Such a theory gives distinctive content to our conception of justice. Yet this distinctiveness seems to be bought at a high price. By assumption, few societies are placed in the appropriate circumstances of justice. Even the common property resource regimes that we took to model just social contracts exhibited, in some cases, inequalities of social and economic advantage by distinguishing between those with property and those who were wage-labourers.

The rarity of societies that meet the equal power condition suggests a serious methodological challenge. Since most societies are marked by inequalities of power, it follows that the observation-set of potentially just societies is small, relative to the total number of societies. That the circumstances of justice in our model societies are not replicated in other societies seems to be a *reductio ad absurdum* of the empirical method. If the circumstances that make for justice are comparatively rare, how is it possible for justice to be promoted outside those circumstances? The same theory that shows how justice emerges under very specific conditions also implies that, where those conditions are absent, the achievement of justice is impossible. When Robert Putnam proposed that the differences in economic performance and governmental efficiency between the north and south of Italy were attributable to long-term, historically determined differences in civic traditions, one reformist regional president is reported to have said that the argument was a counsel of despair and that the 'fate of reform was sealed centuries ago'.[2] If the social contracts that underlie and reinforce the civic community are specific to particular times and places, how can they be a model for social and political organization in general? A social scientific theory explains how economic and political outcomes arise by reference to the conditions that bring them about. It follows that where those conditions are absent, then so will be the outcomes. When Hayek said that social justice was a mirage, he did not have this argument in mind. Yet it is an argument that might seem tailor-made to buttress his conclusions.[3] Social justice seems at best circumstantial.

However, the conclusion is premature. Social conditions predispose rather than determine. Social and economic conditions may inhibit the development of sentiments of justice but they do not entirely prevent their arising and being influential. The barriers are real, but not immovable. Consider the transformation of the British electoral system at the end of the nineteenth century. UK elections in the nineteenth century were typically corrupt, and inspired both satire and popular movements for reform. However, a decisive moment of change came with the 1883 legislation that significantly extended the franchise. Because neither the Liberals nor the Conservatives, as the two major parties, could afford bribery on the scale required in an enlarged electorate, and because neither could predict where the balance of advantage lay with the expansion, they each had an incentive to institutionalize practices that avoided corruption, for fear of giving advantage to the other side. Circumstances conspired to create a veil of ignorance that equalized the power between participants in their negotiations with one another. Supplemented by a reform movement that had for many years been working to create a climate of public opinion in which corruption was seen as unacceptable, rules were established that effectively outlawed electoral abuse.[4] The lesson is that constructive action must take advantage of any windows of opportunity that open from time to time. The price of democratic justice is eternal vigilance in the search for political opportunities.

Originating circumstantially, just practices can become stable. The path-dependence of political institutions means not simply that rules and practices can be traced back to policy decisions but also that the institutions established by those policy decisions establish actors with incentives to maintain and uphold the rules and practices. The institutions that are established become self-reinforcing and create the conditions of assurance between competitive actors that rules will be followed. In electoral practices, once a set of rules is agreed by the parties, electoral officials, with the responsibility for operating the secret ballot and regulating party campaigning, acquire an interest in maintaining the rules. Much, therefore, can be accomplished by institutions. However, rules can never be completely enforced, so the change in institutions needs to be accompanied by a change in attitudes on the part of key actors. Were an institution merely to provide external regulation of a continuing prisoner's dilemma, the assurance to which it gave rise could be self-defeating. The assurance gained by any one party that the other side will keep the rules gives the first party an incentive to take advantage of any lax implementation to break the rules, when it would be to their own advantage to do so. (If the other side is effectively prevented from bribing voters, then I have a greater incentive to bribe them to gain whatever advantage I can, so long as I can get away with it.) To have the assurance that institutions can be relied upon to operate to the general advantage requires assurance that others will abide by the rules, even when they could break them. It requires attitudes to change such that the underlying game ceases to be a prisoner's dilemma. To secure stability, just practices need not only to be externally enforced but to be recognized from the inner point of view.[5] How can we conceptualize the origins, content, and force of this inner point of view?

8.2. From community to association

To say that equality of power can be an occasion for a sense of justice to emerge is not to say that such a contractarian self-understanding is necessary for a sense of justice for members of a society. Conceivably, it might be the case that, when members of a society come to see their social organization as an implicit social contract, that understanding undermines the sense of community on which their commitment to justice depended. Consider a traditional community in which sentiments of loyalty, honesty in dealing, respect for the public interest, and civic pride are high. Members of this community regularly act unself-consciously from a sense of justice. They pay taxes that have been properly levied. They play their part in such onerous social responsibilities as jury duty, environmental protection, or military service. They take part in public debate and deliberation, or at least take an intelligent interest in such debate and deliberation, so that when they come to vote they do so with intelligence and an understanding of the issues at stake. When they hold public office, they act in accordance with the public interest and not the interest of their private pocket. They bring their children up to respect constitutional principles of political and social equality. They are committed to sustainable development and the protection of the interests of future generations. However, they never think of these duties as corresponding to the terms of a social contract that could have been negotiated by political representatives in circumstances of equality of power. Their sense of justice is written into their hearts, not derived from a chain of reasoning in their heads.

It is easy to imagine that, were social contract theory to be promulgated in such a society, it could lead some members to question how well grounded were the duties required. If they come to see society as a reciprocal arrangement for mutual advantage, they may start to question the terms of the advantage that they secure as individuals or social groups, calculating the benefits received in relation to the costs incurred. Inevitably, in a world in which justice is a virtue, its principles will require some members of society to accept delay in the repayment of effort or contribution. Where reciprocity is generalized to anonymous others without any sense of obvious return, individuals may start to doubt that the traditional principles on which they have always acted are well grounded in a calculus of long-term self-interest. Since there is no exact balance in any society between the effort that people expend and the return they receive, even when a society secures justice, the principle of reciprocity, which in general yields a surplus of benefit over costs, may be violated at the individual level. No society is capable of perfect justice. In consequence, some of its members will receive more than they are due, and others less. To have a sense of justice does not preclude one from being a good accountant, and when the accountancy is done with precision there will be net gainers and net losers. Rational and reflective individuals may want to rebalance the books, but in doing so they may find themselves undermining the sentiments of justice upon which their society has been successfully built, as each person seeks a rebalancing that corrects for a presumed deficit in their personal account. Where communitarian tradition once stood, the acids of individualism implicit in viewing society as a scheme for rational mutual advantage eat away at the bonds of society.

The situation is one where an unreflective sense of justice seems more secure than a reasoned sense of justice. The disposition to justice in everyday transactions is a non-calculating disposition requiring individuals not to estimate on each and every occasion whether the practice of justice contributes to their personal well-being, even supposing it to contribute to their overall advantage. If this is so, how can a democratic contract theory be the basis for a just social order? Does the sense of justice not lie in community? This is the burden of the communitarian critique of social contract theory.

As Mulhall and Swift noted, communitarianism offers both a substantive and a methodological critique of social contract theory.[6] By making justice a matter of contract among individuals, it is said that the theory distorts a proper understanding of the relationship between individuals and the communities to which they belong. Individuals depend upon society for constitutive elements of their person, most notably language and the moral conceptions that give them self-understanding and an understanding of the social world in which they live. Mistaken about the sources of the self, social contract theory also misconstrues the content of a plausible political morality, inappropriately giving pride of place to individual rights or individual interests over and above a shared conception of justice or the common good. Sandel criticized Rawls's deontology for its supposition that an individual conception of the self is sufficient, since 'we cannot regard ourselves as independent in this way without great cost to those loyalties and conviction whose moral force consists partly in the fact that living by them is inseparable from understanding ourselves as the particular persons we are'.[7] MacIntyre suggested that in Rawls's theory, 'the only constraints are those that a prudent rationality would impose', so that individuals 'are primary and society secondary, and the identification of individual interests is prior to, and independent of, the construction of any moral or social bonds between them'.[8] Although a mischaracterization of Rawls's theory, something like this is true of democratic contractarianism. Both Sandel and MacIntyre suggest that there is something self-defeating about modern contract theory. The source of that self-defeat is to be found in the way that the theory occludes an understanding of the true pattern of relations between individuals as members of specific communities.

If the supposition that there could be an historically given and unquestionable sense of justice were true, and if some societies were fortunate enough to have inherited a clear and perspicacious set of principles of justice, then doubt about the contractarian basis for justice might be justified. But the supposition is outlandish. Outside the *polis* as idealized by Hegel, in which there is a total coherence of culture, there is always occasion to question the foundation of social relationships upon which established duties rest. Unless a culture automatically harmonized the goals of persons, individuals will always be able to raise the question as to whether their interests are being justly met. As Hegel himself saw, following his reading of the political economy of the Scottish Enlightenment, commercial society produced simultaneously an interdependence of needs and a particularity of ends that required mediation through political authority.[9] Societies do not spontaneously produce justice. Their mode of production entrenches certain inequalities. Their lack of science prevents their having the technology to solve the collective action problems they face. Their religious traditions inculcate beliefs prejudicial to some minority groups. Their neighbours are aggressive. Their various languages breed mutual incomprehension. Behind these local conditions, original sin provokes a pervading disproportionate bias to self. In these circumstances, democratic justice is an achievement against tradition and community; not an expression of it.

Nor does rendering justice through social cooperation require a sentimentalized notion of civic friendship. Although political divisions may run deep, they need not prevent cooperation to mutual advantage. Writing of cooperation in Törbel, Netting noted examples where people worked productively together despite deep political differences. Thus: 'The man who repairs an avalanche-damaged wall on the alp and shares a drink of wine from a wooden flask with his neighbour will speak in private of the humiliations suffered by his great-grandfather at the hands of that same neighbor's ancestor well over a century ago and of the implacable political hostility that still absorbs their respective descendants.'[10] Of course, it is plausible to think that strong associational bonds reaching across different members of a society will create the conditions within which collectively oriented political action will be enhanced, as the theory of social capital suggests.[11] Yet although civic friendship and social capital may enhance the disposition to behave justly, the content of justice must be consistent with mutual advantage, if it is to be justice.

8.3. Equality and the sense of justice

When in Book II of *The Republic*, Glaucon offers the contractarian theory of justice as an answer to the question posed by Socrates, he presents it as a return to the theory first offered by Thrasymachus in Book I. Thrasymachus, also a Sophist, had defined justice as what serves the interest of the stronger. It follows, as Thrasymachus himself acknowledged, that it is typically in the interest of the stronger party to make the selfish appropriation of goods as great as possible, so that others are intimidated into acquiescence.[12] Yet although Glaucon is presented as offering a restatement of this view, his theory is significantly different, because he makes justice a convention arising from a stand-off between those who enjoy an equality of power, not the exercise of power by those who possess an advantage. Justice emerges when each party to a struggle recognizes that mutual restraint is to common advantage and can agree rules by which the exercise of power is suitably constrained.

From the point of view of any particular associate, the obligations of the democratic contract impose self-restraint that is equivalent to the restraint that would be induced by the fear of retaliation of someone equally powerful. One way of seeking to explicate this condition for political associates is to say that it implies a role-reversal test. In their dealings with others, associates should ask themselves how they would judge their action were roles reversed.

Interpreted one way, this is not a strong test, as the example of Hare's 'fanatic' goes to show. Hare considered the case of the Nazi who was willing to persecute others but who said that, should it turn out that he was a member of an 'inferior' group, he would be willing to accept the punishment.[13] A test of equal power in a social contract and a Harean role-reversal test differ in this respect, because within the equal power of the social contract relations between individuals and groups must be defined by reference to the interests of those individuals and groups as those individuals and groups see them, rather than allowing someone more powerful to redefine the weight of those interests under some hypothetical role-reversal. The social contract allows members of a potentially vulnerable group to veto polices that would lead to their being exploited.

Democratic contractarianism therefore implies a role-reversal test akin to the principle offered by Rawls in the earliest (contractarian) presentation of his theory, in 'Justice as Fairness', where he suggested that his principles of justice were those 'a person would keep in mind if he were designing a practice in which his enemy were to assign him his place'.[14] Brian Barry criticized the logic of this test on the grounds that this was to invoke a premiss known to be false into the reasoning of the contracting parties. There is no rationality in designing institutions for a social system on the premiss that your enemy is to assign you your place in that social system if, in fact, your place is determined by personal luck and talent. It would be a bit like always taking a raincoat when you went out, on the assumption that your worst enemy was in control of the weather and would always make it rain.[15] Rawls subsequently accepted this point, but his concession lost an important element in the sense of justice.[16]

Let us agree that it is not sensible to suppose that one's place in the social order is determined by someone with malevolent intent. Nevertheless, justice still requires institutions that constrain those who do have malevolent intent and the power to carry out their intentions. The argument is not to be understood as saying that within a proposed social contract I am going to favour institutional designs that rest on the premiss that my place will be determined by my enemy. Rather the argument is to be understood as the view that, however my place is determined, it makes sense to favour designs that will protect me from the abuse of power by others and I shall assess the extent of that possible abuse by reference to a situation in which power was balanced or roughly equal among affected parties. Where the assigned enemy test is met, then role-reversal arguments can be used freely, for the groundwork of existence of each is protected by the political order. Where associates can agree that, under a role-reversal test, certain social practices are acceptable, then policies in line with that judgement can be pursued. Such a test is particularly important in matters like the control of hazards, where the inevitability of some risks arising from energy production or transport has to be controlled in the light of considerations about the social incidence of such risks. But it can be applied to public reasoning by associates across a wide range of public policies.

Nietzsche wrote that preachers of equality are tarantulas, in whose soul sits revenge.[17] According to Nietzsche, such preachers were soured by self-conceit and repressed their envy—not to mention the self-conceit and envy of their parents. Yet these base motives would keep breaking out in the madness of revenge expressed in the assertion of equality and the hatred of power. On this view, democracy is a slave morality, but the affirmation of life and beauty requires battle and inequality. Philosophical understanding means resisting the temptation to vengefulness. A democrat might want to build political morality upon the fear of power, but that is no reason to embrace the theory in which these elements are central. Rather it is a reason to renounce it.

Though vigorously expressed, the fallacy implicated in Nietzsche's position is obvious. It is an elementary mistake of logical quantification, confusing contraries with contradictories. Black is contrary to white: a box that is black all over cannot be white all over. But that does not mean that black and white are contradictories exhausting the possibilities. A box may be grey. By the same token, power might be the assertion of one group over another; or it might be a situation in which a formerly subjugated group itself takes the place of the leading caste. There might be a vacuum of power. And there can be a balance of power. When a balance of power obtains, we do not have a case of revenge or the expression of envy, but the circumstances in which each can protect their interests. Hannah Arendt, who had to accommodate the twin weight of the Nietzschean existentialism associated with Heidegger and her love of the Periclean *polis*, achieved some sort of reconciliation when she argued that Athenian citizens undertook 'the burden of justification, defense, and administration of public affairs' in exchange for the chance to excel in the public realm against their equals.[18] Thus, a collectivity in which there is a struggle for power can require of its participants that they regard one another as political equals, that is to say as participants in the public realm of political decision making. Though Arendt herself contrasts this situation with justice in the modern sense, it is hard to see why. The sentiment of justice is not a desire for the inversion of inequalities of power, as the Nietzschean position requires; nor should it be represented as a situation where there is no power. Rather it is the situation of collective practical reasoning where power is approximately equal.

If individuals and groups are to break free of domination, including the domination supported by tradition or community, they need a sense of self-assertion.[19] Domination may take the form of the imposition by one social class or group of legal and other constraints on the fortunes of another social class or group, as illustrated in the case of laws imposing racial segregation or the form of marriage contract against which Mill protested. However, it can also take the form of an internalized sense of powerlessness that is the ground of its own fulfilment. The consciousness that is the condition of subjugation may be a consciousness to the effect that there is no subjugation. Many societies are typified by injustice because their members cannot envisage an alternative and this is 'the supreme and most insidious act of power'. Loyalty to unjust social norms is a core form of human exploitation.[20] In these circumstances, the sense of justice requires an assertion of one's own claims rather than a suppression of a sense of personal advantage. The forms that this can take are various, involving not only outright political competition and revolt but on occasion the invocation of an alternative tradition against a dominant political culture. Thus Cécile Laborde has shown in the case of the *hijab* controversy in France that the wearing of traditional dress can be interpreted not as a restriction of freedom but as a distinctive form of autonomy, which draws its strength from the thought world of those who are wearing the dress, but which also serves to express opposition to injustice.[21]

The sense of justice is not simply the willingness to abide by the terms of reciprocal justice even when to do so would be to one's own disadvantage. It is also shown in a willingness to look others in the eye and assert one's own claims when not to do so would lead to one's being unjustly disadvantaged. To have this sense of justice is to have certain virtues of character. As Joel Feinberg once explained, persons with these virtues do not need to fear persons of superior power or to please others as a condition of their well-being. They possess 'an easy and unaffected dignity'. They are neither small-minded or petty nor haughty and superior.[22] They stand up for themselves. If we are not for ourselves, who will be for us?

Yet, although we must be for ourselves, we cannot only be for ourselves, if the social contract is to be viable. The origin of justice may be in conditions in which power is approximately equal, and the principles of justice may be defined as the outcome of a social contract negotiated in conditions of equal power. Theoretically, we model parties in the contract without supposing that they have a sense of justice, because the work of determining the principles of justice will be done by the specification of the conditions under which the contract is negotiated. However, this gives rise to an obvious problem. To be a just person in a political association is to be the sort of person who acts on considerations of justice.[23] Outside the specific circumstances of the model contract and such real world approximations as there are, what motive have groups and individuals to behave justly, if their only reason for action is a prudent rationality? The Epicureans may have held that the contract to mutual advantage did not issue in a view of cynical compliance but implied that one should practise justice by convention as though it were justice by nature.[24] However, is there any reason to agree with them on this point?

To address this question, let us consider what principles of practical rationality must motivate those who are disposed to act justly in line with the social contract. Even in societies that are relatively just, some associates will often find themselves in situations of superior power. In a negotiation, one side may have more relevant information than another or have access to greater resources so that they can be more patient when bargaining or can bring some threat-advantage to the table that is not matched by the threat-advantage of the other side. In these contexts a sense of justice is required so that actors do not exploit their one-sided power. To act on the principles of justice that emerge from democratic social contracts negotiated within the circumstances of justice when those circumstances are absent therefore requires motives that are other than the motive to find the best contractual terms for oneself subject to the constraint that other equally powerful actors are also seeking to obtain the best terms for themselves. It requires a sense of democratic justice.

At the core of the sense of democratic justice is a principle of reciprocity. The basic logic of reciprocity is that of a willingness to act cooperatively, conditional upon others doing so. However, the reciprocity that is suitable for a social contract is distinct from the conception of reciprocity that is found in bilateral exchange. In the case of bilateral exchange, the principle of reciprocity dictates that one should render some service or provide some good to a specific other in exchange for a benefit bestowed. Democratic reciprocity goes beyond the specificity of such an obligation and means that one should play one's part in a scheme of cooperation to mutual advantage. The obligation to play that part is conditional upon (enough) others, who are also party to the contract, playing their part. Such a scheme may be thought of as a set of interlocking rights and duties that attach to membership of the scheme.

To say that one should play one's part in a scheme of democratic justice might seem to suggest that the obligations to which one is subject were somehow owed to an abstract scheme and inapplicable to interpersonal relations. However, the basic structure of a scheme of social cooperation simply names the aggregated behaviour of individuals solidified into routines, habits, and practices. The support of a market structure, for example, requires participants to deal honestly with one another without force or fraud. Of course, there are local understandings of what force and fraud means, so that in some communities absence of fraud is compatible with a rule of *caveat emptor*, in others it requires utmost good faith, and in yet others something between the two. However, given these understandings, one supports a structure by participating in it according to its rules and conventions. When people render honest bills for work that has been done, pay on terms that correspond to their contractual requirements, or refuse to take advantage of honest mistakes committed by others, they are thereby supporting the structure of the market according to the understandings that are relevant. There is generally no separate thing that one does in supporting fair play in the market over and above conducting oneself in accordance with the relevant rules of the market when transacting with specific others. That is what playing one's part in a just scheme of economic relations means.

As well as not exploiting others when it would be possible to do so, the sense of justice also requires agents to accept the claims of others, even when those others have no power to enforce those claims. It also requires agents to bear the costs of the system of mutual advantage when it is their turn to do so. This obviously covers such obligations as paying one's taxes for public goods and the sorts of shared savings scheme that provide for need. The obligation does not necessarily depend upon the scheme being strictly 'fair', in the actuarial sense, in respect of any particular individual. That is to say, even when there is a common interest in having a scheme of shared savings, there will be some individuals who would find it advantageous from a personal point of view to opt out. The fact that a just scheme of cooperation gives everyone subject to it a right to assert their own claims does not mean that individuals will suffer no disadvantage as a result, and perhaps a disadvantage for which there will be no compensation. For example, a scheme in which everyone serves in the armed forces for a certain period of their lives may well be a scheme of mutual advantage from which everyone gains, but there will be some people who, when their turn to serve comes, will be unlucky because they will end up fighting and being killed in a war. We can still say that such an arrangement is advantageous to them, if only in *ex ante* terms, because they enjoyed the security that comes with military protection, so that it was in their interest to have the scheme even if they personally eventually endured unrequited loss.

8.4. Governance and motives

The sense of democratic justice is revealed in the principles of the practical reasoning exercised by each associate and, in particular, in the extent to which that reasoning is guided by the terms of the social contract. The reflective element of practical rationality enables those caught in dilemmas of collective action to step back and appraise their situation in the light of the understanding available to them. To come to a meaningful collective agreement, those caught in the dilemma also need to be able to give themselves normative self-direction in the form of reasons that others see as credible. They also need to be able to follow a chain of reasoning in a practical syllogism, identifying which actions count as satisfying the conditions implied by the collective agreement. Yet the ability to resolve collective action problems through practical reasoning is not by itself sufficient for justice. Producers often resolve their collective action problems by constructing cartels to the detriment to consumers. As Adam Smith noted, '[p]eople of the same trade seldom meet together, even for merriment and diversion, but the conversation ends in a conspiracy against the publick, or in some contrivance to raise prices'.[25] By the same token, honour among thieves will make the job of the police force harder. Deliberative rationality is only a necessary condition for effective collective action to secure common interests across society, not a sufficient one. How, then, can we suppose that the terms of the social contract can provide with individuals reasons for action?

Some contractualists, like Barry, attempt to solve this problem by positing a motive for acting justly distinct from that of self-interest. According to Barry, such a motive is the outcome of 'the desire to be able to justify one's actions to others on grounds they could not reasonably reject'.[26] Barry regards the desire to be able to justify one's conduct as an original principle of human behaviour, and affirms that 'the equation of rationality with the efficient pursuit of self-interest is . . . pure assertion'.[27] On this account, we simply make the willingness to act in accordance with the principles of justice an axiom of the theory. Positing such a motive to solve the problem of how it is that principles of a social contract can provide associates with reasons for acting justly may seem like the theoretical equivalent of those fairy stories in which the hero, by rubbing a magic lantern, can call upon a superhuman spirit to rescue the situation at a crucial point of danger. However, this would be too quick a conclusion. Positing a motive to behave justly is consistent with the assumption of limited altruism that is one of the circumstances of justice. As Hart put it, human beings are neither angels nor devils.[28] They can take a disinterested view of one another's welfare. We can accept that it is conceptually impossible to collapse entirely the sense of justice into the self-interested motives of political associates, for even when people are willing to concede that their behaviour would be inconsistent with a contractarian role-reversal test, they may still lack the motive to act in accordance with that judgement. However, we cannot infer from this that the motive to act justly is uniform or unresponsive to the situation in which individuals are placed. Accepting the conceptual point still leaves open a number of questions about the empirical conditions in which the motive to behave justly can be activated.

Within the common property resource regimes, an important constraint upon free riding is imposed by the ability of participants to monitor one another's behaviour. Producers are prevented from overfishing or abstracting more than their share of water by the knowledge that others can observe these actions and impose punishment. The constraint was enforceable because punishment or the anticipation of punishment induced compliance in the minds of potential defectors. Governance equals a social contract in the common interest together with its means of monitoring and enforcement. Governance implies punishment—and indeed one of Ostrom's conditions for successful common pool resource regimes is that a system of graduated punishments is in place.[29] In great societies, the corresponding institutions include accounting practices to audit those who handle public finance or private investments, police and the security services to provide surveillance against crime, and political institutions to set ambition against ambition to expose failure in public office. The press and media as well as non-governmental organizations publicize information on poor performance or the misuse of power as a way of bringing public pressure to bear on governments. These institutions and practices provide a system of governance. Although there is no perfect system of monitoring and punishment, the role of governance is to support the motive to justice that is implicit in the assumption of limited altruism, both through the deterrent effect of punishment and by the assurance that such a system gives to those who are compliant that their interests will be maintained.

Some contractarians deny that governance and its associated monitoring are needed, provided that the reasoning of the contracting parties is sound. Cooperation in the social contract can take place within the limits of reason alone. The fool who favours injustice, in a quotation from Hobbes often cited by Gauthier, 'cannot be received into any Society, that unite themselves for Peace and Defence, but by the errour of them that receive him'.[30] The price of being able to reap the benefits of cooperation with others is that one be a reliable cooperator oneself, and the best way of making oneself transparently a reliable cooperator is to be one. To be a transparent cooperator is to be the sort of person who accepts internally the constraints of justice in dealing with others. If you have internalized the sense of justice, there is still, nevertheless, some sense in which opportunistic behaviour is still possible for you, since there is no external constraint that would prevent that behaviour. However, on Gauthier's view, dispositions of justice are so internalized that agents would not act upon their short-term advantage. As Morris and Ripstein say, Gauthier's account of obligation 'is internal and dispositional, rather than external and coercive'.[31] A community of rational agents, all of whose members exhibited such dispositions of justice, could live in conditions of anarchy without governance.

However, transparency of the sort required for this argument to work presupposes deductive, non-defeasible rationality. Agents can credibly commit to agreed terms of a contract provided that they are capable of foreseeing all eventualities, even if only probabilistically. Suppose, for example, that they can see that they have a non-negligible probability of interacting with others in such a way that they will have to play cooperate in a one-shot prisoner's dilemma on some occasions to their own disadvantage. Suppose they accept Gauthier's argument that it would be rational to acquire a disposition to cooperate even when on particular occasions it would be more beneficial to defect. They would, in effect, be incurring the disadvantages associated with the times when they cooperated as others defected as the price for being able to cooperate with others who are willing to reciprocate. The highest net income stream available to agents need not be the income stream with no losses at all. It is simply that there have to be large enough gains to compensate for the losses.

Suppose now that agents cannot foresee all contingencies. It is not simply that they cannot assign (subjective) probabilities to contingencies; it is rather that they cannot anticipate the contingencies at all, as will be the case in conditions of bounded rationality. In such a condition, agents cannot credibly commit to cooperating across a sequence of interactions at all, at least not without having some reserve clause that would allow them exemptions from their obligations under exceptional and unforeseeable circumstances. Agents who are boundedly rational cannot commit to a disposition to cooperate unless they have a get-out clause, since they cannot avoid the prospect of being confronted with a situation that defeated their prior assumptions about the prudence of cooperating. So they are unable to commit, even in the conditional form, by contractarian theory. And if they are unable to commit, then no pretence at commitment is credible. They are locked in a suboptimal situation. A situation of bounded rationality, in which some contingencies remain unknown, makes any agreed contract incomplete, and in the face of incomplete contracts there is no place for credible commitment unless that can be supported by external devices of monitoring and constraint.

It may be argued that governance is not necessary in this case, because in the absence of opportunistic motives, agents who find themselves in unanticipated contingencies under incomplete contracts will simply negotiate in good faith to a mutually agreeable solution.[32] The need for governance, it may be said, arises not as a result of a failure of rationality but as a consequence of having a particular type of motive, namely one that shows willingness to free ride on others if given the opportunity. However, even without opportunism, governance is still necessary. In an unanticipated situation and faced with a dispute, people in good faith may believe that they have the better of the argument, even if they are not being opportunistic in trying to steal the advantage. As Locke said, 'Men being partial to themselves, Passion and Revenge is very apt to carry them too far, and with too much heat, in their own Cases; as well as negligence, and unconcernedness, to make them too remiss, in other Mens.' Locke correctly inferred the need for an 'indifferent Judge'.[33] In other words, even with a willingness to negotiate in good faith, what is needed is judicial authority to adjudicate between competing good faith claims, which is another name for one aspect of governance.

The need for governance to deal with good faith disagreements also arises even if, in a contractualist way, we posit a basic desire among persons to be able to justify their conduct to one another. A sincere desire to be able to justify one's conduct to others does not preclude there being deep differences of view. So, whether we are contractarians or contractualists, there is a need for authoritative resolution of differences and this in turn implies a need to socialize and educate people into the rationale of authoritative governance. It is sometimes said that to recognize that a policy of education is needed to instil the sense of justice is to look at matters from an instrumental point of view.[34] But, in a world of bounded rationality, authoritative resolution will always be called for and so instruction as to the rationale of such authority is needed. There is an instrumental justification for such education.

For political associates to see the need for governance in the form of authoritatively based law is for them to see the social contract as a normative system. Consider a trivial but paradigmatic example. If we do not think of the law as a normative system, then parking fines are not punishment for violating a rule but merely the cost of parking in a convenient place. By contrast, for someone who looks at the normative system from the inner point of view, the fine is a sign of fault and not simply a charge incident to a certain type of action. Some airport taxes are at least as large as fines, but they occupy a different place in the normative order.

A normative system comprises the rules, roles, and relations that constitute a system of governance. To treat those norms as authoritative is not to deny that they can be irksome on some occasions. There is no reason to suppose that there is a happy coincidence of the requirement of justice and the interests of political associates. However, when the sentiments of justice are internalized, they transform a person's sense of themselves. An internal sense of justice brings in its wake notions of commitment and reciprocity as themselves motivating, independently of any penalties that might attach for non-compliance. If someone thinks of themselves as involved in the moral relationships of justice with others, then the character of that relationship becomes an element in their own character. Of course, this does not mean that cooperating parties will always abide by the jointly advantageous rules. It does mean that, when they are punished for breach of those rules, they are being confronted with an understanding of themselves as cooperative beings governed by moral norms on which the system of political governance rests.[35]

Convention can become second nature. When a sense of justice is internalized, it becomes dispositional and will lead people not to exploit the power over others that social conditions and happenstance may bring their way. A sense of justice diffused throughout society will lead people to play their part in a just scheme of cooperation, even when on occasions it would be to their advantage to exploit others or treat them unjustly. Moreover, institutional arrangements, when well designed, can reinforce this internalized sense of justice to the common good. With a well developed sense of justice, the inequalities and corruption inherited from the past can be overcome.

8.5. The civic culture of democratic justice

A society can be rich in public goods, without itself being rich. Even at modest levels of economic development its dwellings can be clean, well built, and well maintained. Its streets can be safe and its standards of hygiene high. Provision can be made for public recreation in squares and parks, as well as for sharing the expenses of ill health and infirmity. Its educational institutions can have high standards. Its public officials and judiciary can be upright. Its money can be sound, its public finances in good order, and its system of taxation effective in raising revenue without unnecessary burden. Its business practices can be honest. It can use non-renewable natural resources prudently and conserve renewable resources for future generations. It can invest in science and research to advance knowledge and support future generations. It can play a constructive role in world affairs, promoting peace and contributing to security where necessary. Unless the desires and wants of its citizens are shaped by frugality as an intrinsic value, such a society would still benefit from economic development. Working hours could be shortened, more time given over to education (at any age) and advances made in health care, as well as the private material consumption of citizens enhanced. As a society becomes richer, it may choose to embody its achievements in museums, art galleries, theatres, public buildings, and fine thoroughfares that are a focus of civic pride to its members.

One cannot take pride in just anything, however. As Philippa Foot once pointed out, it does not make sense to say that a man can feel proud of the sea or the sky or of laying one hand on top of the other three times in an hour.[36] To be able to say intelligibly that one feels pride requires appropriate beliefs and a certain relation to the facts at hand. In particular, as Foot explains, it requires both that the object of pride be an achievement and that in some ways it belongs to the person who expresses a sense of pride.[37] One cannot therefore have civic pride without both being part of a collective with achievements and having oneself made some contribution to those achievements. The outward and visible signs of collective achievements are to be found in the provision of public good and shared savings that are the preconditions for individual interests and fulfilment. To secure political equality, credible political choice, a prudent use of material resources, and the conditions in which all can be as productive in their own way as they are able, has so far proved beyond the capacity of any society. To establish the institutions of a society in line with these principles of democratic justice would be an achievement.

There can be justice without democracy, but there cannot be social justice without democracy. In non-democratic and unjust societies, individuals can act justly. They can discharge their offices, public or private, with diligence and attention to detail, not neglecting the claims of those within their scope of responsibility. They can transact on fair terms with others and not exploit advantages of information or position. They can show respect to all with whom they deal. They can make their contribution to the common good, even when others default They can make provision for their own needs without neglecting the needs of others. They can do justice and they may even love mercy. What they cannot do is be a participant in a regime of social justice. Such regimes are built through cooperation among citizens, as negotiated by those citizens and their representatives. If social justice is not possible without democracy, then as a citizen you cannot be proud of the justice of your society without also being willing to play a part in the construction of those just institutions.

The contract of justice requires democratic political cooperation. Initially such cooperation may only emerge from the retaliation reaped by not according respect to the interests of others in situations of approximate equality of power. Perhaps the mutual fear of retaliation is always an element in maintaining social relations in which no person or group is treated as inferior. However, a culture of democracy in the government of public concerns comes over time to embody the results of successful cooperation, it creates the conditions within which the principle of social equality becomes central to the political culture, replacing a politics of uneasy equilibrium. In such a society, despite differences of income and achievement, as well as the conflicts of interests to which these differences give rise, citizens will value one another as equals sharing the joint public practical rationality that is the essential condition for meeting their common interests. In such a society, individuals can be for themselves; but they will never be only for themselves.

NOTES

Chapter 1

1. Aristotle, *The Politics*, translated by H. Rackham (Cambridge, MA: Harvard University Press, 1944), V.ii.2, 1302a, p. 379.
2. Jean-Jacques Rousseau, *Discourse on the Origin and the Foundations of Inequality among Men*, originally 1755, in *Jean-Jacques Rousseau: The First and Second Discourses*, edited, translated and annotated by Victor Gourevitch (New York: Harper & Row, 1986), p. 170.
3. James Madison,'Federalist Paper No. 10' in *The Federalist Papers*, originally 1788, edited Terence Ball (Cambridge: Cambridge University Press, 2003 edition), p. 42.
4. Henry Sidgwick, *The Elements of Politics* (London: Macmillan, 1891), Chapter V.
5. Plato, *The Republic*, translated by Francis MacDonald Cornford (Oxford: Clarendon Press, 1941), Book II, 3589, pp. 42–3.
6. There is some dispute in among commentators as to whether Glaucon's statement should be understood as being a version of social contract theory. See R.C. Cross and A.D. Woozley, *Plato's Republic: A Philosophical Commentary* (London: Macmillan, 1966), pp. 73–4 and Michael Lessnoff, *Social Contract* (Basingstoke: Macmillan, 1986), p. 21 for sceptical views. I have followed the positive assessment in W.K.C. Guthrie, *History of Greek Philosophy III* (Cambridge: Cambridge University Press, 1969) and Nicholas Denyer, 'The Origins of Justice' in Giovanni Pugliese Carratelli (ed.), *ΣΥΖΗΤΗΣΙΣ. Studi sull'Epicureismo Greco e Romano: Offerti a Marcello Gigante* (Napoli: Gaetano Macchiaroli Editore, 1983), pp. 133–52. See also, Malcolm Schofield, 'Social and Political Thought', in Keimpe Algra, Jonathan Barnes, Jaap Mansfeld, and Malcolm Schofield (eds.), *The Cambridge History of Hellenistic Philosophy* (Cambridge: Cambridge University Press, 1999), 739–70.
7. Denyer, 'The Origins of Justice'.
8. Compare Guthrie, *History of Greek Philosophy III*, Chapter 5.
9. Plato, *Protagoras*, translated by W.C.K. Guthrie, in Edith Hamilton and Huntingdon Cairns (eds.), *The Collected Dialogues of Plato* (Princeton: Princeton University Press, 1973), pp. 308–52, 322b, p. 319.
10. Aristotle, *The Politics*, III.v.11, 1280b10, p. 215. The criticism is consistent with Aristotle's more general view that rule-governed commerce does not make for a state, which requires the exercise of the political virtues.

11. Denyer, 'The Origins of Justice', p. 149.
12. John Stuart Mill, *The Subjection of Women*, original edition 1869, reprinted in John Gray (ed.), *John Stuart Mill On Liberty and Other Essays* (Oxford: Oxford University Press, 1991), p. 478.
13. Brian Barry, *Theories of Justice* (London: Harvester-Wheatsheaf, 1989); *Justice as Impartiality* (Oxford: Oxford University Press, 1995); Ken Binmore, *Playing Fair: Game Theory and the Social Contract Volume I* (Cambridge, MA and London: The MIT Press, 1994); *Just Playing: Game Theory and the Social Contract Volume II* (Cambridge, MA and London: The MIT Press, 1998); David Gauthier, *Morals by Agreement* (Oxford: Clarendon Press, 1986); Russell Grice, *The Grounds of Moral Judgement* (Cambridge: Cambridge University Press, 1967); John Rawls, *Political Liberalism: With a New Introduction and 'Reply to Habermas'* (New York: Columbia University Press, 1996); *A Theory of Justice: Revised Edition* (Oxford: Oxford University Press, 1999); *Justice as Fairness: A Restatement*, edited by Erin Kelly (Cambridge, MA: The Belknap Press, 2001); and T.M. Scanlon, 'Contractualism and Utilitarianism' in A. Sen and B. Williams (eds.), *Utilitarianism and Beyond* (Cambridge: Cambridge University Press, 1982), pp. 101–28; *What We Owe to Each Other* (Cambridge, MA: Belknap Press, 1998).
14. See Barry, *Theories of Justice*.
15. Stephen Darwall, 'Introduction' in Stephen Darwall (ed.), *Contractarianism/Contractualism* (Oxford: Blackwell Publishing, 2003), pp. 1–8, at p. 1; David Gauthier, 'Political Contractarianism', *Journal of Political Philosophy*, 5: 2, (1997), pp. 132–48. See also Samuel Freeman, *Justice and the Social Contract: Essays on Rawlsian Political Philosophy* (New York: Oxford University Press, 2007), p. 4, who has a version of this distinction, though he is not rigid between the terms 'contractarian' and 'contractualist'.
16. Rawls, *A Theory of Justice*, p. 4.
17. Gauthier, 'Political Contractarianism', p. 133–5, contrasting with Scanlon, 'Contractualism and Utilitarianism', p. 128, who notes the concern with protection as fundamental to the grounds of morality on one view and general agreement itself on what morality is about on the other.
18. Barry, *Theories of Justice*, p. 13.
19. Freeman, *Justice and the Social Contract*, pp. 18–19.
20. Darwall, 'Introduction', p. 1.
21. Rawls, *A Theory of Justice*, p. 11.
22. Rawls, *A Theory of Justice*, p. 14.
23. Rawls, *Political Liberalism*, pp. 89–90.

24. Rawls, *Political Liberalism*, p. 26; Barry, *Theories of Justice*, p. 266. Compare Scanlon, 'Contractualism and Utilitarianism', pp. 104–10.
25. Gauthier, 'Political Contractarianism', p. 2.
26. Matt Matravers, *Justice and Punishment: The Rationale of Coercion* (Oxford: Oxford University Press, 2000), p. 100.
27. Brian Barry, 'Something in the Disputation Not Unpleasant', in Paul Kelly (ed.), *Impartiality, Neutrality and Justice: Re-Reading Brian Barry's Justice as Impartiality* (Edinburgh: Edinburgh University Press, 1998), pp. 186–257, at pp. 187–8.
28. Albert Weale, *Democracy*, second edition (Houndmills, Basingstoke: Palgrave Macmillan, 2007), p. 18.
29. Weale, *Democracy*, Chapter 3.
30. James Bohman and William Rehg (eds.), *Deliberative Democracy* (Cambridge, MA: MIT Press, 1997); Maurizio Passerin D'Entrèves, 'Introduction: Democracy as Public Deliberation' in Maurizio Passerin D'Entrèves (ed.) *Democracy as Public Deliberation: New Perspectives* (Manchester: Manchester University Press, 2002), pp. 1–36.
31. Joshua Cohen, 'Deliberation and Democratic Legitimacy' in Alan Hamlin and Philip Pettit (eds.), *The Good Polity: Normative Analysis of the State* (Oxford: Basil Blackwell, 1989), pp. 17–34, at p. 22; John S. Dryzek, 'Legitimacy and Economy in Deliberative Democracy', *Political Theory*, 29: 5, (2001), pp. 651–69, at p. 651.
32. Henry S. Richardson, *Democratic Autonomy: Public Reasoning about the Ends of Policy* (Oxford: Oxford University Press, 2002), pp. 62–5. Compare, as a small sample: John S. Dryzek, *Deliberative Democracy and Beyond: Liberals, Critics, Contestations* (Oxford: Oxford University Press, 2000); Jon Elster (ed.), *Deliberative Democracy* (Cambridge: Cambridge University Press, 1998); James S. Fishkin, *Democracy and Deliberation: New Directions for Democratic Reform* (New Haven and London: Yale University Press, 1991); *The Voice of the People: Public Opinion and Democracy* (New Haven and London: Yale University Press, 1995); James S. Fishkin and Peter Laslett (eds.), *Debating Deliberative Democracy* (Oxford: Blackwell, 2003); Robert E. Goodin, *Reflective Democracy* (Oxford: Oxford University Press, 2003); Amy Gutmann and Dennis Thompson, *Democracy and Disagreement* (Cambridge, MA: Harvard University Press, 1996); *Why Deliberative Democracy?* (Princeton and Oxford: Princeton University Press, 2004); and Jürgen Habermas, *Between Facts and Norms*, translated by William Rehg (Cambridge: Polity Press, 1996).
33. Dryzek, *Deliberative Democracy and Beyond*, 14.
34. Albert Weale, 'Contractarian Theory, Deliberative Democracy and General Agreement', in Keith Dowding, Robert E. Goodin, and

Carole Pateman (eds.), *Justice and Democracy: Essays for Brian Barry* (Cambridge: Cambridge University Press, 2004), pp. 79–96. For a fuller exposition of this argument see Weale, *Modern Social Contract Theory* (forthcoming).

35. Amartya Sen, *The Idea of Justice* (London: Penguin Books, 2009), p. 90.
36. Sen, *The Idea of Justice*, p. 326.
37. Cohen, 'Deliberation and Democratic Legitimacy', p. 20.
38. Kenneth J. Arrow, 'Gifts and Exchanges', *Philosophy and Public Affairs*, 1: 4, (1972), pp. 343–62, at p. 357.
39. Robert D. Putnam, *Making Democracy Work* (Princeton: Princeton University Press, 1993), p. 183.
40. Barrington Moore, Jr, *Injustice: The Social Bases of Obedience and Revolt* (London and Basingstoke: Macmillan, 1978), pp. 16, 22, 32 and 26 respectively.
41. Oran Young, *International Cooperation* (Ithaca, NY: Cornell University Press, 1989), p. 5. For the idea of society as a system of rules, roles, and relations, see Dorothy Emmet, *Rules, Roles and Relations* (London: Macmillan, 1966).
42. H.L.A. Hart, *The Concept of Law*, second edition (Oxford: Clarendon Press, 1994).
43. On positional goods, see Fred Hirsch, *The Social Limits to Growth* (London and Henley: Routledge and Kegan Paul, 1977). For relative deprivation, see W.G. Runciman, *Relative Deprivation and Social Justice: A Study of Attitudes to Social Inequality in Twentieth-Century England* (London, Boston, and Henley: Routledge & Kegan Paul, 1966). The housing example is used in Robert H. Frank, *Luxury Fever: Weighing the Cost of Excess* (Princeton and Oxford: Princeton University Press, 1999).
44. Grice, *The Grounds of Moral Judgement*, p. 100.
45. Gauthier, *Morals by Agreement*, p. 4.
46. Mill, *The Subjection of Women*, p. 478.
47. I have drawn this conception from: Elizabeth S. Anderson, 'What Is the Point of Equality?', *Ethics*, 109: 2, (1999), pp. 287–337, pp. 312–15; David Miller, *Principles of Social Justice* (Cambridge, MA: Harvard University Press, 1999), pp. 239–44; W.G. Runciman, *Sociology in Its Place and Other Essays* (Cambridge University Press, 1970), Chapter 9; and Michael Walzer, *Spheres of Justice: A Defence of Pluralism and Equality* (Oxford: Martin Robertson, 1983), Chapter 11.
48. Herbert A. Simon, *Reason in Human Affairs* (Oxford: Basil Blackwell, 1983), pp. 17–23.
49. Herbert A. Simon, *Administrative Behavior: A Study of Decision-Making Processes in Administrative Organizations*, forward by Chester

I. Barnard, third edition (New York: The Free Press, 1976), Chapter V; *Reason in Human Affairs* (Oxford: Basil Blackwell, 1983), pp. 17–23.

50. Graham Allison and Philip Zelikow, *Essence of Decision*, second edition (New York: Longman, 1999), p. 307.
51. G.L.S. Shackle, *Decision Order and Time in Human Affairs*, second edition (Cambridge: Cambridge University Press, 1969), p. 291. Compare G.L.S. Shackle, *Imagination and the Nature of Choice* (Edinburgh: Edinburgh University Press, 1979), p. 98.
52. Rawls, *A Theory of Justice*, pp. 26–7.
53. H.L.A. Hart, 'Between Utility and Rights' in H.L.A. Hart, *Essays in Jurisprudence and Philosophy* (Oxford: Clarendon Press, 1983), pp. 198–222.
54. P.S. Atiyah, *The Rise and Fall of Freedom of Contract* (Oxford: Clarendon Press, 1979); W.H. Greenleaf, *The British Political Tradition: Volume Two The Ideological Heritage* (London: Methuen & Co., 1983).
55. Cited in Greenleaf, *The British Political Tradition*, p. 274.
56. Graham Wallas, 'Property under Socialism', in G. Bernard Shaw (ed.) *Fabian Essays in Socialism* (London: Walter Scott, Limited, 1899), pp. 131–49, at p. 135.
57. Wallas, 'Property under Socialism', p. 134.
58. See the discussion of liberal, conservative and socialist writers in Greenleaf, *The British Political Tradition*, Chapters 5, 7, and 13. See also Samuel Brittan, *Left or Right: The Bogus Dilemma* (London: Secker & Warburg, 1968); *Capitalism with a Human Face* (Hammersmith, London: Fontana Press, 1996).
59. Albert Weale, *Equality and Social Policy* (London, Henley and Boston: Routledge & Kegan Paul, 1978).
60. Brian Barry, *Why Social Justice Matters* (Cambridge: Polity Press, 2005).
61. David Braybrooke, 'Social Contract Theory's Fanciest Flight', *Ethics*, 97: 4, (1987), pp. 750–64, at pp. 750–1. For reasons that will become apparent in section 3.6, there is in fact a substantial collectivist element in Gauthier's theory with respect to the question of economic rent.
62. Rawls, *A Theory of Justice*, pp. xiv–xvi.
63. Martin O'Neill and Thad Williamson, 'Introduction' in Martin O'Neill and Thad Williamson (eds.) *Property-Owning Democracy: Rawls and Beyond* (Chichester: Wiley-Blackwell, 2012), pp. 1–14, at p. 5.

Chapter 2

1. Ken Binmore, *Playing Fair: Game Theory and the Social Contract Volume I* (Cambridge, MA and London: The MIT Press, 1994), p. 71.

2. John Horton, 'Political Legitimacy, Justice and Consent', *Critical Review of International Social and Political Philosophy*, 15: 2, (2012), pp. 129–48, at pp. 135–6.
3. Barrington Moore, Jr, *Injustice: The Social Bases of Obedience and Revolt* (London and Basingstoke: Macmillan, 1978).
4. John Rawls, *Political Liberalism: With a New Introduction and 'Reply to Habermas'* (New York: Columbia University Press, 1996), p. 23.
5. Albert Weale, 'Contractarian Theory, Deliberative Democracy and General Agreement', in Keith Dowding, Robert E. Goodin, and Carole Pateman (eds.), *Justice and Democracy: Essays for Brian Barry* (Cambridge: Cambridge University Press, 2004), pp. 79–96. My intention is to justify this characterization in detail in Albert Weale, *Modern Social Contract Theory*, forthcoming.
6. John Stuart Mill, *The Subjection of Women*, originally 1869, reprinted in John Gray (ed.) *John Stuart Mill On Liberty and Other Essays* (Oxford: Oxford University Press, 1991), p. 478.
7. Amartya Sen, *The Idea of Justice* (London: Penguin Books, 2009).
8. J.L. Hyland, *Democratic Theory: The Philosophical Foundations* (Manchester: Manchester University Press, 1995), pp. 49–50.
9. Joseph M. Bessette, *The Mild Voice of Reason: Deliberative Democracy and American National Government* (Chicago: Chicago University Press, 1982).
10. Jürg Steiner, André Bächtiger, Markus Spörndli, and Marco. R. Steenbergen, *Deliberative Politics in Action: Analyzing Parliamentary Discourse* (Cambridge: Cambridge University Press, 2004).
11. Brian Barry, *Theories of Justice* (London: Harvester-Wheatsheaf, 1989), pp. 347–8.
12. Brian Barry, *Justice as Impartiality* (Oxford: Oxford University Press, 1995), pp. 100 and 104.
13. Barry, *Justice as Impartiality*, p. 106.
14. A.P.S. Woodhouse (ed.), *Puritanism and Liberty: Being the Army Debates (1647–49) from the Clarke Manuscripts*, new preface by Ivan Roots (London: J.M. Dent & Sons Ltd, 1986), pp. 53–6.
15. Hannah Arendt, *On Revolution* (Harmondsworth: Penguin Books), 1973, p. 174. For an excellent discussion of Hannah Arendt's account of social contract theory, see Helmut Dubiel, 'Hannah Arendt and the Theory of Democracy: A Critical Reconstruction', in Peter Graf Kielmannsegg, Horst Mewes, and Elisabeth Glaser-Schmidt (eds.), *Hannah Arendt and Leo Strauss: German Emigrés and American Political Thought after World War II* (Cambridge: German Historical Institute, Washington D.C. and Cambridge University Press, 1995), pp. 11–28.

16. Alexander Meiklejohn, *Political Freedom: The Constitutional Powers of the People* (New York: Harper and Brothers, 1960), pp. 15–27. For a delightful study of how the New England town meetings can be seen as models of democracy without over-idealizing them, see Frank M. Bryan, *Real Democracy: The New England Town Meeting and How It Works* (Chicago and London: The University of Chicago Press, 2004). On rates of participation in the town meetings, see Joseph F. Zimmerman, *The New England Town Meeting: Democracy in Action* (Westport, Connecticut: Praeger, 1999).
17. Rawls, *Political Liberalism*, pp. 231–40. Compare also Rawls's saying that the idea of the four-stage sequence was suggested by the United States Constitution and its history, John Rawls, *A Theory of Justice: Revised Edition* (Oxford: Oxford University Press, 1999), p. 172, n.1.
18. Kenneth A. Bollen and Robert W. Jackman, 'Economic and Non-economic Determinants of Political Democracy in the 1960s', *Research in Political Sociology*, 1, (1985), pp. 27–48.
19. Matravers, Matt, *Justice and Punishment: The Rationale of Coercion* (Oxford: Oxford University Press, 2000), p. 100.
20. For these criteria, see Robert A. Dahl, *On Democracy* (New Haven and London: Yale University Press, 1998), Chapter 4 and Albert Weale, *Democracy*, second edition (Houndmills, Basingstoke: Palgrave Macmillan, 2007), pp. 18–23.
21. Peter J. Katzenstein, *Small States in World Markets: Industrial Policy in Europe* (Ithaca, NY: Cornell University Press, 1985).
22. F.A. Hayek, *Law, Legislation and Liberty, Volume 1, Rules and Order* (London: Routledge, 1973); *Law, Legislation and Liberty, Volume 2, The Mirage of Social Justice* (London: Routledge, 1976); *Law, Legislation and Liberty, Volume 3, The Political Order of a Free People* (London: Routledge, 1979); Michael Oakeshott, *On Human Conduct* (Oxford: Clarendon Press, 1975); Robert Nozick, *Anarchy, State and Utopia* (Oxford: Basil Blackwell, 1974), chapter 5.
23. Oakeshott, *On Human Conduct*, p. 131.
24. Weale, *Democracy*, p. 56–9.
25. Henry Sidgwick, *The Elements of Politics* (London: Macmillan, 1891), pp. 324–32.
26. This is so, whatever the substantive merit of its views. Isaiah Berlin once claimed that 'men of imagination, originality and creative genius, and, indeed, minorities of all kinds, were less persecuted' in the Prussia of Frederick the Great or the Austria of Josef II than in many earlier or later democracies, Isaiah Berlin, *Four Essays on Liberty* (Oxford: Oxford University Press, 1969), pp. 129–30. So far as I am aware, this claim has never been subjected to thorough statistical test.

My own guess is that the best one can hope for from states without an obligation of democratic accountability is a form of soft authoritarianism, and those would be rare cases.

27. See Dahl, *On Democracy*, p. 38.
28. John Stuart Mill, *Considerations on Representative Government*, original edition 1861, in *On Liberty and Other Essays*, edited with an introduction by John Gray (Oxford: Oxford University Press, 1991), pp. 203–467, at p. 335. Compare Charles R. Beitz, *Political Equality* (Princeton: Princeton University Press, 1989), pp. 32–40.
29. By contrast, say, with the approach found in Thomas Christiano, *The Constitution of Equality: Democratic Authority and Its Limits* (Oxford: Oxford University Press, 2008).
30. Jean-Jacques Rousseau, *The Social Contract*, originally 1762, translated by G.D.H. Cole (London: J.M. Dent and Sons, 1973), p. 247.
31. For accounts of common property resource regimes, see in particular Fikret Berkes (ed.), *Common Property Resources: Ecology and Community-Based Sustainable Development* (London: Belhaven Press, 1989); E. Walter Coward Jr (ed.), *Irrigation and Agricultural Development in Asia; Perspectives from the Social Sciences* (Ithaca and London: Cornell University Press, 1980); Elinor Ostrom, *Governing the Commons: The Evolution of Institutions for Collective Action* (Cambridge: Cambridge University Press, 1990); Robert Wade, *Village Republics: Economic Conditions for Collective Action in South India* (Cambridge: Cambridge University Press, 1988), as well as other sources cited in the discussion.
32. Ostrom, *Governing the Commons*.
33. Garrett Hardin, 'The Tragedy of the Commons', *Science*, 162: 3859, (1968), pp. 1243–8.
34. Fikret Berkes, 'Fishermen and "The Tragedy of the Commons"', *Environmental Conservation*, 12: 3, (1985), pp. 199–206.
35. Ken Binmore, 'Bargaining and Morality' in David Gauthier and Robert Sugden (eds.), *Rationality, Justice and the Social Contract: Themes from Morals by Agreement* (New York: Havester-Wheatsheaf, 1993), pp. 131–56; *Playing Fair*. The latter discusses the various fallacies by which people have sought to get around this tautological feature.
36. Ostrom, *Governing the* Commons, pp. 18–21. See also Fikret Berkes, 'Local-level Management and the Commons Problem: A Comparative Study of Turkish Fisheries', *Marine Policy*, 10: 3, (1986), pp. 215–29, at pp. 221–2, which introduces the example.
37. Oran Young, *International Cooperation* (Ithaca, NY: Cornell University Press, 1989), p. 5.

38. Ostrom, *Governing the* Commons, pp. 62, 65, and 69 respectively. Note that Robert McC. Netting, *Balancing on an Alp: Ecological Change and Continuity in a Swiss Mountain Community* (Cambridge: Cambridge University Press, 1981), p. 60 says that Törbel was regulating its affairs by written statute by 1473.
39. Wade, *Village Republics*, pp. 14 and 183–7.
40. Ostrom, *Governing the Commons*, p. 90.
41. Ostrom, *Governing the Commons*, p. 31.
42. Ostrom, *Governing the Commons*, pp. 60–1.
43. Netting, *Balancing on an Alp*, p. 46.
44. Wade, *Village Republics*.
45. Ostrom, *Governing the Commons*, p. 33.
46. Berkes, 'Local Level Management and the Commons Problem', pp. 222 and 227.
47. Wade, *Village Republics*, pp. 28 and 55.
48. S.E. Finer, *The History of Government: Volume II The Intermediate Ages* (Oxford: Oxford University Press, 1999), Chapter 7.
49. David Hume, *Enquiry Concerning the Principles of Morals*, originally 1751, reprinted in *Essays, Moral, Political, and Literary by David Hume*, edited by T.H. Green and T.H. Grose (London: Longmans, Green, and Co., 1889), pp. 167–287; H.L.A. Hart, *The Concept of Law*, second edition (Oxford: Clarendon Press, 1994), pp. 193–200; J.R. Lucas, *The Principles of Politics* (Oxford: Clarendon Press, 1966); Rawls, *A Theory of Justice*, pp. 109–12.
50. Hume, *Enquiry*, p. 179.
51. Karl Marx, *Capital: A Critique of Political Economy, Volume One*, fourth edition, 1890, translated by Ben Fowkes (Harmondworth: Penguin Books, 1976), pp. 169–70.
52. Adam Smith, *An Enquiry into the Nature and Causes of the Wealth of Nations*, originally 1776 (Oxford: Clarendon Press, 1976 edition), p. 27.
53. Hume, *Enquiry*, pp. 167–287, at p. 182.
54. Hume, *Enquiry*, p. 183.
55. Ostrom, *Governing the Commons*, p. 26.
56. Netting, *Balancing on an Alp*, p. 46.
57. Berkes, 'Fishermen and "The Tragedy of the Commons"'.
58. Wade, *Village Republics*, pp. 155–6.
59. Wade, *Village Republics*, pp. 72–82.
60. A further reason why we may take common pool resource regimes as modelling a contract for justice is that, to the extent to which they achieve environmental sustainability, they help maintain the obligations

of justice that one generation has to subsequent generations. The communities in which the resource regimes are established are stable and persist over time, so that costly investment at one time carries the expectation of return at a later time for the members of that community. The exact logic at work here is hard to identify. It may be that stable communities are also traditional communities, so that techniques that work for one generation are embodied in traditions that are passed down from one generation to the next, making for a type of Burkean inter-generational contract. Alternatively, sustainability in the medium term may turn into longer-run sustainability through a pattern of overlapping generations in which the set of individuals who make up a community at any one time steadily changes in composition but with sufficient continuity such that all gain within their lifetimes. However sustainability is achieved, it expresses a logic in which collectively agreed mutual advantage secures benefits over the long term.

61. Barry, *Theories of Justice*, pp. 160–3.
62. Christopher Hill, *Puritanism and Revolution: Studies in Interpretation of the English Revolution of the 17th Century* (London: Panther Books, 1968), Chapter 3.
63. Thomas Jefferson, 'Notes on the State of Virginia, 1787' Query XIX in *The Portable Thomas Jefferson* (Harmondsworth: Penguin Books, 1977), p. 157. Hill, *Puritanism and Revolution*, p. 98, citing Chinard, who also makes reference to the Narodniks, p. 118.
64. Barry, *Justice as Impartiality*, p. 106.
65. The next few paragraphs draw upon Albert Weale, 'Contractarian Theory, Deliberative Democracy and General Agreement', in K. Dowding, R.E. Goodin, and C. Pateman (eds.), *Justice and Democracy: Essays for Brian Barry* (Cambridge: Cambridge University Press, 2004), pp. 79–96, especially pp. 86–7.
66. For Saltaire see the excellent Saltaire Village Website: http://www.saltairevillage.info/ (last accessed 30 December 2012). On New Earswick, see Nicholas Pevsner, *The Buildings of England. Yorkshire: The North Riding* (Harmondsworth: Penguin, 1966), pp. 266–7 and: http://www.jrht.org.uk/communities/new-earswick/history-of-new-earswick (last accessed 30 December 2012). For Letchworth and Welwyn Garden City, see Nicholas Pevsner, *The Buildings of England. Hertfordshire*, second edition revised by Bridget Cherry (New Haven and London: Yale University Press, 1977), pp. 224–5 and p. 396.
67. Mary Hesse, 'Models and Analogy in Science' in Paul Edwards (ed.), *The Encyclopedia of Philosophy* (London and New York: Macmillan Publishing and The Free Press, 1967), volume 5, pp. 354–59.

68. See the discussion on this formal sense of model in Ernest Nagel and James R. Newman, *Gödel's Proof* (New York: New York University Press, 1958), who note Bertrand Russell's famous epigram about pure mathematics thought of in an axiomatized way, that it is the only subject in which we do not know what we are talking about or whether what we say is true.
69. David M. Estlund, *Democratic Authority: A Philosophical Framework* (Princeton and Oxford: Princeton University Press, 2008), Chapter XIII.
70. Rawls, *Political Liberalism*, 89–90.
71. P.J.D. Wiles, *Economic Institutions Compared* (Oxford: Basil Blackwell, 1977). pp. 99–102.
72. Rawls, *A Theory of Justice*, p. 111 and pp. 255–6.
73. Susan Moller Okin, *Justice, Gender, and the Family* (New York: Basic Books, Inc., 1989).

Chapter 3

1. Jean-Jacques Rousseau, *Discourse on the Origin and the Foundations of Inequality among Men* in *Jean-Jacques Rousseau: The First and Second Discourses*, originally 1755, edited, translated, and annotated by Victor Gourevitch (New York: Harper & Row, 1986), p. 170.
2. Thomas Hobbes, *Leviathan*, originally 1651, edited with an introduction by Michael Oakeshott (Oxford: Basil Blackwell, n.d.), p. 82.
3. John Locke, *Two Treatises of Government*, originally 1690, edited Peter Laslett (New York: Mentor, 1965), Chapter V; Thomas Hodgskin, *The Natural and Artificial Right of Property Contrasted*, originally 1832, (Clifton, New Jersey: A.M. Kelley, 1973); Robert Nozick, *Anarchy, State and Utopia* (Oxford: Basil Blackwell, 1974), p. 166.
4. John Stuart Mill, *Principles of Political Economy with Some of Their Applications to Social Philosophy, Books I–II*, originally 1871, Introduction by V.W. Bladen, textual editor J.M. Robson (Toronto and Buffalo: University of Toronto Press, 1965), pp. 199–200.
5. John Rawls, *A Theory of Justice: Revised Edition* (Oxford: Oxford University Press, 1999), p. 87.
6. David Gauthier, *Morals by Agreement* (Oxford: Clarendon Press, 1986), especially at pp. 272–80.
7. Robert McC. Netting, *Balancing on an Alp: Ecological Change and Continuity in a Swiss Mountain Community* (Cambridge: Cambridge University Press, 1981), p. 15.

8. Fikret Berkes, 'Local-level Management and the Commons Problem: A Comparative Study of Turkish Fisheries', *Marine Policy*, 10: 3, (1986), pp. 215–29.
9. Robert Wade, *Village Republics: Economic Conditions for Collective Action in South India* (Cambridge: Cambridge University Press, 1988).
10. For these examples, see Elinor Ostrom, *Governing the Commons: The Evolution of Institutions for Collective Action* (Cambridge: Cambridge University Press, 1990).
11. Netting, *Balancing on an Alp*, p. 60.
12. Berkes, 'Local-level Management and the Commons Problem'.
13. Hobbes, *Leviathan*, p. 81.
14. Hobbes, *Leviathan*, p. 85, importantly cited by Gauthier, *Morals by Agreement*, p. 159.
15. David Hume, *Enquiry Concerning the Principles of Morals*, originally 1751, reprinted in *Essays, Moral, Political, and Literary by David Hume*, edited by T.H. Green and T.H. Grose (London: Longmans, Green, and Co., 1889), pp. 167–287, at p. 185.
16. W.N. Hohfeld, *Fundamental Legal Conceptions* (New Haven: Yale University Press, 1923).
17. Locke, *Two Treatises*, Chapter V.
18. Michael Lipton, *Land Reform in Developing Countries: Property Rights and Property Wrongs* (London and New York, 2009), 50–1.
19. Rawls, *A Theory of Justice*, p. 87.
20. Abhinay Muthoo, *Bargaining Theory with Applications* (Cambridge: Cambridge University Press, 1999), pp. 336–8.
21. Thomas C. Schelling, *The Strategy of Conflict* (London: Oxford University Press, 1960), p. 75.
22. H.L.A. Hart, 'Are There Any Natural Rights?' *Philosophical Review* 64: 2, (1955), pp. 175–91, reprinted in Anthony Quinton (ed.), *Political Philosophy* (Oxford: Oxford University Press, 1967), pp. 53–66, at p. 61.
23. Locke, *Two Treatises*, p. 330.
24. Locke, *Two Treatises*, p. 330.
25. The move from 'no injustice' to 'no need to require permission of others' is rather too quick. All may have an interest in conserving their labour and not wasting it in a fruitless search for what others are going to appropriate, even when they recognize that others will have the right to appropriate should they get to the resource first. Even if there really is enough and as good for all to appropriate, all will often benefit from coordinating their efforts. Considerations other than justice may imply a right for the community to exercise control over the appropriation of individuals.

26. Locke, *Two Treatises*, p. 332.
27. Locke, *Two Treatises*, p. 333.
28. Hodgskin, *The Natural and Artificial Right of Property Contrasted*, pp. 24–6.
29. Hodgskin, *The Natural and Artificial Right of Property Contrasted*, pp. 61–2.
30. Hodgskin, *The Natural and Artificial Right of Property Contrasted*, p. 41.
31. Anton Menger, *The Right to the Whole Produce of Labour: The Origin and Development of Labour's Claim to the Whole Product of Industry*, translated by M.E. Tanner with an Introduction and Bibliography by H.S. Foxwell, (London: Macmillan, 1899), pp. 5–6.
32. For the notion of full liberal ownership and alternatives, see A.M. Honoré, 'Ownership' in A.G. Guest (ed.) *Oxford Essays in Jurisprudence* (Oxford: Oxford University Press, 1961), pp. 107–47.
33. Rawls, *A Theory of Justice*, 266.
34. Rawls, *A Theory of Justice*, pp. 54 and 65.
35. Nozick, *Anarchy, State and Utopia*, p. 155.
36. Rawls, *A Theory of Justice*, p. 89. Italics added.
37. John Rawls, *A Theory of Justice* (Oxford: Oxford University Press, 1972), p. 104.
38. In connection with this line of argument, it is worth noting Musgrave's comment that implementation of maximin leads to a redistributive system that, among individuals with a high earnings capacity, favours those who have a preference for leisure. See R.A. Musgrave, 'Maximin, Uncertainty, and the leisure Trade-Off', *Quarterly Journal of Economics*, 88: 4, (1974), pp. 625–32, at p. 632.
39. Nozick, *Anarchy, State and Utopia*, p. 169.
40. Albert Weale, 'Justice, Social Union and the Separateness of Persons' in David Gauthier and Robert Sugden (eds.), *Rationality, Justice and the Social Contract: Themes from Morals by Agreement* (New York: Havester-Wheatsheaf, 1993), pp. 75–94, at pp. 81–2.
41. Rawls, *A Theory of Justice*, revised edition, p. 87.
42. G.A. Cohen, *If You're an Egalitarian, How Come You're So Rich?* (Cambridge, MA and London: Harvard University Press, 2000), pp. 126–7; compare G.A. Cohen, *Rescuing Justice and Equality* (Cambridge, MA and London: Harvard University Press, 2008), Chapter 1.
43. Menger, *The Right to the Whole Produce of Labour*, pp. 165–6. See also Albert Fried, *Socialism in America: From the Shakers to the Third International* (New York: Columbia University Press, 1992), pp. 26–30.
44. G.A. Cohen, *Why Not Socialism?* (Princeton and Oxford: Princeton University Press, 2009). Compare Miriam Ronzoni, 'Life Is Not a

Camping Trip—On the Desirability of Cohenite Socialism', *Politics, Philosophy and Economics*, 11: 2, (2012), pp. 171–85.
45. Gauthier, *Morals by Agreement*.
46. It is not clear to me that there is no equivalent of rent in a Crusoe-type economy. Suppose one would climb the tree to shake down the coconuts for four coconuts, and eight will actually come down. Suppose also that you know this in advance. Is this not a form of rent?
47. Gauthier, *Morals by Agreement*, p. 276.
48. Gauthier originally thought that the solution to the bargain would respect the principle of minimax relative concession, according to which each party to the contract concedes an equal proportionate loss of the surplus earned through cooperation, although he subsequently conceded that a solution should be consistent with the Nash product. See *Morals by Agreement*, Chapter V and David Gauthier, 'Uniting Separate Persons' in David Gauthier and Robert Sugden (eds.), *Rationality, Justice and the Social Contract: Themes from Morals by Agreement* (New York: Havester-Wheatsheaf, 1993), pp. 176–92, at pp. 177–8. However, this point does not bear on the argument about the justifiability of rent; it would merely be a different principle for distributing rent were there such a case to be made.
49. Weale, 'Justice, Social Union and the Separateness of Persons'.
50. Abram Bergson, 'Market Socialism Revisited', *Journal of Political Economy*, 75: 5, (1967), pp. 655–73, at pp. 662–3.
51. David Braybrooke, 'Social Contract Theory's Fanciest Flight', *Ethics*, 97: 4, (1987), pp. 750–64.
52. Ronald Dworkin, 'What Is Equality? Part 2: Equality of Resources', *Philosophy and Public Affairs*, 10: 4, (1981), pp. 283–345, reprinted in *Sovereign Virtue: The Theory and Practice of Equality* (Cambridge, MA: Harvard University Press, 2000), Chapter 2.
53. Dworkin, *Sovereign Virtue*, pp. 73–4.
54. Keith Dowding, 'Luck, Equality and Responsibility', *Critical Review of International Social and Political Philosophy*, 13: 1, (2010), pp. 71–92, especially p. 81.
55. David Miller, *Principles of Social Justice* (Cambridge, MA: Harvard University Press, 1999), pp. 61–92; 203–29.
56. Menger, whose discussion still has much to commend it, thought that the historical tendency was to give priority to the right to subsistence, *The Right to the Whole Produce of Labour*, p. 176.
57. Cohen, *If You're an Egalitarian, How Come You're So Rich?*, p. 108.

Chapter 4

1. S.E. Finer, *Comparative Government* (Harmondsworth: Penguin, 1970), p. 15. The centrality of disagreement to the practise of politics has been stressed by Richard Bellamy, *Political Constitutionalism: A Republican Defence of the Constitutionality of Democracy* (Cambridge: Cambridge University Press, 2007) and Jeremy Waldron, *Law and Disagreement* (Oxford: Oxford University Press, 1999), pp. 101–3.
2. For the idea of compossibility in political theory, see Hillel Steiner, *An Essay on Rights* (Oxford: Blackwell, 1994), Chapter 3(c).
3. John Stuart Mill, *Utilitarianism*, originally 1861, in *On Liberty and Other Essays*, edited with an introduction by John Gray (Oxford: Oxford University Press, 1991), pp. 129–201, p. 190. Compare, H.L.A. Hart, 'Between Utility and Rights' in H.L.A. Hart, *Essays in Jurisprudence and Philosophy* (Oxford: Clarendon Press, 1983), pp. 198–222, at pp. 187–91.
4. Barrington Moore, Jr, *Injustice: The Social Bases of Obedience and Revolt* (London and Basingstoke: Macmillan, 1978).
5. Mancur Olson, *Power and Prosperity: Outgrowing Communist and Capitalist Dictatorships* (New York: Basic Books, 2000), pp. 6–12.
6. Cited in Christopher Hill, *Puritanism and Revolution: Studies in Interpretation of the English Revolution of the 17th Century* (London: Panther Books, 1968), p. 103.
7. Amartya Sen, *The Idea of Justice* (London: Penguin Books, 2009), Chapters 12 and 13.
8. For a pure version of this approach, see Ken Binmore, *Playing Fair: Game Theory and the Social Contract Volume I* (Cambridge, MA and London: The MIT Press, 1994) and *Just Playing: Game Theory and the Social Contract Volume II* (Cambridge, MA and London: The MIT Press, 1998). Gauthier generally relies upon the pure theory, but departs from it in his distinction between choice and preference: David Gauthier, *Morals by Agreement* (Oxford: Clarendon Press, 1986), pp. 29–32. For an orthodox criticism of this approach, see Ken Binmore, 'Bargaining and Morality' in David Gauthier and Robert Sugden (eds.), *Rationality, Justice and the Social Contract: Themes from Morals by Agreement* (New York: Havester-Wheatsheaf, 1993), pp. 131–56.
9. As in John C. Harsanyi, *Essays on Ethics, Social Behavior, and Scientific Explanation* (Dordrecht: D. Reidel, 1976), despite his being a contract theorist only in an extended sense.

10. Brian Barry, *Theories of Justice* (London: Harvester-Wheatsheaf, 1989) and *Justice as Impartiality* (Oxford: Oxford University Press, 1995); T.M. Scanlon, 'Contractualism and Utilitarianism' in Amartya Sen and Bernard Williams (eds.), *Utilitarianism and Beyond* (Cambridge: Cambridge University Press, 1982), pp. 101–28.
11. Donald Davidson, 'How Is Weakness of the Will Possible?' in Joel Feinberg (ed.), *Moral Concepts* (Oxford: Oxford University Press, 1969), pp. 93–133; Russell Grice, *The Grounds of Moral Judgement* (Cambridge: Cambridge University Press, 1967), pp. 10–12.
12. Aristotle, *The Nicomachean Ethics*, revised edition, translated by H. Rackham (Cambridge, MA and London: Harvard University Press, 1934), 1112a, 17, pp. 132–3.
13. G.H. von Wright, 'On So-Called Practical Inference' in Joseph Raz (ed.), *Practical Reasoning* (Oxford: Oxford University Press, 1978), pp. 46–62.
14. Binmore, 'Bargaining and Morality', pp. 136–40; *Playing Fair*, p. 162.
15. For the importance of modelling the terms on which agents cooperate, as well as whether they cooperate, and therefore the relevance of the battle of the sexes game, see Fritz W. Scharpf, 'Decision Rules, Decision Styles, and Policy Choices', *Journal of Theoretical Politics*, 1: 2, pp. 149–76, especially p. 162.
16. Robert Axelrod, *The Evolution of Cooperation* (London: Penguin, 1984). For the conditions relating time-horizons to the willingness to cooperate, see Michael Taylor, *Anarchy and Cooperation* (London: John Wiley and Sons, 1976).
17. John Maynard Smith, *The Theory of Evolution* (Harmondsworth: Penguin, 1975). See also, Brian Skyrms, *Evolution of the Social Contract* (Cambridge: Cambridge University Press, 1996) and Robert Sugden, *The Economics of Rights, Co-operation and Welfare* (Oxford: Basil Blackwell, 1986).
18. von Wright, 'On So-Called Practical Inference', p. 57.
19. Anthony Kenny, *Will, Freedom and Power* (Oxford: Basil Blackwell, 1975), Chapter V.
20. Joseph Raz, 'Introduction' in Joseph Raz (ed.), *Practical Reasoning* (Oxford: Oxford University Press, 1978), pp. 1–17, at p. 11.
21. Respectively Hannah Arendt, *The Human Condition* (Chicago: University of Chicago Press, 1958), p. 178 and G.L.S. Shackle, *Imagination and the Nature of Choice* (Edinburgh: Edinburgh University Press, 1979), p. 10. There must be an article to be written comparing two such contrasting thinkers who both make creativity the centrepiece of their account of human action!

22. Kenny, *Will, Freedom and Power*, p. 20.
23. Matthew L. Ginsberg, 'AI and Nonmonotonic Reasoning' in Dov M. Gabbay, C.J. Hogger, J.A. Robinson, and D. Nute (eds.), *Handbook of Logic in Artificial Intelligence and Logic Programming: Volume 3, Nonmonotonic Reasoning and Uncertain Reasoning* (Oxford: Clarendon Press, 1994), pp. 1–33, at p. 3.
24. Some writers refer to it as 'monotony' but this has an unfortunate resonance and does not accord with the name of an analogous property in social choice theory.
25. Ginsberg, 'AI and Nonmonotonic Reasoning'; Isaac Levi, *For the Sake of the Argument: Ramsey Test Conditionals, Inductive Inference, and Nonmonotonic Reasoning* (Cambridge: Cambridge University Press, 1996); Witold Łukaszewicz, *Non-Monotonic Reasoning: Formalization of Commonsense Reasoning* (New York: Ellis Horwood, 1990); David Makinson, 'General Patterns in Nonmonotonic Reasoning' in Dov M. Gabbay, C.J. Hogger, J.A. Robinson, and D. Nute (eds.), *Handbook of Logic in Artificial Intelligence and Logic Programming, Volume 3, Nonmonotonic Reasoning and Uncertain Reasoning* (Oxford: Clarendon Press, 1994), pp. 35–110; and Donal Nute, 'Defeasible Logic' in Dov M. Gabbay, C.J. Hogger, J.A. Robinson and D. Nute (eds.), *Handbook of Logic in Artificial Intelligence and Logic Programming, Volume 3, Nonmonotonic Reasoning and Uncertain Reasoning* (Oxford: Clarendon Press, 1994), pp. 353–95.
26. For a valuable classification of a range of cases, see Łukaszewicz, *Non-Monotonic Reasoning*, pp. 84–7.
27. Robert B. Brandom, *Making It Explicit* (Cambridge, MA: Havard University Press, 2000), pp. 87–9.
28. Nute, 'Defeasible Logic', p. 363.
29. Thomas C. Schelling, *The Strategy of Conflict* (London: Oxford University Press, 1960).
30. I am indebted here to Brian Barry, *Democracy, Power and Justice: Essays in Political Theory* (Oxford: Clarendon Press, 1989), Chapters 8 and 11, and to Peter Morriss, *Power: A Philosophical Analysis* (Manchester: Manchester University Press, 1988).
31. For the refinements of this analysis, see Steven Lukes, *Power: A Radical View*, second edition (Houndmills Basingstoke: Palgrave Macmillan, 2005).
32. David Hume, 'Of the First Principles of Government' in *Essays, Moral, Political, and Literary*, originally 1742, edited T.H. Green and T.H. Grose (London: Longmans, Green and Co., 1889 edition), pp. 109–13, at p. 110.

33. For the notion of harm as a setback to interests, see Joel Feinberg, *The Moral Limits of the Criminal Law, Volume One: Harm to Others* (Oxford: Oxford University Press, 1984), Chapter 1.
34. Schelling, *The Strategy of Conflict*, p. 6.
35. Joseph S. Nye, *The Paradox of American Power* (Oxford: Oxford University Press, 2002).
36. Jürgen Habermas, *Between Facts and Norms*, translated by William Rehg (Cambridge: Polity Press, 1996), pp. 15–16.
37. Butler's idea seems to be that there are only certain frames of mind in which important truths can be understood. See, for example, Joseph Butler, *Fifteen Sermons Preached at the Rolls Chapel*, originally 1726, with Introduction, Analyses, and Notes by The Very Rev. W.R. Matthews (London: G. Bell & Sons Ltd, 1969), Sermon XI, 'Upon the Love of Our Neighbour', paragraph 20.
38. Compare Gauthier, *Morals by Agreement*, 143–4: 'Each person must be willing to entertain a concession in relation to a feasible concession point if its relative magnitude is no greater than that of the greatest concession that he supposes some rational person is willing to entertain', explicating this condition by saying that it 'expresses the equal rationality of the bargainers. Since each person, as a utility-maximizer, seeks to minimize his concession, then no one can expect any other rational person to be willing to make a concession if he would not be willing to make a similar concession.'
39. Onora O'Neill, *Constructions of Reason: Explorations in Kant's Practical Philosophy* (Cambridge: Cambridge University Press, 1989), Chapter 2.
40. Albert Weale, *Democracy*, second edition, (Houndmills, Basingstoke: Palgrave Macmillan, 2007), Chapter 3.
41. Ostrom, Elinor, *Governing the Commons: The Evolution of Institutions for Collective Action* (Cambridge: Cambridge University Press, 1990), p. 31.
42. John Rawls, *Political Liberalism: With a New Introduction and 'Reply to Habermas'* (New York: Columbia University Press, 1996), p. 226.
43. Rawls, *Political Liberalism*, pp. xxiv–xxvii.
44. Hans Daalder, 'The Netherlands: Opposition in a Segmented Society', in Robert A. Dahl (ed.), *Political Opposition in Western Democracies* (New Haven and London: Yale University Press, 1966); Arend Lijphart, *The Politics of Accommodation: Pluralism and Democracy in the Netherlands* (Berkeley and Los Angeles: University of California Press, 1968).
45. Ian O'Flynn, *Deliberative Democracy and Divided Societies* (Edinburgh: Edinburgh University Press, 2006).

46. See David M. Estlund, *Democratic Authority: A Philosophical Framework* (Princeton and Oxford: Princeton University Press, 2008), especially Chapter II.
47. Henry S. Richardson, *Democratic Autonomy: Public Reasoning about the Ends of Policy* (Oxford: Oxford University Press, 2002), p. 76.
48. For a clear statement of the sceptical position, see J.L. Mackie, *Ethics: Inventing Right and Wrong* (Harmondsworth: Penguin Books, 1977), pp. 27–30. On 'justified, correct or well grounded' reasons, see Joseph Raz, *Practical Reason and Norms* (Princeton, New Jersey: Princeton University Press, 1990), p. 29.
49. Simone Chambers, 'Behind Closed Doors: Publicity, Secrecy, and the Quality of Deliberation', *Journal of Political Philosophy* 12: 4, (2004), pp. 389–410.
50. Ian Hacking, 'Lakatos's Philosophy of Science', in Ian Hacking (ed.), *Scientific Revolutions* (Oxford: Oxford University Press, 1981), pp. 128–43, p. 131. The whole essay is a *tour de force*.
51. Habermas, *Between Facts and Norms*, p. 15.
52. Charles Sanders Peirce, 'The Fixation of Belief' in *Collected Papers of Charles Sanders Peirce, Volumes V and VI*, edited by Charles Hartshorne and Paul Weiss (Cambridge, MA: Harvard University Press, 1934), pp. 223–47, at pp. 242–3. Compare A.J. Ayer, *The Origins of Pragmatism. Studies in the Philosophy of Charles Sanders Peirce and William James* (London and Basingstoke: Macmillan, 1968), pp. 17–40 and Mary Hesse, 'Science and Objectivity', in John B. Thompson and David Held (eds.), *Habermas: Critical Debates* (London and Basingstoke: Macmillan, 1982), pp. 98–115, at p. 98. For a more extended discussion of these arguments, see Weale, *Democracy*, pp. 83–90.
53. Richard Bevan Braithwaite, *Scientific Explanation: A Study of the Function of Theory, Probability and Law in Science* (Cambridge: Cambridge University Press, 1968), pp. 272–3.
54. John Stuart Mill, *Considerations on Representative Government*, original edition 1861, in *On Liberty and Other Essays*, edited with an introduction by John Gray (Oxford: Oxford University Press, 1991), pp. 203–467, Chapter III.
55. Ginsberg, 'AI and Nonmonotonic Reasoning', 5–7.
56. Amy Gutmann and Dennis Thompson, *Democracy and Disagreement* (Cambridge, MA: Harvard University Press, 1996), Chapter 2; *Why Deliberative Democracy?* (Princeton and Oxford: Princeton University Press, 2004), pp. 178–81.
57. Gutmann and Thompson, *Why Deliberative Democracy?*, p. 29.

Chapter 5

1. Rawls, John *A Theory of Justice: Revised Edition* (Oxford: Oxford University Press, 1999), p. xv.
2. Robert Wade, *Village Republics: Economic Conditions for Collective Action in South India* (Cambridge: Cambridge University Press, 1988).
3. F.A. Hayek, *Law, Legislation and Liberty, Volume II, The Mirage of Social Justice* (London: Routledge, 1976), p. 67.
4. For the centrality of the concept of the rule of law in Hayek and other neo-liberal writers, see Raymond Plant, *The Neo-Liberal State* (Oxford: Clarendon Press, 2010), Chapter 2.
5. Hayek, *Law, Legislation and Liberty, Volume I, Rules and Order* (London: Routledge, 1973), pp. 8–9.
6. Hayek, *Law, Legislation and Liberty, Volume I*, p. 9.
7. Hayek, *Law, Legislation and Liberty, Volume I*, p. 20.
8. Hayek, *Law, Legislation and Liberty, Volume I*, p. 14.
9. Hayek, *Law, Legislation and Liberty, Volume I*, p. 150, n. 19.
10. P.S. Atiyah, *The Rise and Fall of Freedom of Contract* (Oxford: Clarendon Press, 1979), pp. 562–7.
11. Hayek, *Law, Legislation and Liberty, Volume II*, p. 100.
12. F.A. Hayek, *The Constitution of Liberty* (London and Henley: Routledge & Kegan Paul, 1960), pp. 285–6.
13. Hayek, *Law, Legislation and Liberty, Volume II*, p. 4.
14. Hayek, *Law, Legislation and Liberty, Volume II*, pp. 80–1.
15. Hayek, *Law, Legislation and Liberty, Volume I*, p. 128.
16. F.A. Hayek, *Law, Legislation and Liberty, Volume III, The Political Order of a Free People* (London: Routledge, 1979), 5.
17. Hayek, *Law, Legislation and Liberty, Volume III*, p. 99.
18. Hayek, *Law, Legislation and Liberty, Volume III*, p. 113.
19. Karl Polanyi, *The Great Transformation: The Political and Economic Origins of Our Time* (Boston: Beacon Press, 1957).
20. Sanford Lakoff, *Democracy: History, Theory, Practice* (Boulder: Westview Press, 1996), p. 41.
21. Anthony Birch, *The Concepts and Theories of Modern Democracy*, second edition, (London and New York: Routledge, 2001), p. 13.
22. The material on the character of the modern state owes much to S.E. Finer, *The History of Government from the Earliest Times Volume III: Empires, Monarchies, and the Modern State* (Oxford: Oxford University Press, 1997), Book V.
23. Peter Flora, Stein Kuhnle, and Derek Urwin (eds.), *State Formation, Nation-Building, and Mass Politics in Europe: The Theory of Stein Rokkan* (Oxford: Oxford University Press, 1999).

24. S.E. Finer, *The History of Government from the Earliest Times Volume II: The Intermediate Ages* (Oxford: Oxford University Press, 1997), pp. 912–13 and 926–7 respectively.
25. H.L.A. Hart, *The Concept of Law*, second edition, (Oxford: Clarendon Press, 1994), p. 75.
26. Elie Kedourie, *Nationalism*, fourth edition, (Oxford: Blackwell, 1993). See also, Ernest Gellner, *Nations and Nationalism* (Oxford: Blackwell, 1983).
27. Michael Freeden, *Ideologies and Political Theory: A Conceptual Approach* (Oxford: Clarendon Press, 1996), p. 3.
28. David B. Truman, *The Governmental Process: Political Interests and Public Opinion* (New York: Alfred A. Knopf, 1951), p. 322.
29. Arend Lijphart, *Electoral Systems and Party Systems* (Oxford: Oxford University Press, 1994); *Patterns of Democracy: Government Forms and Performance in Thirty-Six Countries* (New Haven and London: Yale University Press, 1999) and G. Bingham Powell Jr, *Contemporary Democracies. Participation, Stability, and Violence* (Cambridge, MA: Harvard University Press, 1982); 'Constitutional Design and Electoral Control', *Journal of Theoretical Politics*, 1: 2, (1989), pp. 107–30, *Elections as Instruments of Democracy. Majoritarian and Proportional Visions* (New Haven and London: Yale University Press, 2000).
30. Powell, 'Constitutional Design and Electoral Control', p. 113; *Elections as Instruments of Democracy*, p. 39.
31. See Albert Weale, *Democracy*, second edition, (Houndmills, Basingstoke: Palgrave Macmillan, 2007), pp. 30–4 for the reasons to adopt these terms.
32. Lijphart, *Electoral Systems and Party Systems*.
33. Anthony King, *The Founding Fathers v. the People* (Cambridge, MA: Harvard University Press, 2012).
34. Thomas McKeown, *The Modern Rise of Population* (London: Edward Arnold, 1976).
35. Oliver E. Williamson, *The Economic Institutions of Capitalism: Firms, Markets, Relational Contracting* (New York: The Free Press, 1985), Chapter 9 offers an interesting account.
36. Williamson, *The Economic Institutions of Capitalism*, pp. 223–5.
37. Kenneth J. Arrow, *Social Choice and Justice: Collected Papers Volume 1* (Oxford: Basil Blackwell, 1984), p. 188.
38. Adam Smith, *An Enquiry into the Nature and Causes of the Wealth of Nations*, originally 1776, (Oxford: Clarendon Press, 1976), pp. 28–9.
39. For the notion of asset-specificity, see Williamson, *The Economic Institutions of Capitalism*, pp. 52–6 and *passim*.
40. R.H. Coase, *The Firm, the Market and the Law* (Chicago and London: University of Chicago Press, 1988), p. 35.

41. P.J.D. Wiles, *Economic Institutions Compared* (Oxford: Basil Blackwell, 1977), p. 64.
42. Alfred Marshall, *Principles of Economics*, eighth edition 1920 (London and Basingstoke: Macmillan, 1979), p. 520.
43. Polanyi, *The Great Transformation*, p. 37.
44. Peter Laslett, Peter, *The World We Have Lost: Further Explored*, third edition, (London: Routledge, 1983), p. 12.
45. Marshall, *Principles of Economics*, pp. 365–6.
46. Marshall, *Principles of Economics*, p. 360.
47. Laslett, *The World We Have Lost*, pp. 16; 190–1.
48. Laslett, *The World We Have Lost*, p. 34.
49. Arrow, *Social Choice and Justice*, p. 188.
50. Wiles, *Economic Institutions Compared*, pp. 99–102. Compare Laslett, *The World We Have Lost*, p. 78.
51. Carole Pateman, *The Sexual Contract* (Cambridge: Polity Press, 1988).
52. Pateman, *The Sexual Contract*, particularly Chapter 5.
53. Rawls, *A Theory of Justice*, pp. 6 and 405.
54. Rawls, *A Theory of Justice*, p. 111, compare pp. 255–6.
55. Susan Moller Okin, *Justice, Gender, and the Family* (New York: Basic Books, Inc., 1989), pp. 90–3.
56. Okin, *Justice, Gender, and the Family*, Chapter 5. See also Sebastiano Maffettone, *Rawls: An Introduction* (Cambridge: Polity Press, 2010), pp. 30–3.
57. John Rawls, *Justice as Fairness: A Restatement*, edited by Erin Kelly (Cambridge, MA: The Belknap Press, 2001), § 50.
58. Carole Pateman and Charles Mills, *Contract and Domination* (Cambridge: Polity Press, 2007), p. 21.
59. Laslett, *The World We Have Lost*, pp. 1–2.
60. Laslett, *The World We Have Lost*, p. 2.
61. Peter Laslett, 'The Family as a Knot of Individual Interests' in Robert McC. Netting, Richard R. Wilk and Eric J. Arnould (eds.), *Households: Comparative and Historical Studies of the Domestic Group* (Berkeley: University of California Press, 1984), pp. 353–79, at p. 371.
62. Laslett, *The World We Have Lost*, p. 8.
63. Laslett, *The World We Have Lost*, p. 120.
64. Alan Macfarlane, *The Origins of English Individualism* (Cambridge: Cambridge University Press, 1979).
65. Laslett, 'The Family as a Knot of Individual Interests', p. 353.
66. Laslett, *The World We Have Lost*, p. 119.
67. Sir Henry Sumner Maine, *Ancient Law: Its Connection with the Early History of Society and Its Relation to Modern Ideas*, with an Introduction and Notes by Sir Frederick Pollock, fourth American edition from

the tenth London edition (New York: Henry Holt and Co., 1906), Chapter V; Ferdinand Tönnies, *Community and Association*, translated by Charles P. Loomis (London: Routledge & Kegan Paul, 1955).

68. For an important argument that there was much more individualism before the great transformation than is commonly supposed, see Macfarlane, *The Origins of English Individualism.*

Chapter 6

1. Robert McC. Netting, *Balancing on an Alp: Ecological Change and Continuity in a Swiss Mountain Community* (Cambridge: Cambridge University Press, 1981), p. 188.
2. John S. Dryzek, 'Legitimacy and Economy in Deliberative Democracy', *Political Theory*, 29: 5, (2001), pp. 651–69, at p. 651.
3. Henry S. Richardson, *Democratic Autonomy: Public Reasoning about the Ends of Policy* (Oxford: Oxford University Press, 2002), pp. 62–5.
4. Joshua Cohen, 'Deliberation and Democratic Legitimacy' in Alan Hamlin and Philip Pettit (eds.), *The Good Polity: Normative Analysis of the State* (Oxford: Basil Blackwell, 1989), pp. 17–34, at p. 22.
5. Budge, Ian, *The New Challenge of Direct Democracy* (Cambridge: Polity Press, 1996).
6. Compare Horton's worries about the slippage in liberal theories of legitimacy from 'consent' to 'reasonable consent': John Horton, 'Political Legitimacy, Justice and Consent', *Critical Review of International Social and Political Philosophy*, 15: 2, (2012), pp. 129–48. See also James Bohman and Henry S. Richardson, 'Liberalism, Deliberative Democracy, and "Reasons that All Can Accept"', *Journal of Political Philosophy*, 17: 3, (2009), pp. 253–74.
7. Jürgen Habermas, *Between Facts and Norms*, translated by William Rehg (Cambridge: Polity Press, 1996).
8. See John Parkinson and Jane Mansbridge (eds.), *Deliberative Systems* (Cambridge: Cambridge University Press, 2012).
9. Graham Smith, *Democratic Innovations: Designing Institutions for Citizen Participation* (Cambridge: Cambridge University Press, 2009).
10. Brian Barry, *Theories of Justice* (London: Harvester-Wheatsheaf, 1989), pp. 347–8; *Justice as Impartiality* (Oxford: Oxford University Press, 1995), p. 106.
11. John Rawls, *Political Liberalism: With a New Introduction and 'Reply to Habermas'* (New York: Columbia University Press, 1996), pp. 231–40.

12. Albert Weale, *Democracy*, second edition (Houndmills, Basingstoke: Palgrave Macmillan, 2007), p. 132.
13. Hanna Fenichel Pitkin, *The Concept of Representation* (Berkeley: University of California Press, 1967).
14. Thomas Hobbes, *Leviathan*, originally 1651, edited with an introduction by Michael Oakeshott (Oxford: Basil Blackwell, n.d.).
15. Andrew Rehfeld, 'Towards A General Theory of Political Representation', *The Journal of Politics* 68: 1, (2006), pp. 1–21.
16. Pitkin, *The Concept of Representation*, pp. 225–6.
17. Pitkin, *The Concept of Representation*, p. 209.
18. D.A. Lloyd Thomas, Review of Hanna Fenichel Pitkin, *The Concept of Representation*, *Philosophical Quarterly*, 19, no.75, (1969), pp. 186–7; Andrew Rehfeld, *The Concept of Constituency* (Cambridge: Cambridge University Press, 2005), pp. 180–92.
19. Pitkin, *The Concept of Representation*, pp. 221–5.
20. James F. Bohman, 'The Coming Age of Deliberative Democracy', *Journal of Political Philosophy*, 6: 4, (1998), pp. 418–443.
21. Joshua Cohen, 'Deliberation and Democratic Legitimacy' in Alan Hamlin and Philip Pettit (eds.), *The Good Polity: Normative Analysis of the State* (Oxford: Basil Blackwell, 1989), pp. 17–34, at p. 22.
22. Anthony McGann, *The Logic of Democracy: Reconciling Equality, Minority Protection and Deliberation* (Michigan: University of Michigan Press, 2006).
23. Compare Eliora van der Hout and Anthony J. McGann, 'Proportional Representation Within the Limits of Liberalism Alone', *British Journal of Political Science*, 39: 4, (2009), pp. 735–54.
24. McGann, *The Logic of Democracy*, pp. 41–3; 55–9.
25. Black, Duncan, *The Theory of Committees and Elections* (Cambridge: Cambridge University Press, 1958). Reprinted in *The Theory of Committees and Elections by Duncan Black and Committee Decisions with Complementary Valuation by Duncan Black and R.A. Newing*, revised second editions, edited by Iain McLean, Alistair McMillan and Burt L. Monroe, with a Foreword by Ronald H. Coase (Boston/Dordrecht/London: Kluwer Academic Publishers, 1998).
26. Kenneth O. May, 'A Set of Independent, Necessary and Sufficient Conditions for Simple Majority Decision', *Econometrica*, 20, (1952), pp. 680–4.
27. Iain McLean, *Rational Choice and British Politics* (Oxford: Oxford University Press, 2001); Jack H. Nagel, 'Social Choice in a Pluritarian Democracy: The Politics of Market Liberalization in New Zealand', *British Journal of Political Science*, 28: 2, (1998), pp. 225–70; 'Occam no, Archimedes yes' in Judith Bara and Albert Weale (eds.), *Democratic*

Politics and Party Competition: Essays in Honour of Ian Budge (London and New York: Routledge, 2006), pp. 143–58; William H. Riker, *Liberalism against Populism* (San Francisco: Freeman and Co., 1982); *The Strategy of Rhetoric: Campaigning for the American Constitution*, edited by Randall L. Calvert, John Mueller, and Rick K. Wilson, (New Haven & London: Yale University Press, 1996).

28. Mikael Skou Andersen, *Governance by Green Taxes* (Manchester: Manchester University Press, 1997), p. 265.
29. Kaare Strøm, *Minority Government and Majority Rule* (Cambridge: Cambridge University Press, 1990).
30. John S. Dryzek, and Christian List, 'Social Choice Theory and Deliberative Democracy: A Reconciliation', *British Journal of Political Science*, 33: 1, (2003), pp. 1–28; David Miller, 'Deliberative Democracy and Social Choice' in David Held (ed.) *Prospects for Democracy* (Cambridge: Polity Press, 1993), pp. 74–92.
31. Hugh Ward and Albert Weale, 'Is Rule by Majorities Special?', *Political Studies*, 58: 1, (2010) pp. 26–46.
32. Kenneth J. Arrow, *Social Choice and Individual Values*, second edition, (New Haven and London: Yale University Press, 1963). For an understanding of Arrow's theorem as exhibiting the tension between coherence ('logicality') and fairness, see William H. Riker, *Liberalism against Populism* (San Francisco: Freeman and Co., 1982), Chapter 5.
33. McGann, *The Logic of Democracy*, pp. 66–7.
34. David Chinitz, Matthias Wismar, and Claude Le Pen, 'Governance and Self-Regulation in Social Health Insurance Schemes', in Richard B. Saltman, Reinhard Busse, and Josep Figueras (eds.), *Social Health Insurance Systems in Western Europe* (Maidenhead: Open University Press, 2004), pp. 155–69.
35. Nicholas R. Miller, 'A New Solution Set for Tournaments and Majority Voting: Further Graph-Theoretical Approaches to the Theory of Voting', *American Journal of Political Science*, 24: 1, (1980), pp. 68–96. See also McGann, *The Logic of Democracy*, pp. 67–70.
36. Nicholas R. Miller, 'Pluralism and Social Choice', *American Political Science Review*, 77: 3, (1983), pp. 734–47. See also Peter C. Ordeshook, *Game Theory and Political Theory: An Introduction* (Cambridge: Cambridge University Presss, 1986), pp. 180–7.
37. John Rawls, *Political Liberalism: With a New Introduction and 'Reply to Habermas'* (New York: Columbia University Press, 1996), pp. 231–40.
38. Rawls, *Political Liberalism*, p. 232.
39. Rawls, *Political Liberalism*, p. 237.
40. Rawls, *Political Liberalism*, pp. 238–9.
41. Rawls, *A Theory of Justice*, p. 172.

42. Bruce Ackerman, *We the People 1. Foundations* (Cambridge, MA: Belknap Press of Harvard University Press, 1991); *We the People 2. Transformations* (Cambridge, MA: Belknap Press of Harvard University Press, 1998).
43. David R. Mayhew, *Electoral Realignments: A Critique of an American Genre* (New Haven and London: Yale University Press, 2002).
44. Ronald Dworkin, *Law's Empire* (London: Fontana Press, 1986), pp. 228–32.
45. Richard Bellamy, *Political Constitutionalism: A Republican Defence of the Constitutionality of Democracy* (Cambridge: Cambridge University Press, 2007).
46. On advocacy coalitions, see Hank C. Jenkins-Smith and Paul A. Sabatier, 'Evaluating the Advocacy Coalition Framework' *Journal of Public Policy* 14, (1994), pp. 175–203; Paul A. Sabatier, 'Knowledge, Policy-Oriented Learning and Policy Change: An Advocacy Coalition Framework' *Knowledge: Creation, Diffusion, Utilization* 8: 4, (1987), pp. 64–92; Paul A. Sabatier and Hank C. Jenkins-Smith (eds.), *Policy Change and Learning: An Advocacy Coalition Approach* (Oxford: Westview Press, 1993).
47. Ian Budge, Hans-Dieter Kingerman, Andrea Volkens, Judith Bara, and Eric Tanenbaum, *Mapping Policy Preferences: Estimates for Parties, Electors, and Governments* 1945–98 (Oxford: Oxford University Press, 2001).
48. William H. Riker, *The Strategy of Rhetoric: Campaigning for the American Constitution*, edited by Randall L. Calvert, John Mueller, and Rick K. Wilson (New Haven & London: Yale University Press, 1996), pp. 99–125.
49. Amy Gutmann and Dennis Thompson, *Why Deliberative Democracy?* (Princeton and Oxford: Princeton University Press, 2004), especially pp. 7–12.
50. Albert Weale, Aude Bicquelet, and Judith Bara, 'Debating Abortion, Deliberative Reciprocity and Parliamentary Advocacy', *Political Studies*, 60: 3, (2012), pp. 643–67.
51. Sabatier, 'Knoweldge, Policy-Oriented Learning and Policy Change'; Albert Weale, 'Close Encounters of the Third Sector Kind', in Shaun Hargreaves Heap and Angus Ross (eds.), *Understanding the Enterprise Culture: Themes in the Work of Mary Douglas* (Edinburgh: Edinburgh University Press, 1992), pp. 203–18.
52. John Stuart Mill, *Considerations on Representative Government*, original edition 1861, in *On Liberty and Other Essays*, edited with an introduction by John Gray (Oxford: Oxford University Press, 1991), pp. 203–467, Chapter III.

53. Jürgen Habermas, *Between Facts and Norms*, translated by William Rehg (Cambridge: Polity Press, 1996), p. 179.
54. Brian Barry, *Political Argument* (London: Routledge & Kegan Paul, 1965), Chapter XIV and Fritz W. Scharpf, 'The Joint-Decision Trap: Lessons from German Federalism and European Union' *Public Administration* 66: 3, (1989), pp. 229–78.
55. Richard Bellamy, *Liberalism and Pluralism: Towards A Politics of Compromise* (London: Routledge, 1999), p. 104; *Political Constitutionalism: A Republican Defence of the Constitutionality of Democracy* (Cambridge: Cambridge University Press, 2007), pp. 192–3. See also Ian O'Flynn, *Deliberative Democracy and Divided Societies* (Edinburgh: Edinburgh University Press, 2006), p. 91 and Jane Mansbridge with James Bohman, Simone Chambers, David Estlund, Andreas Føllesdal, Archon Fung, Cristina Lafont, Bernard Manin, and José Luis Martí, 'The Place of Self-Interest and the Role of Power in Deliberative Democracy', *Journal of Political Philosophy*, 18: 1, (2010), pp. 64–100.
56. Jürg Steiner, André Bächtiger, Markus Spörndli, and Marco R. Steenbergen, *Deliberative Politics in Action: Analyzing Parliamentary Discourse* (Cambridge: Cambridge University Press, 2004).
57. Steiner et al., *Deliberative Politics in Action*, p. 135.
58. Gøsta Esping-Andersen, *The Three Worlds of Welfare Capitalism* (Cambridge: Polity Press, 1990).

Chapter 7

1. Frank, Robert H. *Choosing the Right Pond: Human Behavior and the Quest for Status* (New York and Oxford: Oxford University Press, 1985), pp. 40–1.
2. G.A. Cohen, *Rescuing Justice and Equality* (Cambridge, MA and London: Harvard University Press, 2008), p. 73.
3. Cohen, *If You're an Egalitarian, How Come You're So Rich?*, p. 108.
4. David Miller, *Principles of Social Justice* (Cambridge, MA: Harvard University Press, 1999).
5. R.H. Coase, *The Firm, the Market and the Law* (Chicago and London: University of Chicago Press, 1988), p. 35.
6. P.J.D. Wiles, *Economic Institutions Compared* (Oxford: Basil Blackwell, 1977), p. 64.
7. Alfred Marshall, *Principles of Economics*, eighth edition 1920 (London and Basingstoke: Macmillan, 1979), p. 520.

8. Oliver E. Williamson, *The Economic Institutions of Capitalism: Firms, Markets, Relational Contracting* (New York: The Free Press, 1985), pp. 52–3.
9. Robert H. Frank, *Choosing the Right Pond: Human Behavior and the Quest for Status* (New York and Oxford: Oxford University Press, 1985).
10. Marshall, Principles of Economics, pp. 115–16
11. Robert Michels, *Political Parties: A Sociological Study of the Oligarchical Tendencies of Modern Democracy*, translated by Eden and Cedar Paul, (Kitchener, Ontario: Batoche Books, 2001), p. 241. Michels' observation is remarkable for the fact that it generalized a study of the German Social Democratic Party, which aspired at the time to be an egalitarian organization.
12. For the notions of opportunistic behaviour and asymmetric information and their centrality in organizational processes, see Oliver E. Williamson, *The Economic Institutions of Capitalism: Firms, Markets, Relational Contracting* (New York: The Free Press, 1985).
13. Robert H. Frank and Philip J. Cook, *The Winner-Take-All Society* (New York: The Free Press, 1995), Chapter 4.
14. Marshall, Principles of Economics, pp. 365–9.
15. Kenneth J. Arrow, *Social Choice and Individual Values*, second edition (New Haven and London: Yale University Press, 1963), p. 188.
16. R.H. Coase, *The Firm, the Market and the Law* (Chicago and London: University of Chicago Press, 1988), Chapter 4.
17. For the discussion of public opinion evidence, together with a theoretical discussion, see Miller, *Principles of Justice*. See also, David Braybrooke, *Meeting Needs* (Princeton, New Jersey: Princeton University Press, 1987); Alan Gewirth, *Reason and Morality* (Chicago: University of Chicago Press, 1978); Raymond Plant, *Modern Political Thought* (Oxford: Basil Blackwell, 1991), Chapter 5, offers a valuable survey of the main arguments.
18. For empirical treatments of the welfare state, see: Gøsta Esping-Andersen, *The Three Worlds of Welfare Capitalism* (Cambridge: Polity Press, 1990); Peter Flora and Arnold J. Heidenheimer, eds.), *The Development of Welfare States in Europe and America* (New Brunswick and London: Transaction Books, 1981): Theodore Marmor, Jerry L. Mashaw, and Philip L. Harvey, *America's Misunderstood Welfare State: Persistent Myths, Enduring Realities* (New York: Basic Books, 1990). For an excellent account of the ethical principles, see J. Donald

Moon, 'The Moral Basis of the Welfare State', in Amy Gutmann (ed.) *Democracy and the Welfare State* (Princeton: Princeton University Press), pp. 27–52.

19. Joseph White, *Competing Solutions: American Health Care Proposals and International Experience* (Washington DC: The Brookings Institution, 1995).
20. See Amartya Sen, *The Idea of Justice* (London: Penguin Books, 2009), Part III.
21. Results from research are usefully summarized in Richard H. Thaler and Cass R. Sunstein, *Nudge: Improving Decisions about Health, Wealth and Happiness* (Harmondsworth: Penguin Books, 2008).
22. Nicholas Barr, *The Welfare State as Piggy Bank: Information, Risk, Uncertainty and the Role of the State* (Oxford: Oxford University Press, 2001), p. 1.
23. Jane Falkingham and John Hills, 'Redistribution Between People or Across the Life Cycle?', in Jane Falkingham and John Hills (eds.), *The Dynamic of Welfare: The Welfare State and the Life Cycle* (New York: Prentice Hall/Harvester Wheatsheaf, 1995), pp. 137–49, quotation at p. 149.
24. This objection was raised by an anonymous referee on a report on an earlier version of this work.
25. Peter Laslett, 'The Family as a Knot of Individual Interests' in Robert McC. Netting, Richard R. Wilk, and Eric J. Arnould (eds.), *Households: Comparative and Historical Studies of the Domestic Group* (Berkeley: University of California Press, 1984), pp. 353–79, at p. 353.
26. This is not deny that some forms of reproductive work are marketable, even in small-scale communities. Nursing, including wet nursing, has been a marketable activity in some societies, and surrogacy goes back at least as far as Hagar (*Genesis*, 16: 1). In an even more striking example of the way in which market-like activity can pervade reproduction, Macfarlane cites the existence of contracts in the late middle ages between children and their parents by which the parents agreed to bring up the children in exchange for being looked after during their old age (Alan Macfarlane, *The Origins of English Individualism* (Cambridge: Cambridge University Press, 1979)). However, such arrangements are typically at the edges of the bulk of the work that parents put into rearing their children.
27. Mary D. Stocks, *Eleanor Rathbone: A Biography* (London: Victor Gollancz Ltd, 1950), pp. 62–4 and Chapter VIII.
28. Stocks, *Eleanor Rathbone*, p. 99.
29. David Gauthier, *Morals by Agreement* (Oxford: Clarendon Press, 1986), p. 18, n. 30 and p. 268.
30. Brian Barry, *Theories of Justice* (London: Harvester-Wheatsheaf, 1989), pp. 245–7.

31. Robert Wade, *Village Republics: Economic Conditions for Collective Action in South India* (Cambridge: Cambridge University Press, 1988), pp. 28 and 55.
32. John Rawls, *A Theory of Justice: Revised Edition* (Oxford: Oxford University Press, 1999), p. xv.
33. John Stuart Mill, *Principles of Political Economy with Some of Their Applications to Social Philosophy, Books III–V*, originally 1871, Introduction by V.W. Bladen, textual editor J.M. Robson (Toronto and Buffalo: University of Toronto Press, 1965), p. 767.
34. Mill, *Principles of Political Economy*, p. 768.
35. Mill, *Principles of Political Economy*, pp. 775–94.
36. Carole Pateman, *Participation and Democratic Theory* (Cambridge: Cambridge University Press, 1970); Waheed Hussain, 'Nurturing the Sense of Justice: The Rawlsian Argument for Democratic Corporatism', in Martin O'Neill and Thad Williamson (eds.) *Property-Owning Democracy: Rawls and Beyond* (Chichester: Wiley-Blackwell, 2012), pp. 180–200.
37. James E. Meade, *Efficiency, Equality, and the Ownership of Property* (London: George Allen and Unwin, 1964); *The Intelligent Radical's Guide to Economic Policy: The Mixed Economy* (London: George Allen & Unwin Ltd, 1975).
38. See the criticisms in James E. Meade, *Planning and the Price Mechanism* (London: Allen & Unwin, 1948).
39. For the lack of opposition in general between the principles of the property-owning democracy and the principles of the welfare state, see Albert Weale, 'The Property-Owning Democracy *versus* the Welfare State?', *Analyse und Kritik*, forthcoming. See the discussion in Thad Williamson, 'Realizing Property-Owning Democracy: A 20-Year Strategy to Create an Egalitarian Distribution of Assets in the United States', in Martin O'Neill and Thad Williamson (eds.) *Property-Owning Democracy: Rawls and Beyond* (Chichester: Wiley-Blackwell, 2012), pp. 225–48, with its proposals for securing $50,000 to each adult, but where other policies to deal with risk across the life-course are also endorsed.

Chapter 8

1. John Stuart Mill, *The Subjection of Women*, original edition 1869, reprinted inJohn Gray (ed.) *John Stuart Mill On Liberty and Other Essays*, (Oxford: Oxford University Press, 1991), p. 478.

2. Robert D. Putnam, *Making Democracy* Work (Princeton: Princeton University Press, 1993), p. 183.
3. F.A. Hayek, *Law, Legislation and Liberty, Volume II, The Mirage of Social Justice* (London: Routledge, 1976).
4. Cornelius O'Leary, *The Elimination of Corrupt Practices in British Elections, 1868 to 1911* (Oxford: Clarendon Press, 1962).
5. The importance of the inner point of view and the role of a rule of recognition in the validity of a legal system was, of course, stressed by Hart. See H.L.A. Hart, *The Concept of Law*, second edition, (Oxford: Clarendon Press, 1994), especially Chapter VI. See also Martin Hollis, *Trust within Reason* (Cambridge: Cambridge University Press, 1998), Chapter 8.
6. Stephen Mulhall and Adam Swift, *Liberals and Communitarians* (Oxford: Blackwell, 1992), pp. 14–16.
7. Michael J. Sandel, *Liberalism and the Limits of Justice* (Cambridge: Cambridge University Press, 1982), p. 179.
8. Alasdair MacIntyre, *After Virtue: A Study in Moral Theory* (London: Duckworth, 1981), pp. 232–3.
9. G.W.F. Hegel, *The Philosophy of Right*, originally 1821, translated by T.M. Knox in *Hegel's Philosophy of Right* (Oxford: Clarendon Press, 1952), Third Part: Ethical Life. For a lucid account of Hegel's persistent attempt to overcome what he saw as the fragmentation of contemporary German political and social culture, see Raymond Plant, *Hegel* (London: George Allen & Unwin, 1973). Plant is particularly interesting in tracing the influence of James Steuart's *Inquiry Concerning the Principles of Political Economy* on Hegel (pp. 64–8; 114–16) with its idea of commercial society as a tacit contract and its stress upon the importance of the statesman in dealing with the collectively harmful unintended effects of economic change.
10. Robert McC. Netting, *Balancing on an Alp: Ecological Change and Continuity in a Swiss Mountain Community* (Cambridge: Cambridge University Press, 1981), pp. 186–7.
11. Putnam, *Making Democracy Work*.
12. Plato, *The Republic*, translated by Francis MacDonald Cornford (Oxford: Clarendon Press, 1941), I. 343, p. 24.
13. R.M. Hare, *Freedom and Reason* (Oxford: Clarendon Press, 1963), Chapter 9.
14. John Rawls, 'Justice as Fairness', *Philosophical Review*, 64: 1, (1958), pp. 164–94. Reprinted in John Rawls, *Collected Papers*, edited by Samuel Freeman (Cambridge, MA: Harvard University Press), pp. 47–72, from which references are taken: see p. 54.

15. Brian Barry, (1973) *The Liberal Theory of Justice. A Critical Examination of the Principal Doctrines in* A Theory of Justice *by John Rawls* (Oxford: Clarendon Press, 1973), pp. 87–8.
16. John Rawls, *A Theory of Justice* (Oxford: Oxford University Press, 1972), p. 153.
17. Friedrich Nietzsche, *Thus Spoke Zarathustra: A Book for Everyone and No One*, translated with an introduction by R.J. Hollingdale, (Harmondsworth: Penguin Books, 1969), pp. 123–6.
18. Hannah Arendt, *The Human Condition* (Chicago: University of Chicago Press, 1958), p. 41.
19. Compare John Stuart Mill, *On Liberty*, in *On Liberty and Other Essays*, originally 1859, edited with an introduction by John Gray (Oxford: Oxford University Press, 1991), pp. 1–128, at p. 69.
20. On the insidiousness of tacit power, see Barrington Moore, Jr, *Injustice: The Social Bases of Obedience and Revolt* (London and Basingstoke: Macmillan, 1978) and Steven Lukes, *Power: A Radical View*, second edition (Houndmills Basingstoke: Palgrave Macmillan, 2005), p. 28. On loyalty to unjust norms and the potential for exploitation, see David Gauthier, *Morals by Agreement* (Oxford: Clarendon Press, 1986), p. 11.
21. Cécile Laborde, *Critical Republicanism: The Hijab Controversy and Political Philosophy* (Oxford: Oxford University Press, 2008).
22. Joel Feinberg, *Rights, Justice, and the Bounds of Liberty* (Princeton, New Jersey: Princeton University Press, 1980), p. 16. Pettit shows how such a set of virtues is built into the republican conception of the person: Philip Pettit, *Republicanism: A Theory of Freedom and Government* (Oxford: Oxford University Press, 1997), pp. 71–2.
23. Philippa Foot, *Natural Goodness* (Oxford: Clarendon Press, 2001), p. 12.
24. Nicholas Denyer, 'The Origins of Justice' in Giovanni Pugliese Carratelli (ed.), *ΣΥΖΗΤΗΣΙΣ. Studi sull'Epicureismo Greco e Romano: Offerti a Marcello Gigante* (Napoli: Gaetano Macchiaroli Editore, 1983), pp. 133–52, at p. 149.
25. Adam Smith, *An Enquiry into the Nature and Causes of the Wealth of Nations*, originally 1776, (Oxford: Clarendon Press, 1976 edition), p. 145.
26. Brian Barry, *Theories of Justice* (London: Harvester-Wheatsheaf, 1989) p.284, citing T.M. Scanlon, 'Contractualism and Utilitarianism', in Amartya Sen and Bernard Williams (eds.), *Utilitarianism and Beyond* (Cambridge: Cambridge University Press, 1982), pp. 101–28.
27. Barry, *Theories of Justice*, p. 285.

28. H.L.A. Hart, *The Concept of Law*, second edition (Oxford: Clarendon Press, 1994), p. 196.
29. Elinor Ostrom, *Governing the Commons: The Evolution of Institutions for Collective Action* (Cambridge: Cambridge University Press, 1990), pp. 60–1.
30. See, for example, Gauthier, *Morals by Agreement*, p. 161.
31. Christopher W. Morris and Arthur Ripstein, 'Practical Reason and Preference' in Christopher W. Morris and Arthur Ripstein (eds.), *Practical Rationality and Preference: Essays for David Gauthier* (Cambridge: Cambridge University Press, 2001), pp. 1–10, at p. 6.
32. This adapts an argument of Oliver E. Williamson, *The Economic Institutions of Capitalism. Firms, Markets, Relational Contracting* (New York: The Free Press, 1985), p. 31.
33. John Locke, *Two Treatises of Government*, originally 1690, edited Peter Laslett (New York: Mentor, 1965), p. 396.
34. This seems to be the implication of Scanlon's view about the relationship between general agreement and self-protection in the theory of morality. See Scanlon, 'Contractualism and Utilitarianism', p. 128.
35. Matt Matravers, *Justice and Punishment: The Rationale of Coercion* (Oxford: Oxford University Press, 2000), p. 251.
36. Philippa Foot, 'Moral Beliefs', in Philippa Foot (ed.), *Theories of Ethics* (Oxford: Oxford University Press, 1967), pp. 83–100, at pp. 85–6.
37. What of parents who feel proud of their children or teachers who are proud of their pupils? Here there is achievement, but the achievement is not that of the parents or the teachers. This is a case where ordinary language is ambiguous. When parents and teachers say that they are proud, they must either mean that they are proud for what they have done to enable the achievements, which is a related form of achievement, or vicariously proud *for* the children or pupils.

BIBLIOGRAPHY

Acheson, James M., 'Where Have All the Exploiters Gone? Co-Management of the Maine Lobster Industry', in Fikret Berkes (ed.), *Common Property Resources: Ecology and Community-Based Sustainable Development* (London: Belhaven Press, 1989), pp. 199–217.

Ackerman, Bruce, *We the People 1. Foundations* (Cambridge, MA: Belknap Press of Harvard University Press, 1991).

Ackerman, Bruce, *We the People 2. Transformations* (Cambridge, MA: Belknap Press of Harvard University Press, 1998).

Allison, Graham and Philip Zelikow, *Essence of Decision*, second edition (New York: Longman, 1999).

Anderson, Elizabeth S., 'What Is the Point of Equality?', *Ethics*, 109: 2, (1999), pp. 287–337.

Arendt, Hannah, *The Human Condition* (Chicago: University of Chicago Press, 1958).

Arendt, Hannah, *On Revolution* (Harmondsworth: Penguin Books, 1973).

Aristotle, *The Politics*, translated by H. Rackham (Cambridge, MA: Harvard University Press, 1944).

Aristotle, *The Nicomachean Ethics*, revised edition, translated by H. Rackham (Cambridge, MA and London: Harvard University Press, 1934).

Arrow, Kenneth J., *Social Choice and Individual Values*, second edition (New Haven and London: Yale University Press, 1963).

Arrow, Kenneth J., 'Gifts and Exchanges', *Philosophy and Public Affairs*, 1: 4, (1972), pp. 343–62.

Arrow, Kenneth J., *Social Choice and Justice: Collected Papers Volume 1* (Oxford: Basil Blackwell, 1984).

Atiyah, P.S., *The Rise and Fall of Freedom of Contract* (Oxford: Clarendon Press, 1979).

Axelrod, Robert, *The Evolution of Cooperation* (London: Penguin, 1984).

Ayer, A.J., *The Origins of Pragmatism. Studies in the Philosophy of Charles Sanders Peirce and William James* (London and Basingstoke: Macmillan, 1968).

Barr, Nicholas, *The Welfare State as Piggy Bank: Information, Risk, Uncertainty and the Role of the State* (Oxford: Oxford University Press, 2001)

Barry, Brian, *Political Argument* (London: Routledge & Kegan Paul, 1965).

Barry, Brian, *The Liberal Theory of Justice: A Critical Examination of the Principal Doctrines in* A Theory of Justice *by John Rawls* (Oxford: Clarendon Press, 1973).

Barry, Brian, *Democracy, Power and Justice: Essays in Political Theory* (Oxford: Clarendon Press, 1989).

Barry, Brian, *Theories of Justice* (London: Harvester-Wheatsheaf, 1989).

Barry, Brian, *Justice as Impartiality* (Oxford: Oxford University Press, 1995).

Barry, Brian, 'Something in the Disputation Not Unpleasant', in Paul Kelly (ed.), *Impartiality, Neutrality and Justice: Re-Reading Brian Barry's Justice as Impartiality* (Edinburgh: Edinburgh University Press, 1998), pp. 186–257.

Barry, Brian, *Why Social Justice Matters* (Cambridge: Polity Press, 2005).

Beitz, Charles R., *Political Equality* (Princeton: Princeton University Press, 1989).

Bellamy, Richard, *Liberalism and Pluralism: Towards A Politics of Compromise* (London: Routledge, 1999).

Bellamy, Richard, *Political Constitutionalism: A Republican Defence of the Constitutionality of Democracy* (Cambridge: Cambridge University Press, 2007).

Bergson, Abram, 'Market Socialism Revisited', *Journal of Political Economy*, 75: 5, (1967), pp. 655–73.

Berkes, Firket, 'Fishermen and "The Tragedy of the Commons"', *Environmental Conservation*, 12: 3, (1985), pp. 199–206.

Berkes, Firket, 'Local-level Management and the Commons Problem: A Comparative Study of Turkish Fisheries', *Marine Policy*, 10: 3, (1986), pp. 215–29.

Berkes, Fikret (ed.), *Common Property Resources: Ecology and Community-Based Sustainable Development* (London: Belhaven Press, 1989).

Berkes, Fikret and Farvar M. Taghi, 'Introduction and Overview' in Fikret Berkes (ed.), *Common Property Resources: Ecology and Community-Based Sustainable Development* (London: Belhaven Press, 1989), pp. 1–17.

Berlin, Isaiah, *Four Essays on Liberty* (Oxford: Oxford University Press, 1969).

Bessette, Joseph M., *The Mild Voice of Reason: Deliberative Democracy and American National Government* (Chicago: Chicago University Press, 1982).

Binmore, Ken, 'Bargaining and Morality' in David Gauthier and Robert Sugden (eds.), *Rationality, Justice and the Social Contract: Themes from Morals by Agreement* (New York: Havester-Wheatsheaf, 1993), pp. 131–56.

Binmore, Ken, *Playing Fair: Game Theory and the Social Contract Volume I* (Cambridge, MA and London: The MIT Press, 1994).

Binmore, Ken, *Just Playing: Game Theory and the Social Contract Volume II* (Cambridge, MA and London: The MIT Press, 1998).

Birch, Anthony H., *The Concepts and Theories of Modern Democracy*, second edition (London and New York: Routledge, 2001).

Black, Duncan, *The Theory of Committees and Elections* (Cambridge: Cambridge University Press, 1958). Reprinted in *The Theory of Committees and Elections by Duncan Black and Committee Decisions with Complementary Valuation by Duncan Black and R.A. Newing*, revised second editions, edited by Iain McLean, Alistair McMillan, and Burt L. Monroe, with a Foreword by Ronald H. Coase (Boston/Dordrecht/London: Kluwer Academic Publishers, 1998).

Bohman, James F., 'The Coming Age of Deliberative Democracy', *Journal of Political Philosophy*, 6: 4, (1998), pp. 418–43.

Bohman, James and William Rehg (eds.), *Deliberative Democracy* (Cambridge, MA: MIT Press, 1997).

Bohman, James and Henry S. Richardson, 'Liberalism, Deliberative Democracy, and "Reasons that All Can Accept"', *Journal of Political Philosophy*, 17: 3, (2009), pp. 253–74.

Bollen, Kenneth A. and Robert W. Jackman, 'Economic and Noneconomic Determinants of Political Democracy in the 1960s', *Research in Political Sociology*, 1, (1985), pp. 27–48.

Brandom, Robert B., *Making It Explicit* (Cambridge, MA: Havard University Press, 2000).

Braybrooke, David, *Meeting Needs* (Princeton, NJ: Princeton University Press, 1987).

Braybrooke, David, 'Social Contract Theory's Fanciest Flight', *Ethics*, 97: 4, (1987), pp. 750–64.

Brittan, Samuel, *Left or Right: The Bogus Dilemma* (London: Secker & Warburg, 1968).

Brittan, Samuel, *Capitalism with a Human Face* (Hammersmith, London: Fontana Press, 1996).

Bryan, Frank M., *Real Democracy: The New England Town Meeting and How It Works* (Chicago and London: The University of Chicago Press, 2004).

Budge, Ian, *The New Challenge of Direct Democracy* (Cambridge: Polity Press, 1996).

Butler, Joseph, *Fifteen Sermons Preached at the Rolls Chapel*, originally 1726, with Introduction, Analyses, and Notes by The Very Rev. W.R. Matthews (London: G. Bell & Sons Ltd, 1969).

Chambers, Simone, 'Behind Closed Doors: Publicity, Secrecy, and the Quality of Deliberation', *Journal of Political Philosophy* 12: 4, (2004), pp. 389–410.

Chinitz, David, Matthias Wismar, and Claude Le Pen 'Governance and Self-Regulation in Social Health Insurance Schemes', in Richard B. Saltman, Reinhard Busse and Josep Figueras (eds.), *Social Health Insurance Systems in Western Europe* (Maidenhead: Open University Press, 2004), pp. 155–69.

Christiano, Thomas, *The Constitution of Equality: Democratic Authority and Its Limits* (Oxford: Oxford University Press, 2008).

Coase, R.H., *The Firm, the Market and the Law* (Chicago and London: University of Chicago Press, 1988).

Cohen, G.A., *If You're an Egalitarian, How Come You're So Rich?* (Cambridge, MA and London: Harvard University Press, 2000).

Cohen, G.A., *Rescuing Justice and Equality* (Cambridge, MA and London: Harvard University Press, 2008).

Cohen, G.A., *Why Not Socialism?* (Princeton and Oxford: Princeton University Press, 2009).

Cohen, Joshua, 'Deliberation and Democratic Legitimacy' in Alan Hamlin and Philip Pettit (eds.), *The Good Polity: Normative Analysis of the State* (Oxford: Basil Blackwell, 1989), pp. 17–34.

Coward Jr, E. Walter (ed.), *Irrigation and Agricultural Development in Asia; Perspectives from the Social Sciences* (Ithaca and London: Cornell University Press, 1980).

Cross, R.C. and A.D. Woozley, *Plato's Republic: A Philosophical Commentary* (London: Macmillan, 1966).

D'Entrèves, Maurizio Passerin, 'Introduction: Democracy as Public Deliberation' in Maurizio Passerin D'Entrèves (ed.) *Democracy as Public Deliberation: New Perspectives* (Manchester: Manchester University Press, 2002), pp. 1–36.

Daalder, Hans, 'The Netherlands: Opposition in a Segmented Society', in Robert A. Dahl (ed.), *Political Opposition in Western Democracies* (New Haven and London: Yale University Press, 1966).

Dahl, Robert A. *On Democracy* (New Haven and London: Yale University Press, 1998).

Dancy, Jonathan, *Ethics without Principles* (Oxford: Clarendon Press, 2004).

Darwall, Stephen, 'Introduction' in Stephen Darwall (ed.), *Contractarianism/Contractualism* (Oxford: Blackwell Publishing, 2003), pp. 1–8.

Davidson, Donald, 'How Is Weakness of the Will Possible?' in Joel Feinberg (ed.), *Moral Concepts* (Oxford: Oxford University Press, 1969), pp. 93–133.

Denyer, Nicholas, 'The Origins of Justice' in Giovanni Pugliese Carratelli (ed.), *ΣΥΖΗΤΗΣΙΣ. Studi sull'Epicureismo Greco e Romano: Offerti a Marcello Gigante* (Napoli: Gaetano Macchiaroli Editore, 1983), pp. 133–52.

Dowding, Keith, 'Luck, Equality and Responsibility', *Critical Review of International Social and Political Philosophy*, 13: 1, (2010), pp. 71–92.

Dryzek, John S., *Deliberative Democracy and Beyond: Liberals, Critics, Contestations* (Oxford: Oxford University Press, 2000).

Dryzek, John S., 'Legitimacy and Economy in Deliberative Democracy', *Political Theory*, 29: 5, (2001), pp. 651–69.

Dryzek, John S. and Christian List, 'Social Choice Theory and Deliberative Democracy: A Reconciliation', *British Journal of Political Science*, 33: 1, (2003), pp. 1–28.

Dubiel, Helmut, 'Hannah Arendt and the Theory of Democracy: A Critical Reconstruction', in Peter Graf Kielmannsegg, Horst Mewes, and Elisabeth Glaser-Schmidt (eds.), *Hannah Arendt and Leo Strauss: German Emigrés and American Political Thought after World War II* (Cambridge: German Historical Institute, Washington D.C. and Cambridge University Press, 1995), pp. 11–28.

Dworkin, Ronald, 'What Is Equality? Part 2: Equality of Resources', *Philosophy and Public Affairs*, 10: 4, (1981), pp. 283–345.

Dworkin, Ronald, *Law's Empire* (London: Fontana Press, 1986).

Dworkin, Ronald, *Sovereign Virtue: The Theory and Practice of Equality* (Cambridge MA: Harvard University Press, 2000).

Elster, Jon (ed.), *Deliberative Democracy* (Cambridge: Cambridge University Press, 1998).

Emmet, Dorothy, *Rules, Roles and Relations* (London: Macmillan, 1966).

Esping-Andersen, Gøsta, *The Three Worlds of Welfare Capitalism* (Cambridge: Polity Press, 1990).

Estlund, David M. (2008) *Democratic Authority: A Philosophical Framework* (Princeton and Oxford: Princeton University Press, 2008).

Falkingham, Jane and John Hills, 'Redistribution Between People or Across the Life Cycle?', in Jane Falkingham and John Hills (eds.), *The Dynamic of Welfare: The Welfare State and the Life Cycle* (New York: Prentice Hall/Harvester Wheatsheaf, 1995), pp. 137–49.

Feinberg, Joel, *Rights, Justice, and the Bounds of Liberty* (Princeton, NJ: Princeton University Press, 1980).

Feinberg, Joel, *The Moral Limits of the Criminal Law, Volume One: Harm to Others* (Oxford: Oxford University Press, 1984).

Finer, S.E., *Comparative Government* (Harmondsworth: Penguin, 1970).

Finer, S.E., *The History of Government from the Earliest Times Volume II: The Intermediate Ages* (Oxford: Oxford University Press, 1997)

Finer, S.E., *The History of Government from the Earliest Times Volume III: Empires, Monarchies, and the Modern State* (Oxford: Oxford University Press, 1997).
Fishkin, James S., *Democracy and Deliberation: New Directions for Democratic Reform* (New Haven and London: Yale University Press, 1991).
Fishkin, James S., *The Voice of the People: Public Opinion and Democracy* (New Haven and London: Yale University Press, 1995).
Fishkin, James S. and Peter Laslett (eds.), *Debating Deliberative Democracy* (Oxford: Blackwell, 2003).
Flora, Peter and Arnold J. Heidenheimer, (eds.), *The Development of Welfare States in Europe and America* (New Brunswick and London: Transaction Books, 1981).
Flora, Peter, Stein Kuhnle, and Derek Urwin (eds.), *State Formation, Nation-Building, and Mass Politics in Europe: The Theory of Stein Rokkan* (Oxford: Oxford University Press, 1999).
Foot, Philippa, 'Moral Beliefs', in Philippa Foot (ed.), *Theories of Ethics* (Oxford: Oxford University Press, 1967), pp. 83–100.
Foot, Philippa, *Natural Goodness* (Oxford: Clarendon Press, 2001).
Frank, Robert H., *Choosing the Right Pond: Human Behavior and the Quest for Status* (New York and Oxford: Oxford University Press, 1985).
Frank, Robert H., *Luxury Fever: Weighing the Cost of Excess* (Princeton and Oxford: Princeton University Press, 1999).
Frank, Robert H. and Philip J. Cook, *The Winner-Take-All Society* (New York: The Free Press, 1995).
Freeden, Michael, *Ideologies and Political Theory: A Conceptual Approach* (Oxford: Clarendon Press, 1996).
Freeman, Samuel, *Justice and the Social Contract: Essays on Rawlsian Political Philosophy* (New York: Oxford University Press, 2007).
Fried, Albert, *Socialism in America: From the Shakers to the Third International* (New York: Columbia University Press, 1992).
Gauthier, David, *Morals by Agreement* (Oxford: Clarendon Press, 1986).
Gauthier, David, 'Morality, Rational Choice, and Semantic Representation: A Reply to My Critics' in Ellen Frankel Paul, Fred D. Miller Jr, Jeffrey Paul, and John Ahrens (eds.) *The New Social Contract: Essays on Gauthier* (Oxford: Basil Balckwell, 1988), pp. 173–221.
Gauthier, David, 'Why Contractarianism?' in Peter Vallentyne (ed.), *Contractarianism and Rational Choice: Essays on David Gauthier's Morals by Agreement* (Cambridge: Cambridge University Press, 1991), pp. 15–30.
Gauthier, David, 'Uniting Separate Persons' in David Gauthier and Robert Sugden (eds.), *Rationality, Justice and the Social Contract: Themes from*

Morals by Agreement (New York: Havester-Wheatsheaf, 1993), pp. 176–92.

Gauthier, David, 'Political Contractarianism', *Journal of Political Philosophy*, 5: 2, (1997), pp. 132–48.

Gauthier, David, 'Mutual Advantage and Impartiality' in Paul Kelly (ed.), *Impartiality, Neutrality and Justice: Re-reading Brian Barry's Justice as Impartiality* (Edinburgh: Edinburgh University Press, 1998), pp. 120–36.

Gellner, Ernest, *Nations and Nationalism* (Oxford: Blackwell, 1983).

Gewirth, Alan, *Reason and Morality* (Chicago: University of Chicago Press, 1978).

Ginsberg, Matthew L., 'AI and Nonmonotonic Reasoning' in Dov M. Gabbay, C.J. Hogger, J.A. Robinson, and D. Nute (eds.), *Handbook of Logic in Artificial Intelligence and Logic Programming, Volume 3, Nonmonotonic Reasoning and Uncertain Reasoning* (Oxford: Clarendon Press, 1994), pp. 1–33.

Goodin, Robert E., *Reflective Democracy* (Oxford: Oxford University Press, 2003).

Gough, J.W. (1936) *The Social Contract: A Critical Study of Its Development* (Oxford: Clarendon Press).

Greenleaf, W.H., *The British Political Tradition: Volume Two The Ideological Heritage* (London: Methuen & Co., 1983).

Grice, Russell, *The Grounds of Moral Judgement* (Cambridge: Cambridge University Press, 1967).

Guthrie, W.K.C., *History of Greek Philosophy III* (Cambridge: Cambridge University Press, 1969).

Gutmann, Amy and Dennis Thompson, *Democracy and Disagreement* (Cambridge, MA: Harvard University Press, 1996).

Gutmann, Amy and Dennis Thompson, *Why Deliberative Democracy?* (Princeton and Oxford: Princeton University Press, 2004).

Habermas, Jürgen, *The Philosophical Discourse of Modernity*, translated by Frederick Lawrence (Cambridge: Polity Press, 1985).

Habermas, Jürgen, *Between Facts and Norms*, translated by William Rehg (Cambridge: Polity Press, 1996).

Hacking, Ian, 'Lakatos's Philosophy of Science', in Ian Hacking (ed.) *Scientific Revolutions* (Oxford: Oxford University Press, 1981), pp. 128–43.

Hardin, Garrett, 'The Tragedy of the Commons', *Science*, 162: 3859, (1968), pp. 1243–8.

Hare, R.M., *Freedom and Reason* (Oxford: Clarendon Press, 1963).

Hargreaves Heap, Shaun, Bruce Lyons, Martin Hollis, Robert Sugden, and Albert Weale, *The Theory of Choice: A Critical Guide* (Oxford: Blackwell, 1992).

Harsanyi, John C., *Essays on Ethics, Social Behavior, and Scientific Explanation* (Dordrecht: D. Reidel, 1976).

Hart, H.L.A., 'Are There Any Natural Rights?' *Philosophical Review* 64: 2, (1955), pp. 175–91, reprinted in Anthony Quinton (ed.), *Political Philosophy* (Oxford: Oxford University Press, 1967), pp. 53–66, especially at pp. 61–2.

Hart, H.L.A., 'Between Utility and Rights' in H.L.A. Hart, *Essays in Jurisprudence and Philosophy* (Oxford: Clarendon Press, 1983), pp. 198–222.

Hart, H.L.A., *The Concept of Law*, second edition (Oxford: Clarendon Press, 1994).

Hayek, F.A., *The Constitution of Liberty* (London and Henley: Routledge & Kegan Paul, 1960).

Hayek, F.A., *Law, Legislation and Liberty, Volume I, Rules and Order* (London: Routledge, 1973).

Hayek, F.A., *Law, Legislation and Liberty, Volume II, The Mirage of Social Justice* (London: Routledge, 1976).

Hayek, F.A., *Law, Legislation and Liberty, Volume III, The Political Order of a Free People* (London: Routledge, 1979).

Hegel, G.W.F., *The Philosophy of Right*, originally 1821, translated by T.M. Knox in *Hegel's Philosophy of Right* (Oxford: Clarendon Press, 1952).

Hesse, Mary, 'Models and Analogy in Science' in P. Edwards (ed.), *The Encyclopedia of Philosophy* (London and New York: Macmillan Publishing and The Free Press, 1967), volume 5, pp. 354–9.

Hesse, Mary, 'Science and Objectivity', in John B. Thompson and David Held (eds.), *Habermas: Critical Debates* (London and Basingstoke: Macmillan, 1982), pp. 98–115.

Hesse, Mary B., *Models and Analogies in Science* (Notre Dame: University of Notre Dame Press, 1966).

Hill, Christopher, *Puritanism and Revolution: Studies in Interpretation of the English Revolution of the 17th Century* (London: Panther Books, 1968).

Hirsch, Fred, *The Social Limits to Growth* (London and Henley: Routledge and Kegan Paul, 1977).

Hobbes, Thomas, *Leviathan*, originally 1651, edited with an introduction by Michael Oakeshott (Oxford: Basil Blackwell, n.d.).

Hodgskin, Thomas, *The Natural and Artificial Right of Property Contrasted*, originally 1832 (Clifton: Augutus M. Kelley, 1973 edition).

Hohfeld, W.N., *Fundamental Legal Conceptions* (New Haven: Yale University Press, 1923).

Hollis, Martin, *Trust within Reason* (Cambridge: Cambridge University Press, 1998).

Honoré, A.M., 'Ownership' in A.G. Guest (ed.) *Oxford Essays in Jurisprudence* (Oxford: Oxford University Press, 1961), pp. 107–47.

Horton, John, 'Political Legitimacy, Justice and Consent', *Critical Review of International Social and Political Philosophy*, 15: 2, (2012), pp. 129–48.

Hout, Eliora van der and Anthony J. McGann, 'Proportional Representation Within the Limits of Liberalism Alone', *British Journal of Political Science*, 39 4, (2009), pp. 735–54.

Hume, David, *Enquiry Concerning the Principles of Morals*, originally 1751, reprinted in *Essays, Moral, Political, and Literary by David Hume*, edited by T.H. Green and T.H. Grose (London: Longmans, Green, and Co., 1889), pp. 167–287.

Hume, David, 'Of the First Principles of Government' in *Essays, Moral, Political, and Literary*, originally 1742, edited T.H. Green and T.H. Grose (London: Longmans, Green and Co., 1889 edition), pp. 109–13.

Hussain, Waheed, 'Nurturing the Sense of Justice: The Rawlsian Argument for Democratic Corporatism', in Martin O'Neill and Thad Williamson (eds.) *Property-Owning Democracy: Rawls and Beyond* (Chichester: Wiley-Blackwell, 2012), pp. 180–200.

Hyland, J.L., *Democratic Theory: The Philosophical Foundations* (Manchester: Manchester University Press, 1995).

Jefferson, Thomas, *The Portable Thomas Jefferson*, ed. Merrill D. Peterson (Harmondsworth: Penguin Books, 1977).

Jenkins-Smith, Hank C. and Paul A. Sabatier, 'Evaluating the Advocacy Coalition Framework' *Journal of Public Policy* 14, (1994), pp. 175–203.

Katzenstein, Peter J., *Small States in World Markets: Industrial Policy in Europe* (Ithaca, NY: Cornell University Press, 1985).

Kedourie, Elie, *Nationalism*, fourth edition (Oxford: Blackwell, 1993).

Kelly, Jerry S., *Arrow Impossibility Theorems* (New York: Academic Press, 1978).

Kenny, Anthony, *Will, Freedom and Power* (Oxford: Basil Blackwell, 1975).

King, Anthony, *The Founding Fathers v. the People* (Cambridge, MA: Harvard University Press, 2012).

Laborde, Cécile, *Critical Republicanism: The Hijab Controversy and Political Philosophy* (Oxford: Oxford University Press, 2008).

Lakoff, Sanford, *Democracy: History, Theory, Practice* (Boulder: Westview Press, 1996).

Laslett, Peter, *The World We Have Lost: Further Explored*, third edition (London: Routledge, 1983).

Laslett, Peter, 'The Family as a Knot of Individual Interests' in Robert McC. Netting, Richard R. Wilk and Eric J. Arnould (eds.), *Households:*

Comparative and Historical Studies of the Domestic Group (Berkeley: University of California Press, 1984), pp. 353–79.

Lessnoff, Michael, *Social Contract* (Basingstoke: Macmillan, 1986).

Levi, Isaac, *For the Sake of the Argument: Ramsey Test Conditionals, Inductive Inference, and Nonmonotonic Reasoning* (Cambridge: Cambridge University Press, 1996).

Lijphart, Arend, *The Politics of Accommodation: Pluralism and Democracy in the Netherlands* (Berkeley and Los Angeles: University of California Press, 1968).

Lijphart, Arend, *Electoral Systems and Party Systems* (Oxford: Oxford University Press, 1994).

Lijphart, Arend, *Patterns of Democracy: Government Forms and Performance in Thirty-Six Countries* (New Haven and London: Yale University Press, 1999).

Lipton, Michael, 'The Prisoners' Dilemma and Coase's Theorem: A Case for Democracy in Less Developed Countries?', in R.C.O. Matthews (ed.) *Economy and Democracy* (Houndmills: Macmillan, 1985), pp. 49–109.

Lipton, Michael, *Land Reform in Developing Countries: Property Rights and Property Wrongs* (London and New York: Routledge, 2009).

Lloyd Thomas, D.A., A review of Hanna Fenichel Pitkin, *The Concept of Representation*, *Philosophical Quarterly*, 19, no.75, (1969), pp. 186–7.

Locke, John, *Two Treatises of Government*, originally 1690, edited Peter Laslett (New York: Mentor, 1965).

Lucas, J.R., *The Principles of Politics* (Oxford: Clarendon Press, 1966).

Łukaszewicz, Witold, *Non-Monotonic Reasoning: Formalization of Commonsense Reasoning* (New York: Ellis Horwood, 1990).

Lukes, Steven, *Power: A Radical View*, second edition (Houndmills Basingstoke: Palgrave Macmillan, 2005).

Macfarlane, Alan, *The Origins of English Individualism* (Cambridge: Cambridge University Press, 1979).

MacIntyre, Alasdair, *After Virtue: A Study in Moral Theory* (London: Duckworth, 1981).

Madison, James, 'Federalist Paper No. 10' in *The Federalist Papers*, originally 1788, edited Terence Ball (Cambridge: Cambridge University Press, 2003 edition).

Maffettone, Sebastiano, *Rawls: An Introduction* (Cambridge: Polity Press, 2010).

Maine, Sir Henry Sumner, *Ancient Law: Its Connection with the Early History of Society and Its Relation to Modern Ideas*, with an Introduction and Notes by Sir Frederick Pollock, fourth American edition from the tenth London edition (New York: Henry Holt and Co., 1906).

Makinson, David, 'General Patterns in Nonmonotonic Reasoning' in Dov M. Gabbay, C.J. Hogger, J.A. Robinson, and D. Nute (eds.), *Handbook of Logic in Artificial Intelligence and Logic Programming, Volume 3, Nonmonotonic Reasoning and Uncertain Reasoning* (Oxford: Clarendon Press, 1994), pp. 35–110.

Mansbridge, Jane, with James Bohman, Simone Chambers, David Estlund, Andreas Føllesdal, Archon Fung, Cristina Lafont, Bernard Manin, and José Luis Martí, 'The Place of Self-Interest and the Role of Power in Deliberative Democracy' *Journal of Political Philosophy*, 18: 1, (2010), pp. 64–100.

Marmor, Theodore, Jerry L. Mashaw, and Philip L. Harvey, *America's Misunderstood Welfare State: Persistent Myths, Enduring Realities* (New York: Basic Books, 1990).

Marshall, Alfred, *Principles of Economics*, eighth edition 1920 (London and Basingstoke: Macmillan, 1979).

Marx, Karl, *Capital: A Critique of Political Economy, Volume One*, fourth edition, 1890, translated by Ben Fowkes (Harmondworth: Penguin Books, 1976).

Matravers, Matt, *Justice and Punishment: The Rationale of Coercion* (Oxford: Oxford University Press, 2000).

Mayhew, David R., *Electoral Realignments: A Critique of an American Genre* (New Haven and London: Yale University Press, 2002).

Maynard Smith, John, *The Theory of Evolution* (Harmondsworth: Penguin, 1975).

McClennen, Edward F. (1988) 'Constrained Maximization and Resolute Choice' in Ellen Frankel Paul, Fred D. Miller Jr, Jeffrey Paul, and John Ahrens (eds.) *The New Social Contract: Essays on Gauthier* (Oxford: Basil Balckwell), pp. 95–118.

McGann, Anthony, *The Logic of Democracy: Reconciling Equality, Minority Protection and Deliberation* (Michigan: University of Michigan Press, 2006).

McKeown, Thomas, *The Modern Rise of Population* (London: Edward Arnold, 1976).

McLean, Iain, *Rational Choice and British Politics* (Oxford: Oxford University Press, 2001).

Meade, James E., *Planning and the Price Mechanism* (London: Allen & Unwin, 1948).

Meade, James E., *Efficiency, Equality, and the Ownership of Property* (London: George Allen and Unwin, 1964).

Meade, James E., *The Intelligent Radical's Guide to Economic Policy: The Mixed Economy* (London: George Allen & Unwin Ltd, 1975).

Meiklejohn, Alexander, *Political Freedom: The Constitutional Powers of the People* (New York: Harper and Brothers, 1960).

Menger, Anton, *The Right to the Whole Produce of Labour: The Origin and Development of Labour's Claim to the Whole Product of Industry*, translated by M.E. Tanner with an Introduction and Bibliography by H.S. Foxwell (London: Macmillan, 1899).

Michels, Robert, *Political Parties: A Sociological Study of the Oligarchical Tendencies of Modern Democracy*, translated by Eden and Cedar Paul (Kitchener, Ontario: Batoche Books, 2001).

Mill, John Stuart, *Principles of Political Economy with Some of Their Applications to Social Philosophy, Books I–II*, originally 1871, Introduction by V.W. Bladen, textual editor J.M. Robson (Toronto and Buffalo: University of Toronto Press, 1965).

Mill, John Stuart, *Principles of Political Economy with Some of Their Applications to Social Philosophy, Books III–V*, originally 1871, Introduction by V.W. Bladen, textual editor J.M. Robson (Toronto and Buffalo: University of Toronto Press, 1965).

Mill, John Stuart, *Considerations on Representative Government*, original edition 1861, in *On Liberty and Other Essays*, edited with an introduction by John Gray (Oxford: Oxford University Press, 1991), pp. 203–467.

Mill, John Stuart, *On Liberty*, in *On Liberty and Other Essays*, originally 1859, edited with an introduction by John Gray (Oxford: Oxford University Press, 1991), pp. 1–128.

Mill, John Stuart, *The Subjection of Women*, original edition 1869, reprinted in *On Liberty and Other Essays*, edited with an introduction by John Gray (Oxford: Oxford University Press, 1991).

Mill, John Stuart, *Utilitarianism*, originally 1861, in *On Liberty and Other Essays*, edited with an introduction by John Gray (Oxford: Oxford University Press, 1991), pp. 129–201.

Miller, David, 'Deliberative Democracy and Social Choice' in David Held (ed.) *Prospects for Democracy* (Cambridge: Polity Press, 1993), pp. 74–92.

Miller, David, *Principles of Social Justice* (Cambridge, MA: Harvard University Press, 1999).

Miller, Nicholas R., 'A New Solution Set for Tournaments and Majority Voting: Further Graph-Theoretical Approaches to the Theory of Voting', *American Journal of Political Science*, 24: 1, (1980), pp. 68–96.

Miller, Nicholas R., 'Pluralism and Social Choice', *American Political Science Review*, 77: 3, (1983), pp. 734–47.

Moon, J. Donald, 'The Moral Basis of the Welfare State, in in Amy Gutmann (ed.) *Democracy and the Welfare State* (Princeton: Princeton University Press, 1988), pp. 27–52.

Moore, Jr, Barrington, *Injustice: The Social Bases of Obedience and Revolt* (London and Basingstoke: Macmillan, 1978).

Morris, Christopher W. and Arthur Ripstein, 'Practical Reason and Preference' in Christopher W. Morris and Arthur Ripstein (eds.), *Practical Rationality and Preference: Essays for David Gauthier* (Cambridge: Cambridge University Press, 2001), pp. 1–10.

Morriss, Peter, *Power: A Philosophical Analysis* (Manchester: Manchester University Press, 1988).

Mueller, Dennis C. (2003) *Public Choice III* (Cambridge: Cambridge University Press).

Mulhall, Stephen and Adam Swift, *Liberals and Communitarians* (Oxford: Blackwell, 1992).

Musgrave, R.A., 'Maximin, Uncertainty, and the Leisure Trade-Off', *Quarterly Journal of Economics*, 88: 4, (1974), pp. 625–32.

Muthoo, Abhinay, *Bargaining Theory with Applications* (Cambridge: Cambridge University Press, 1999).

Nagel, Ernest and James R. Newman, *Gödel's Proof* (New York: New York University Press, 1958).

Nagel, Jack H., 'Occam no, Archimedes yes' in Judith Bara and Albert Weale (eds.), *Democratic Politics and Party Competition: Essays in Honour of Ian Budge* (London and New York: Routledge, 2006), pp. 143–58.

Netting, Robert McC., *Balancing on an Alp: Ecological Change and Continuity in a Swiss Mountain Community* (Cambridge: Cambridge University Press, 1981).

Nietzsche, Friedrich, *Thus Spoke Zarathustra: A Book for Everyone and No One*, translated with an introduction by R.J. Hollingdale (Harmondsworth: Penguin Books, 1969).

Nozick, Robert, *Anarchy, State and Utopia* (Oxford: Basil Blackwell, 1974).

Nute, Donald, 'Defeasible Logic' in Dov M. Gabbay, C.J. Hogger, J.A. Robinson, and D. Nute (eds.), *Handbook of Logic in Artificial Intelligence and Logic Programming, Volume 3, Nonmonotonic Reasoning and Uncertain Reasoning* (Oxford: Clarendon Press, 1994), pp. 353–95.

Nye, Joseph S., *The Paradox of American Power* (Oxford: Oxford University Press, 2002).

O'Flynn, Ian, *Deliberative Democracy and Divided Societies* (Edinburgh: Edinburgh University Press, 2006).

O'Leary, Cornelius, *The Elimination of Corrupt Practices in British Elections, 1868 to 1911* (Oxford: Clarendon Press, 1962).

O'Neill, Martin and Thad Williamson, 'Introduction' in Martin O'Neill and Thad Williamson (eds.) *Property-Owning Democracy: Rawls and Beyond* (Chichester: Wiley-Blackwell, 2012), pp. 1–14.

O'Neill, Onora, *Constructions of Reason: Explorations in Kant's Practical Philosophy* (Cambridge: Cambridge University Press, 1989).

Oakeshott, Michael, *On Human Conduct* (Oxford: Clarendon Press, 1975).

Oakeshott, Michael, *Rationalism in Politics and Other Essays*, with a Foreword by Timothy Fuller (Indianapolis: Liberty Fund, new and expanded edition, 1991).

Okin, Susan Moller, *Justice, Gender, and the Family* (New York: Basic Books, Inc., 1989).

Olson, Mancur, *The Rise and Decline of Nations* (New Haven and London: Yale University Press, 1982).

Olson, Mancur, *Power and Prosperity: Outgrowing Communist and Capitalist Dictatorships* (New York: Basic Books, 2000).

Ordeshook, Peter C., *Game Theory and Political Theory: An Introduction* (Cambridge: Cambridge University Presss, 1986).

Ostrom, Elinor, *Governing the Commons: The Evolution of Institutions for Collective Action* (Cambridge: Cambridge University Press, 1990).

Parkinson, John and Jane Mansbridge (eds.), *Deliberative Systems* (Cambridge: Cambridge University Press, 2012).

Pateman, Carole, *Participation and Democratic Theory* (Cambridge: Cambridge University Press, 1970).

Pateman, Carole, *The Sexual Contract* (Cambridge: Polity Press, 1988).

Pateman, Carole and Charles Mills, *Contract and Domination* (Cambridge: Polity Press, 2007).

Peirce, Charles Sanders, 'The Fixation of Belief' in *Collected Papers of Charles Sanders Peirce, Volumes V and VI*, edited Charles Hartshorne and Paul Weiss (Cambridge, MA: Harvard University Press, 1934), pp. 223–47.

Pettit, Philip, *Republicanism: A Theory of Freedom and Government* (Oxford: Oxford University Press, 1997).

Pevsner, Nicholas, *The Buildings of England. Yorkshire: The North Riding* (Harmondsworth: Penguin, 1966).

Pevsner, Nicholas, *The Buildings of England. Hertfordshire*, second edition revised by Bridget Cherry (New Haven and London: Yale University Press, 1977).

Pitkin, Hanna Fenichel, *The Concept of Representation* (Berkeley: University of California Press, 1967).

Plant, Raymond, *Hegel* (London: George Allen & Unwin, 1973).

Plant, Raymond, *Modern Political Thought* (Oxford: Basil Blackwell, 1991).

Plant, Raymond, *The Neo-Liberal State* (Oxford: Clarendon Press, 2010).

Plato, *The Republic*, translated by Francis MacDonald Cornford (Oxford: Clarendon Press, 1941).

Plato, *Protagoras*, translated by W.C.K. Guthrie, in Edith Hamilton and Huntingdon Cairns (eds.), *The Collected Dialogues of Plato* (Princeton: Princeton University Press, 1973), pp. 308–52, 322b, p. 319.

Polanyi, Karl, *The Great Transformation: The Political and Economic Origins of Our Time* (Boston: Beacon Press, 1957).

Powell Jr, G. Bingham, *Contemporary Democracies. Participation, Stability, and Violence* (Cambridge, MA: Harvard University Press, 1982).

Powell Jr, G. Bingham, 'Constitutional Design and Electoral Control', *Journal of Theoretical Politics*, 1: 2, (1989), pp. 107–30.

Powell Jr, G. Bingham, *Elections as Instruments of Democracy. Majoritarian and Proportional Visions* (New Haven and London: Yale University Press, 2000).

Przeworski, Adam 'Democracy as a Contingent Outcome of Conflicts', in Jon Elster and Rune Slagstad (eds.), *Constitutionalism and Democracy* (Cambridge: Cambridge University Press, 1988), pp. 59–80.

Putnam, Robert D., *Making Democracy* Work (Princeton: Princeton University Press, 1993).

Rawls, John, 'Justice as Fairness', *Philosophical Review*, 64: 1, (1958), pp. 164–94. Reprinted in John Rawls, *Collected Papers*, edited by Samuel Freeman (Cambridge, MA: Harvard University Press), pp. 47–72, from which references are taken.

Rawls, John, *A Theory of Justice* (Oxford: Oxford University Press, 1972).

Rawls, John, *Political Liberalism: With a New Introduction and 'Reply to Habermas'* (New York: Columbia University Press, 1996).

Rawls, John, *A Theory of Justice: Revised Edition* (Oxford: Oxford University Press, 1999).

Rawls, John, *Justice as Fairness: A Restatement*, edited by Erin Kelly (Cambridge, MA: The Belknap Press, 2001).

Raz, Joseph, 'Introduction' in Joseph Raz (ed.) *Practical Reasoning* (Oxford: Oxford University Press, 1978), pp. 1–17.

Raz, Joseph, *Practical Reason and Norms* (Princeton, NJ: Princeton University Press, 1990).

Rehfeld, Andrew, *The Concept of Constituency* (Cambridge: Cambridge University Press, 2005).

Rehfeld, Andrew, 'Towards A General Theory of Political Representation', *The Journal of Politics* 68: 1, (2006), pp. 1–21.

Richardson, Henry S., *Democratic Autonomy: Public Reasoning about the Ends of Policy* (Oxford: Oxford University Press, 2002).

Riker, William H., *Liberalism against Populism* (San Francisco: Freeman and Co., 1982).
Riker, William H., *The Strategy of Rhetoric: Campaigning for the American Constitution*, edited by Randall L. Calvert, John Mueller, and Rick K. Wilson (New Haven & London: Yale University Press, 1996).
Ronzoni, Miriam, 'Life Is Not a Camping Trip—On the Desirability of Cohenite Socialism', *Politics, Philosophy and Economics*, 11: 2, (2012), pp. 171–85.
Rousseau, Jean-Jacques, *The Social Contract*, originally 1762, translated by G.D.H. Cole (London: J.M. Dent and Sons, 1973).
Rousseau, Jean-Jacques, *Discourse on the Origin and the Foundations of Inequality among Men* in *Jean-Jacques Rousseau: The First and Second Discourses*, edited, translated, and annotated by Victor Gourevitch (New York: Harper & Row, 1986), originally 1755.
Rueschemeyer, Dietrich, Evelyne Huber Stephens, and John D. Stephens *Capitalist Development and Democracy* (Cambridge: Polity Press, 1992).
Runciman, W.G., *Relative Deprivation and Social Justice: A Study of Attitudes to Social Inequality in Twentieth-Century England* (London, Boston and Henley: Routledge & Kegan Paul, 1966).
Runciman, W.G., *Sociology in Its Place and Other Essays* (Cambridge: Cambridge University Press, 1970).
Ryan, Alan, *Property and Political Theory* (Oxford: Basil Blackwell, 1984).
Sabatier, P.A., 'Knowledge, Policy-Oriented Learning and Policy Change: An Advocacy Coalition Framework' *Knowledge: Creation, Diffusion, Utilization* 8: 4, (1987), pp. 64–92.
Sabatier, P.A. and H.C. Jenkins-Smith (eds.), *Policy Change and Learning: An Advocacy Coalition Approach* (Oxford: Westview Press, 1993).
Sandel, Michael J., *Liberalism and the Limits of Justice* (Cambridge: Cambridge University Press, 1982).
Scanlon, T.M., 'Contractualism and Utilitarianism' in Amartya Sen and Bernard Williams (eds.), *Utilitarianism and Beyond* (Cambridge: Cambridge University Press, 1982), pp. 101–28.
Scanlon, T.M., *What We Owe to Each Other* (Cambridge, MA: Belknap Press, 1998).
Scharpf, Fritz W., 'The Joint-Decision Trap: Lessons from German Federalism and European Union' *Public Administration* 66: 3, (1989), pp. 229–78.
Scharpf, Fritz W., 'Decision Rules, Decision Styles, and Policy Choices', *Journal of Theoretical Politics*, 1: 2, (1988), pp. 149–76.
Schelling, Thomas C., *The Strategy of Conflict* (London: Oxford University Press, 1960).
Schofield, Malcolm, 'Social and Political Thought', in Keimpe Algra, Jonathan Barnes, Jaap Mansfeld, and Malcolm Schofield (eds.), *The*

Cambridge History of Hellenistic Philosophy (Cambridge: Cambridge University Press, 1999), 739–70.

Sen, Amartya, *The Idea of Justice* (London: Penguin Books, 2009).

Sen, Amartya K., *Collective Choice and Social Welfare* (San Francisco: Holden-Day, 1970).

Shackle, G.L.S. *Decision Order and Time in Human Affairs* (Cambridge: Cambridge University Press, second edition, 1969).

Shackle, G.L.S. *Imagination and the Nature of Choice* (Edinburgh: Edinburgh University Press, 1979).

Sidgwick, Henry, *The Elements of Politics* (London: Macmillan, 1891).

Sidgwick, Henry, *The Methods of Ethics*, originally 1907, foreword by John Rawls (Indianapolis and Cambridge: Hackett Publishing Company, reprint 1981).

Simon, Herbert A., *Administrative Behavior: A Study of Decision-Making Processes in Administrative Organizations*, foreword by Chester I. Barnard (New York: The Free Press, third edition, 1976).

Simon, Herbert A., *Reason in Human Affairs* (Oxford: Basil Blackwell, 1983).

Skyrms, Brian, *Evolution of the Social Contract* (Cambridge: Cambridge University Press, 1996).

Smith, Adam, *An Enquiry into the Nature and Causes of the Wealth of Nations*, originally 1776 (Oxford: Clarendon Press, 1976 edition).

Smith, Graham, *Democratic Innovations: Designing Institutions for Citizen Participation* (Cambridge: Cambridge University Press, 2009).

Steiner, Hillel, *An Essay on Rights* (Oxford: Blackwell, 1994).

Steiner, Jürg, André Bächtiger, Markus Spörndli, and Marco R. Steenbergen, *Deliberative Politics in Action: Analyzing Parliamentary Discourse* (Cambridge: Cambridge University Press, 2004).

Stocks, Mary D., *Eleanor Rathbone: A Biography* (London: Victor Gollancz Ltd, 1950).

Strøm, Kaare, *Minority Government and Majority Rule* (Cambridge: Cambridge University Press, 1990).

Sugden, Robert, *The Economics of Rights, Co-Operation and Welfare* (Oxford: Basil Blackwell, 1986).

Sugden, Robert (1993) 'Rationality and Impartiality: Is the Contractarian Enterprise Possible?' in David Gauthier and Robert Sugden (eds.), *Rationality, Justice and the Social Contract: Themes from Morals by Agreement* (New York: Havester-Wheatsheaf), pp. 157–75.

Sunstein, C.R. (1991) 'Preferences and Politics', *Philosophy and Public Affairs*, 20: 1, pp. 3–34.

Taylor, Michael, *Anarchy and Cooperation* (London: John Wiley and Sons, 1976).

Thaler, Richard H. and Cass R. Sunstein, *Nudge: Improving Decisions about Health, Wealth and Happiness* (Harmondsworth: Penguin Books, 2008).

Tönnies, Ferdinand, *Community and Association*, translated by Charles P. Loomis (London: Routledge & Kegan Paul, 1955).

Truman, David B., *The Governmental Process: Political Interests and Public Opinion* (New York: Alfred A. Knopf, 1951).

Wade, Robert, *Village Republics: Economic Conditions for Collective Action in South India* (Cambridge: Cambridge University Press, 1988).

Waldron, Jeremy, *Law and Disagreement* (Oxford: Oxford University Press, 1999).

Waldron, Jeremy, *God, Locke, and Equality* (Cambridge: Cambridge University Press, 2002).

Wallas, Graham, 'Property under Socialism', in G. Bernard Shaw (ed.) *Fabian Essays in Socialism* (London: Walter Scott, Limited, 1899), pp. 131–49.

Walzer, Michael, *Spheres of Justice: A Defence of Pluralism and Equality* (Oxford: Martin Robertson, 1983).

Ward, Hugh and Albert Weale, 'Is Rule by Majorities Special?', *Political Studies*, 58: 1, (2010) pp. 26–46.

Weale, Albert, *Equality and Social Policy* (London, Henley and Boston: Routledge & Kegan Paul, 1978).

Weale, Albert, 'Close Encounters of the Third Sector Kind', in Shaun Hargreaves Heap and Angus Ross (eds.), *Understanding the Enterprise Culture: Themes in the Work of Mary Douglas* (Edinburgh: Edinburgh University Press, 1992), pp. 203–18.

Weale, Albert, 'Justice, Social Union and the Separateness of Persons' in David Gauthier and Robert Sugden (eds.), *Rationality, Justice and the Social Contract: Themes from Morals by Agreement* (New York: Havester-Wheatsheaf, 1993), pp. 75–94.

Weale, Albert, 'Contractarian Theory, Deliberative Democracy and General Agreement', in Keith Dowding, Robert E. Goodin and Carole Pateman (eds.), *Justice and Democracy: Essays for Brian Barry* (Cambridge: Cambridge University Press, 2004), pp. 79–96.

Weale, Albert, *Democracy*, second edition (Houndmills, Basingstoke: Palgrave Macmillan, 2007).

Weale, Albert, Aude Bicquelet, and Judith Bara, 'Debating Abortion, Deliberative Reciprocity and Parliamentary Advocacy', *Political Studies*, 60: 3, (2012), pp. 643–67.

Weale, Albert (forthcoming) *Modern Social Contract Theory.*

Weale, Albert, 'The Property-Owning Democracy *versus* the Welfare State?', *Analyse und Kritik*, forthcoming.

White, Joseph, *Competing Solutions: American Health Care Proposals and International Experience* (Washington DC: The Brookings Institution, 1995).

Wiles, P.J.D., *Economic Institutions Compared* (Oxford: Basil Blackwell, 1977).

Williamson, Oliver E., *The Economic Institutions of Capitalism: Firms, Markets, Relational Contracting* (New York: The Free Press, 1985).

Williamson, Thad, 'Realizing Property-Owning Democracy: A 20-Year Strategy to Create an Egalitarian Distribution of Assets in the United States', in Martin O'Neill and Thad Williamson (eds.) *Property-Owning Democracy: Rawls and Beyond* (Chichester: Wiley-Blackwell, 2012), pp. 225–48.

Woodhouse, A.P.S. (ed.), *Puritanism and Liberty: Being the Army Debates (1647–49) from the Clarke Manuscripts*, new preface by Ivan Roots (London: J.M. Dent & Sons Ltd, 1986).

Wright, G.H. von, 'On So-Called Practical Inference' in Joseph Raz (ed.) *Practical Reasoning* (Oxford: Oxford University Press, 1978), pp. 46–62.

Young, Oran, *International Cooperation* (Ithaca, NY: Cornell University Press, 1989).

Zimmerman, Joseph F., *The New England Town Meeting: Democracy in Action* (Westport, CT: Praeger, 1999).

INDEX